The Postmodern in Latin and Latino American Cultural Narratives

LATIN AMERICAN STUDIES
VOLUME 3
GARLAND REFERENCE LIBRARY OF THE HUMANITIES
VOLUME 1728

LATIN AMERICAN STUDIES

DAVID WILLIAM FOSTER, *Series Editor*

The Postmodern in Latin and Latino American Cultural Narratives

Collected Essays and Interviews

Edited by
Claudia Ferman

Garland Publishing, Inc.
New York and London
1996

Library of Congress Cataloging-in-Publication Data

The postmodern in Latin and Latino American cultural narratives : collected
    essays and interviews / edited by Claudia Ferman.
            p.   cm. — (Garland reference library of the humanities ; vol.
    1728. Latin American studies ; v. 3)   (Latin American studies ; v. 3)
        Includes bibliographical references and index.
        ISBN 0-8153-1330-6 (alk. paper)
            1. Latin America—Civilization—20th century—Philosophy.
    2. Postmodernism—Latin America.   3. Latin American literature—
    20th century—History and criticism.   4. Pan-Americanism.   5. Interviews—
    Latin America.   I. Title.   II. Series: Garland reference library of the
    humanities ; vol. 1728.   III. Series: Garland reference library of the
    humanities. Latin American studies ; vol. 3.
    F1414.2.F44   1996
    980.03'3—dc20   95-39197
                                                                            CIP

Printed on acid-free, 250-year-life paper
Manufactured in the United States of America

CONTENTS

INTRODUCTION

Despite the ominous foreboding, the debate over postmodernity in Latin America is alive and well.[1] That does not mean that it does not suffer from some endemic problems: subjects are often talked about and debated with little or no awareness that in reality various aspects of the postmodern debate are being discussed; moreover, a lot of heated debate about the term takes place without it having much to do with the questions raised by the postmodern debate. In any case, the importance of this debate does not lie in the amount of ink spilled over it but in the presence of new cultural phenomena and in the vitality and high level of discussion associated with it, a vitality which has enabled the debate to expand in several directions at a rapid pace.

I believe that for Latin America this debate now contains two big areas of controversy, which are deeply rooted in its history and which have profound cultural and political significance. First, the postmodern debate encompasses a series of aesthetico-cultural subjects, such as questions related to literary genre (the remodeling of textual forms), the processes of literaturization and deliteraturization,[2] or the questions of gender associated with textual production. Secondly, the postmodern debate relates to considerations about the processes of the transnationalization of economic and cultural production,[3] and their complex implications concerning questions of identity and cultural production in Latin America. The dissolution of boundaries and the vast global flow of peoples and cultures are forcing us to confront the very terms that have defined much of our past academic debates: for instance, can we still speak of the "foreign," the "alien,"

---

[1] A good indication of its relevance can be found in publications such as *Boundary 2* 20.3, which Duke University Press published in book form in 1993.

[2] See my book, *Política y posmodernidad. Hacia una lectura de la Anti-Modernidad en Latinoamérica*. Miami: Iberian Studies Institute, 1993; and Buenos Aires: Almagesto, 1994.

[3] I am currently working on a project entitled *New Localities for Cultural Production: Transnational Languages and Texts*, which examines the relationships between diasporic processes in Argentina in the last thirty years and its cultural production.

in terms of cultural production? In the "global flows of people and things" (Appadurai),[4] cultural objects—even those that are specifically literary—become emancipated from the categories in which we previously contained them. Free from the exclusive and excluding boundaries of national origins and cultural heritage, these objects sail free in spaces without borders, for Appadurai "fractal" and "non-euclidean." Within the general context of globalization and homogenization, one must revise concepts of national and regional lineage of contemporary Latin American cultural production; it is necessary to incorporate as well the new questions of identity that permeate these productions (cf. Bartra, Benítez-Rojo).

Each one of these questions is profoundly significant since they allude to phenomena which are played out in the daily cultural life of Latin American countries—independently of its more or less fortunate label—involving real people and institutions with real problems of survival and growth. Thus, the distrust of the discussion framed by postmodernity has been marked by considerable triviality and bias. It should not come as any surprise, then, that the respose to that rejection occupies an important place in this book, specifically when the researchers who live in Latin America express their ideas (cf. N. Richard, R. Bartra, N. Casullo, J. Juanes, but also C. Tompkins and S. Colás).

The political implications of each position assume crucial importance. Guided by the claim that the conglomerate of continental and extra-continental Latin American societies have not gained access to modernity (they are still "premodern" and therefore "non-post-modern"), the term "primitive" inadvertently slips in, that is, what is different is described as preceding a certain "superior" formulation. The same phenomenon occurs when one speaks of "native" or "precolonial," or also "post-colonial" in this context. What this disqualification (which is nothing but another variant of eurocentrist thinking) basically does is to remove the cultural production of this conglomerate, from the general space of consideration and debate to a subsidiary space in which it is necessary to make clarifications and compromising actions (literature versus "national" or "regional literatures," etc.).[5]

---

[4]Arjun Appadurai, "Disjunctures and Difference in the Global Cultural Economy," *Public Culture* 2.2 (1990): 1-24.

[5]For a discussion of the foundations that could inform this debate (which exceed the scope of this book) in terms of Latin America, see Enrique Dussel, *1492, El encubrimiento del otro. (Hacia el origen del "mito de la Modernidad")*, Santa Fe de Bogotá: Ediciones Anthropos, 1992; Walter Mignolo, "Linguistics, Maps and Literary Geographies: Nations, Languages and Migrations," (forthcom-

The criticism of the use of concepts such as "center" and "periphery" represents an important articulation of the response to these notions. While these concepts describe the problems of political and economic power of Latin American reality, they cannot express the nature of a cultural production. Cultural productions are neither "central" nor "peripheral." Indeed, the political systems and powers are capable of "marginalizing" cultural expressions, that is, of disregarding them, or with effective marketing strategies, of silencing them. Nevertheless, from the standpoint of the producers and consumers of that cultural production, that product is always central, however inappropriate it may seem in relation to different cultural interests and dogmas. The role of the "gurus" of culture (as Roger Bartra describes them) who decree what must be done in the domain of culture, what is most advisable, what can be accepted as Latin American, and what must be rejected because "it does not belong to it," has not been immune to this politicization of cultural production. On the threshold of the twenty-first century, the "masters of the Latin American" have lost a good number of battles while a diverse, heterogeneous and free cultural production has multiplied.

Another perspective on the same question appears in the area of aesthetic questions. What the postmodern debate introduces as the presence of cultural products in which there is a visible irruption of the popular into the "high culture's" domain (the effacement of the limits between *low brow* and *high brow*) represents a long-standing question in Latin American literature. Since the inception of colonization, "high culture" has been represented by the models of the European artistic tradition. The result is that the combination of these models and the vernacular ones (in terms of the debate which concerns us, those perceived as "low brow," and designated as handicrafts, folklore, etc.) became one of the most important spaces of conflict in terms of the development of cultures in Latin American countries. Beverley's article specifically revisits this aspect of the question and does it in terms of what seems to be the voice of the 90s: cultural criticism.

The emergence of Cultural Studies as a field is in part the product of the impact of the commodification of culture in late capitalism on the human sciences, the same commodification that postmod-

---

ing in *Modern Language Quarterly*), and Stuart Hall, "Cultural Identity and Diaspora," in *Identity, Community, Culture, Difference*, Jonathan Rutherford, ed. (London: Lawrence & Wishart, 1990).

ernist ideology celebrates (or diagnoses) in its sense of the breakdown of the distinction between high and mass culture. (421)

The elements contained in his line of argument clearly show the questions which are at stake: the rejection of the apocalyptic vision of a Latin America invaded culturally and silenced (a vision cherished by the cultural thinking of Marxist origins); the re-foundation of the critical object, as long as the literary object seems to have drifted away from the places where it was normally found (writing losing its predominance over every other cultural artifact); the notions of "hybridity, nomadism and transvestism," [224] which are necessary to describe contemporary cultural production, the offspring of strong waves of globalization; the new theoretical concepts which must accompany these changes in cultural practices. For their part, all these new critical parameters make up a good portion of the methodological space in which cultural criticism is situated. On the other hand, this question of the postmodern debate—the neutralization of canonic, generic and formal hierarchies of the European tradition—is necessarily associated with the debates at the center of postcolonial criticism. The long history which this question has had in Latin American countries enables us to point to an area of contact of enormous richness and activity, once the discourses of a certain disparity of origin and vocabulary find spaces of intelligibility.

Now then, if it is unquestionable that the postmodern debate and cultural criticism mutually inform each other, it is still not equally clear in what space literary criticism develops which deals with the analysis of contemporary Latin American production, and within which parameters it accomplishes it. I have the impression that since the explosion of criticism which accompanied the so-called narrative of the **Boom**, literary criticism has still not attempted to produce a generalized reflection which would provide globalizing categories like those which accompanied the **Boom**; in general terms, the thinking devoted to the **Postboom** had little strength and did not turn out to be theoretically productive. And it has not stopped doing it for fear of relapsing into macrotheories in conflict with this new postmodern *episteme*; or, at least, not only because of it: other questions seem to have engendered this silence. The origin of this phenomenon is not located in the field of literary criticism but in the change in the conditions of production and reading (reception): after the **Boom** Latin American literary production could no longer capture the attention of the readers in the publishing market on a massive scale. Not because it was of less interest or quality—at least not in my opinion—but because the conditions of production and reading changed so considerably that they made a phenomenon of massive access like the **Boom** unattainable. The Spanish American textual tradition exceeded its "borders" (with which criticism had successfully played), and the analysis applied to that textuality started to express other necessities and other interests.

As we have seen, the globalizing discussions which recently have captured the interest of criticism center on phenomena which transcend the chronological and movementist aspects (such as those which defined the **Boom**), that is, a certain body of literature produced within a certain time period in a specific geographical space. The application of these globalizing postmodern configurations manifests itself in the works which deal with aspects relative to *género*, in the double meaning which the word entails in Spanish: *el género* as a discursive category and therefore also literary (**genre**); and *el género* as a category of intercultural differentiation between social, political and economic roles associated with sexual determinations (**gender**). The result of such critical practices are categories such as *el testimonio* (cf. Colás) or *la escritura de la mujer* (cf. Arias and Tompkins) that we described above as the aesthetico-cultural questions with which the postmodern debate deals. These categories have enabled the movement across borders and temporal contexts, giving rise to a critical reflection which relates more closely to the cultural debates than to the idiosyncracies of authors, styles, periods or movements, and have produced perceptive illuminations. In the context of the postmodern debate these globalizing gestures have not fallen into the trap of the universal, but much of their agility and interest stems from their translocal and transtemporal condition. Because of this migratory condition, I would like to designate them *horizontal categories.*[6]

We shall call the complementary class, *vertical categories.* A vertical category demarcates a chronological space, and by means of the parameters of a movement: a certain temporal cut, a more or less defined aesthetic resolve, a group of authors, a body of production, a history, that is, a cluster of events associated with that production. This methodology of generalization would be represented by categories such as the "literature of the Boom," or, in Mexico, "la Onda": the critical (logical) system concretizes an aesthetico-cultural-social phenomenon, and attributes characteristics of the same works and authors to it.

---

[6]The spatial metaphor intended here proposes a content for the term "horizontal" which is very different (even contradictory) from the one proposed by Homi Bhabha to describe the "empty time of the nation's narrative" ("DissemiNation," *The Location of Culture* [London and New York: Routledge, 1994], 152-53). In the present work, the horizontal is associated with the line (trail) marked out by a route (like the lights of moving vehicles in a photograph taken at night) and therefore with the dynamic; whereas the vertical is seen as static.

The horizontal categories show more self-awareness of their *reading* role, that is, of the fact that they offer themselves insofar as they are working with comprehensive spaces of debate which are not necessarily located in the area where literature is happening. Hence the slow removal of theoretical reflection from the strictly literary domain (the book) to an extended field, that of cultural criticism, and the multiplicity of its object.

> The choice of research practices depends upon the questions that are asked, and the questions depend on their context. . . . Thus, for example, although there is no prohibition against close textual readings in cultural studies, they are also not required. Moreover, textual analysis in literary studies carries a history of convictions that texts are properly understood as wholly self-determined and independent objects as well as a bias about which kinds of texts are worthy of analysis. That burden of association cannot be ignored. (Grossberg *Cultural Studies* 2).[7]

This methodology of "close textual readings" seems to be the natural space of literary criticism, and undoubtedly that is what this practice has been doing without interruption. On the other hand, there is no doubt that said "bias," foreign to cultural criticism, is still present in the space of Latin American literary criticism. When textual analysis is practiced, the chosen object corresponds to the canonic Gutenbergian model (which can be associated with the *print capitalism* of Anderson);[8] even today, after several years of postmodern debate, of the influence and spread of cultural studies. For that reason, this book has given adequate space to these practices; it has not rejected them, because they are also part of the configuration of the thinking about Latin American cultures.

The result is that within the postmodern debate it is still possible to produce new *horizontal categories* which account for other conglomerates of cultural production which have still not made their entry into Latin American criticism for the reasons which we have noted. For example, the space of the

---

[7]Lawrence Grossberg. Introduction, in *Cultural Studies*, Lawrence Grossberg, Cary Nelson, Paula A. Treichler, eds. (New York, London: Routledge, 1992).

[8]See Benedict Anderson, *Imagined Communities* (London: Verso, 1991).

intersection of youth poetics, electronic communication and urban cultures,[9] which are undoubtedly associated with the eminently postmodern phenomena of "literaturization and deliteraturization."

The main thrust of this book is summed up in the attempt to develop a space of interplay between academic instances which are not necessarily identical: that of researchers working in Latin American countries, and that of those who are working in the United States. Certainly, such an effort is a response to the new conditions of communication and exchange of information which are produced by the cybernetic revolution (cf. Martín-Barbero). As we know, forms of communication shape us. In the same vein, every *data bank* shapes our knowledge. Academic discussions rely more and more on access to and the participation in those *data banks*. A new map of communications organizes the dialogues and exchanges in the passage toward the twenty-first century. This map is composed of a congested intersection of channels (modes and media of communication). One of the properties of this intersection is that its congestion is reproductive. That is, the larger the intersection the larger the generation of communicational alternatives. In other words, the number of terminals to which an individual, community or enclave is exposed constitutes the coefficient of reproductivity of these terminals. The higher the profusion of communication channels, there exists an increased possibility of access to new channels. If the number of terminals is low, or zero, chances are that it will remain the same unless other chaos coefficients intervene. Literary salons of today cross boundaries and oceans, this time with new class conditioning: an X number of nodes. In these conditions, without a conscious and continuous effort, thinking in the Latin American field runs the risk of being transformed into a space of enormous exclusivism, dissociated and schizophrenic, in the permanent attempt to interpret and translate to the languages which are presumed to be authentic.

On the other hand, the same places recognize unparalleled conditions of hybridization. Hence the title of this book, *The Postmodern in Latin and Latino American Cultural Narratives*, which communicates the very field of geography as an unstable, hybrid space which is opened to new demarcations, which in itself simultaneously contains limits and the transcendence of those limits, their problematization (cf. Olalquiaga).

---

[9]John Beverley as well as George Yúdice, among others, have successfully ventured into this field without there yet existing, however, a widespread awareness of its importance for Latin American cultural production.

By way of conclusion: the present imbrication of aesthetic forms of the Hispanic and pre-Hispanic literary tradition and mass culture (which in Latin America is associated with the different and massive migratory waves, plus the processes of globalization) stands in close relationship to the new conceptions that we have been discussing. In them we can verify the use of the array of models which appear at the disposal of cultural producers, in the rejection of concepts such as high and low culture, external and indigenous, typical and foreign, also in the context of a radical critique of the cultural and political models which specifically established those categories and those limits and borders for cultural production. Within the postmodern debate there appears a formulation of this cultural crossroads. On the other hand, this formulation does not (only) set out to delineate a group of works associated with a set of traits (vertical categories), but it also travels along the length and breadth of cultural production, in its effort to identify and participate in the current cultural debates (horizontal categories).

Translated by Robert Sims

ACKNOWLEDGMENTS

I would like to thank David William Foster, who encouraged me to take on this project and supported me throughout its progress; Robert Sims, for his unparalleled enthusiasm with the vast responsibility of the translation; Lisa Ayres and Stephen Booth for their invaluable help on the editing process; Kerran Kempton, for her help with some of the endless typing; and to all the contributors for their interest in the project.

Voices in the South

IN CHILE:

CULTURAL ALTERITY AND DECENTERING
Nelly Richard

Is it really valid to speak of postmodernity in Latin America or do we just relapse into the imitative vice of peripheral dependence when we use a term which is oversignified because of its core countries' inscription and hence a co-conspirator of the first-worldist discursivity? Is postmodernism only an alien-alienating reference which distorts Latin American consciousness of "its own" or does it serve as a **guide** so that we can "a-propriate" it through the decolonizing gesture of cultural refunctionalization? What are the alternatives for Latin American thinking that a contextualized—**situational**—rereading of the postmodern debate liberates and strengthens as peripheral strategies of resistance to and questioning of the core countries' centralizations? What controversies of that debate revitalize a regional reflection about **our** problems: modernity, culture, democracy, etc.?

These constitute some of the questions which traverse continental reflection about the derivations, adaptations and reformulations of the postmodern theme in Latin America. Questions whose answers to the circulation of international discourses put into operation by the core countries' propositions establish the difference between acritical consumption (passive, mimetic) and differential reception (transformative, questioning).

The arguments which explain Latin American reticence before the postmodern theme are well known. First, the disparities between the regularity of the pattern of the historical development of European modernity and the startling nature of its Latin American replicas, which produce a clash of always heterogeneous temporalities, would render abusive any recourse to a uniform and superimposed nomenclature (that which is regulated by the consecutivity of "pres" and "posts"), because its linear ordering and comprehensiveness of uniform sequences prove incompatible with Latin American discontinuity and fragmentarity. It would be inappropriate to speak of postmodernity in Latin America since the same modernity manifests itself here not only as variable but also as **inconclusive**, and therefore does not conform to the definitive label of a "post" which endeavors to convert the modern into an "after" (completion and transcendence).

There would be no possible match between that serial finalizing "post" which offers an epochal transcendence, and the failed Latin American materialization of a truncated modernity. But the incongruity does not only come from the experiential disparity (continuity, discontinuity) which the historical record of verdicts fabricates about each type of modernity: the central and the peripheral. This disharmony also refers to the impossibility of Latin America recognizing itself in postmodernity as an epochal manifestation of a cluster of traits which arise from the capitalistic hyperdevelopment of the postindustrial North: a North saturated with consumer goods and mediatic images which clashes with the underdeveloped economies of the South stigmatized by critical shortages. That contrast dramatized by the Left would render impudent any reference to post-modernism in Latin America: a postmodernism indissolubly linked with the market reverberations of neoliberal abuse that therefore scandalizes Latin American morality of underdevelopment which lent its ethico-revolutionary support to the militant intelligentsia of the 60s.

It is easy to provide evidence which supports an incongruity between the self-centered realization of the European-dominant modernity and its precarious and frustrated peripheral transcriptions, or else between the standard model of the structural dominant Euro-North American postmodernism and its dissonant gleamings dispersed along the axis of the periphery. But this evidence does not provide sufficient reason to invalidate the relevance of the postmodern debate in Latin America. The significativity of that debate is not limited to having a harmonization of processes serve as a referential guarantor in order to authorize the symmetry-conceived interpretation of experiences.[1] The postmodern as **register** (and not as a phase) strays in every direction from the confirmation that a new "order of things" seeks to displace and replace the finite sequence of the modern. Modernity and postmodernity gain more by being read not as **stages** in a tempo-

---

[1] It seems much more stimulating to me to treat the matter with the following freedom of choice: "What advantages or problems are presented by the inscription of a particular sensibility (Latin American) in the ledger of the 'postmodern'? Does it perhaps prove to be a useful and operational concept, or does it only involve a compulsory fashion for being 'terminologically' up-to-date? Perhaps the different areas of the 'post' horizon are mutually sustaining? Perhaps the presence of postmodern aesthetic operating in our midst implies that we are living in a postmodern or postindustrial context, from the point of view of social theory? Can one really speak of postmodernism in a country in which premodern enclaves still persist? Or say that we are living a postmodern condition when this sensibility is only one among others?" (Bernardo Subercaseaux 142).

ral logic of historical successions, but as problematizations of the reading and rereading of the vocabulary (in crisis) of universal reason: retrospective and **introspective** readings of modernity which propel the historico-cultural energies of each collision of contexts in directions not envisioned by the linear programming of a single historical rationality; heterodox readings of modernity which change the emphases (and the tendentialities) of the history-progress-subject-reason configuration upon redistributing the emphases of the singular and plural, of the one and the many, of the centered and the decentered. Undoubtedly, the first critical dividend of the postmodern theme in Latin America comes from the disruptive nature of these rereadings which strew the scene with the fragmented and broken pieces of the universal rationality of the Western-dominant modernity. A scene which permits rearticulating reflexive tensions between the dominant modernity and the **others** which have been marginalized from its rationalist abstraction (for example: "childhood, woman's culture, the experience of the vanquished and of limits" [Buci-Glucksmann 25]). Latin America—a geographic fringe but, above all, an **enunciative figure** on the defenseless, unprotected edge from hegemonic pacts—has much to gain from the postmodern questioning of the central hierarchies of the dominant universal reason. Here I intend to underscore two of postmodern reformulations (identity/alterity, center/periphery)which challenge traditional Latin American thinking with their new critical articulations.

Rebounderization I: Identity/Alterity

Modernity designed "the great control panel of clear and distinct identities which overlays the scrambled, indefinite, faceless, and as though indifferent, background of differences" (Foucault)[2] in order to separate the Same (the self-centered consciousness of transcendent rationality) from the Other: the negative and clandestine heterogeneity of the other sides—madness, death, sexuality, etc.—censured by universal Logos. The metaphor of the chess game with black and white pieces illustrates the dualistic distribution of identities in a relationship of opposites which modernity performs in order to separate the clear (the distinct) from the dark (the in-distinct) and to delimit the order of reason by protecting it against the dis-order (the confusion) of nonreason or reasonlessness. A whole chain of connections based on similarities and analogies weaves kinships

---

[2]As quoted in Oscar Terán's *Michel Foucault: el discurso del poder*, from the preface of *The Order of Things: An Archeology of the Human Sciences*.

of inclusion (the Same) and exclusion (the Other) that divide the subjects into the representatives of the luminous (the human, the Christian, the European, the civilized, the masculine) and the representatives of the dark (the animal, the pagan, the Indian, the savage, the feminine). Classic rationalism will marginalize and diminish everything which does not correspond to the identity-similarity model which guarantees the homogeneity of its culture, subject and language categories: categories which are self-transparent and self-founded on a discourse of authority for which the Center symbolizes the Totality.

Postmodern fragmentation derives from the systematicity crisis of entire bodies of knowledge and the finite truths of the single reason of dominant-Western modernity. That postmodern explosion shatters the images of totality and the representations of the Whole which served Western logocentric thought as a tool to repress singularisms and particularisms in the name of the abstract-generalizing reason of universal modernity. It is certain that the postmodern criticism of the Eurocentrist legacy of the dominant modernity is formulated within the same perimeter of pronouncements (the perimeter of core countries' culture) which the tradition of that legacy had forged by preserving its exclusive privileges. But even so, that criticism can be recast by us in a gesture which combines the anti-hegemonic protest of the periphery with the interpretations of the fissures engendered within the system of cultural authority of core countries' thinking. In the midst of the stream of proposals which flows from the core countries' culture, to discern those which are already susceptible to a discussion of the defects of their tendential vices,[3] is a special skill which favors the periphery by giving it something concrete in order to **reintentionalize** the meaning of the defects of the center. In that way, "this dissolution of modern representations, of its patriarchal narratives" (Casullo, "Modernidad" 19), thematized by postmodernity, promotes the construction of alternative and dissident forms of cultural thought whose anti-establishment potential the periphery must not relinquish under the pretext that its design has been theoretically formulated from the center. The postmodern problematic of the "other" (of the different) is a problematic which we can rearticulate in a new poetics and politics of the peripheries which continues to drive the subordinated and decentered voices to take the canon of cultural authority by

---

[3]"The **independence** trend which we have indicated as the guiding principle of the Latin American cultural process has always tended to select the non-conformist elements of the European and North American systems which were produced in the core countries, wrenching them from their context and making them their own in a risky, abstract manner" (Rama 39).

storm—whoever their representatives may be and above all when they are the misleading mouthpieces of that "aestheticizing marginocentrality" (Yúdice 30) which abounds in the texts of international postmodernism. Despite the assimilative maneuvers of official postmodernism which seeks to reduce the "other" to a simple piece of multicultural scenery, the conflicts of points of view unleashed at the center by the players of the new social practices who denounce and answer the dominant narratives of the superior culture (white, masculine, learned, core countries) succeeded in creating new cultural positions from which to draw support in order to destabilize the repertory of authority. The critical potential of these new positions raised against the regime of institutional seizure must be fostered and reinterpreted by the cultural periphery in its polemic against the reterritorializations of the center.

The detotalizing turn of postmodernity which splintered the logic of the One has led the **different** to multiply itself and to subdivide the figure of the Other into "others" which no longer remain external but reach across the dominant cultural system. The differential multiplicity of these "others" un-founds the founding mythologies of the Other in which Latin American culture continued to inscribe its emblems of identity-ownership.

The problematics of the colonial subject reveals a double gesture: the colonizing gesture of parceling out identity according to the Westernized norm of the Same (identity by imposition) and the anticolonialist gesture of reaffirming itself through negation (identity by opposition). The design in negative of the Other delineated by the dominant culture is reinverted by the colonial subject into counter-identity without leaving the logocentric tendency "to dichotomize the human continuum into we-they contrasts and to essentialize the resultant 'other'" (Clifford 258). The essentialization of himself/herself as the Other of colonization to which the colonized subject resorts in an inverted pose, his/her essentialist quest for a profound and true (authentic) identity sanctioned by a myth of origin, attempt to fill the void which the lack of "our own" leaves in cultures of estrangement: in borrowing cultures composed of surrogates which signal the deficit of originals and originality. A deficit for which Latin America learned to compensate with the hyper-rhetorization of the **copy** as an allegory of its art of cultural transvestism. "The ambivalence of colonial discourse"[4] is being implanted in this game of mirror images (identities-identifications) played out between **being** and **appearance**: a game dramatized by Latin American cultural thought

---

[4]As in the title of Homi Bhabha's *Of Mimicry and Man: The Ambivalence of Colonial Discourse.*

which always struggled between **substance** (the indigenous origins as the onto-logical foundation of an identity-ownership) and **appearance** (the core countries' touching-up of the mask as an artifice of a borrowed identity). The whole conti-nental discourse of the quest for and definition of the "Latin American identity" long remained the captive of that Manichean schema which set the internal (the profound) against the external (the superficial), the authentic (the native) against the artificial (the foreign), the pure (virgin nature) against the polluting (the vector-progress). All the controversies which informed the history of ideas in Latin America bear the mark of this contrast between regionalism and cosmopoli-tanism (the polemic of modernism and Latin American avant-garde movements), between nationalism and foreignization (the discussion about modernity and the tradition-market confrontation), a conflict articulated by the center-periphery axis with its theories of cultural dependence and anti-imperialist struggle, and by the First World-Third World axis with its myth of resistance to the expansion of capital from sectors which are romantically imagined as still exempt from its traffickings.

The postmetaphysical deconstruction of the thinking of "identity" engen-ders reformulations that challenge in more than one sense the Latin American imaginary of the "our own" by bringing it face to face with the processes of disintegration and heterogeneization of the ranges of cultural identity. By pre-empting the postmodern revalorization of the heterogeneous, a certain current of Latin American thought[5] had already envisaged peripheral modernity as a **col-lage** of pasts and presents which combines signs relating to disjointed memories and experiences: "indigenous traditions, colonial catholic Hispanism, modern political, educational and communicational actions" (García Canclini 71). Those unstable mixtures, through a process of constant recombinations of social textures and historical densities, superimpose and juxtapose spaces and times which are multistratified by discordant tendencies which were continually shaping the processes of hybridization, syncretism and mestization of Latin American culture. The absurdities of that peripheral modernity with its grafts and transplants of never uniform signs were already putting the emphasis on the rereadings of the Latin American which might stress **mixing** as an argument in favor of a multiple identity criss-crossed by dissimilar forces. What postmodernism is doing is un-derscoring—reaccentuating—the cultural expressions which derived from these

---

[5]In particular, see José Joaquín Brunner, *Un espejo trizado: ensayos sobre cultura y políticas culturales* and Néstor García Canclini, *Culturas híbridas: estrategias para entrar y salir de la modernidad.*

hodgepodges and jumbles of signs made up of several sedimentations: expressions of how "in Latin America the rough asymmetricality of the modern assumed instead the form of collage, montage and hybridity" (Casullo, "Posmodernidades" 103). This postmodernist reaccentuation of the heterogeneous immediately allows us to refute the metaphysical thinking of **being** that serves as a foundation for Latin American substantialism of the Origin: a thought pattern which mythologizes and folklorizes the past (roots, sources) as a guardian of a preordained identity. That fundamental traditionalism of the "our own" that archaizes memory as soon as it returns to the origins does not recognize that "ours" is a product of a dialogic interrelationality that traverses multiple and changing registers. Identity is not the ritual repository of a transcendent truth into whose center one can withdraw in search of a sense of belonging. It is a fluid construct that keeps on forming and transforming itself in accordance with the dynamics of clashes and alliances in which the subject plays the leading role in constantly variable circumstances. From this perspective, "authenticity" can only be the creative product of a mixing of pasts and presents selected according to possible futures, by assembling utterances which dialogize the One (our own, ours), by putting it in conflict with the variety of **others'** repertories with which it establishes borrowing and negotiating relationships.[6] Although transculturation may have always shaped Latin American culture as a zone of substitutions and appropriations, its rhetoric of "mixed, relational, appropriative" (Mosquera 537) identity very often remained displaced by the essentialist myth of an identity-ownership that demanded the fixity of origin in order to authenticate being. The postmodern refutation of the sacralization of origin as a transcendental presence (archireference) disinhibited that rhetoric which theatricalizes identity as if it were a **montage** in which the cultural subjects fragment and recombine the set of images which mix the "we" and "the others."

Rebounderization II: Center/Periphery

Just as Identity conceived Alterity in terms of **exteriority**, the Center conceived the Periphery in terms of **distance**. Modernity managed the politico-social order and regulated the geographic exchanges by bringing into play the

---

[6]"Metaphors of continuity and 'survival' do not account for complex historical processes of appropriation, compromise, subversion, masking, invention, and revival" (Clifford, *The Predicament of Culture* 338).

power of the Center in order to create distances, maintain at a distance and control distances. The Cartesian-perspectivist model of Modernity made the understanding of the world revolve around a vantage point called the Center: a point which synthesized a plenitude and coherence of values, and which rationalized the control of space by ruling over proximities and distances from being located **in the middle** of the field of visibility and representation. From the center as the point of the greatest convergence of meaning (light), the periphery (shadow) was envisaged as the edge of the indefinite. Its remoteness from the middle signified a symbolic debasement of the loss of clarity: a fall toward the unrepresentable. The Center symbolized the paradigm of authority that the periphery was supposed to interpret by respecting its value as **original**: as a founding text codified by a single truth.

Postmodernity engenders several redefinitions which modify the center/periphery schema of modernity. Let us cite the first of these: the planetary interdependence of the satellite networking of the real brings about the universal interfacing of all the spaces-times which blurs distances by disseminating the impression that the "multiplicity of images, interpretations and reconstructions" of reality which are now being circulated by the media act independently of any "'central' coordination" (Vattimo 81). Another definition comes from deconstruction which refutes the myth of **presence**: of the self-transparent sign as a theological representative of fundamental and transcendent meaning. Philosophies which discredit the metaphysical hypothesis of the pristine purity of the meaning inscribed in the uniqueness of the Original, then disorganize the Model-Copy relationship of the Latin American imaginary of cultural reproduction, which subordinated the periphery to the center.

The new theories of power (from Foucault onwards) broke with their topography of a centralized referent—located in a visible center—in order to then describe that power as a fluctuating network of scattered points in which multiple antagonisms and pluriconfrontational relationships intersect. This postmodern dissemination of power forces the centers and peripheries to be reconfigured as multi-situated functions and not as fixed locations. The Center has demultiplied itself into function-centers which shift places in accordance with the need for the mechanisms of authority to transfer their pronouncements from one control zone to another. But that nomadism of power does not signify that the marks which depict inequality on the postcolonial map have disappeared.

We know that today the locations of center and periphery escape the simple geographical realism of the North-South opposition in order to subdivide and remultiply themselves into transversal segmentations which recreate "a Third World in every First World" and "First World in every Third World" (Minh-ha

139) by crisscrossing their domination-resistance axes. But even so, the Euro-North American design continues to predominate as the primary blueprint. Postmodernist theory is brought about by that design which articulates academico-institutional discourses and resources for the benefit of the direct representatives of its "American International," a statement which is sufficiently discriminatory so as to refute the ingenuous belief that postmodern theory possesses the "international elasticity" of "a theory for a post-colonial world of products made and sold in different places without a center" similar to "a supermarket of ideas that can be assembled by anyone" (Rajchman 51). This belief assumes: 1) a fluid circulation such that it erases distances; and 2) that the "availability" of cultural material only depends on its being within the physical grasp of the consumer of texts. But we know that any periphery (for example, Chile) experiences the dismembering effect of being situated at a point on the network of exchanges which is far removed from the international decision-making and control centers. We also know that the availability of cultural material—for example, a fragment of postmodernist theory—depends on its being liberated from the overinterpretations of reading which influence its manipulation according to the core countries' preferences. Both of these attributes, the fluidity and the availability of cultural circulation-refunctionalization, continue to be the exclusive property of the center which represents the area of the highest concentration of signs, of the highest circulatory and transactional density of the significations in use.

The "marginal," which had always borne the connotation of the discarded or excluded by the center, is today resemanticized by the postmodern lexicon of the crisis of centrality—a crisis formulated and promoted from the centers of international theory production. This is the new piece of postmodern information which complicates the center/periphery relationship reconverted into center-decentering/periphery. This piece of information requires increased vigilance concerning the stratagems of theoretical power which reinsert the marginal (the decentered) into the exclusive and excluding boundaries of core countries' thought, as if it sufficed to argue about otherness in order to feel that the boundaries of the debate are being pluralized, or—more harshly—as if the debate over the other served "to hide and conceal the power of the voices and movements of the Others" ("Interview" 273). In order for the extent of the opening-up of postmodern discourse to the "others" to be egalitarian and democratizing, what postcolonial theory needs to do is not be satisfied with taking the word as a representative of alterity—even though it is with the good intention of mediating its participation in the academic circuit of the United States. It also needs to renounce certain privileges of delegation-representation (to speak in place of, in the name of) by letting alterity speak to itself and shatter the self-referentiality of the core countries debate with voices from other areas: voices which self-signify from the periphery but which are not satisfied with gaining a place within the concert of the voices of diversity without at the same time resignifying that place and without attempting to transfer their polemic to the forms which organize the core countries' distribution of cultural theorizations on the periphery.

Translated by Robert Sims

Works Cited

Bhabha, Homi. "Of Mimicry and Man: The Ambivalence of Colonial Discourse." *October* 28 (1984): 125-33.

Buci-Glucksmann, Christine. *La Raison baroque: de Baudelaire à Benjamin.* Paris: Ed. Galilée, 1984.

Casullo, Nicolás. "Modernidad, biografía del ensueño y la crisis (introducción a un tema)." *El debate modernidad posmodernidad.* Buenos Aires: Ediciones Punto Sur, 1989. 9-63.

——. "Posmodernidad de los orígenes." *Nuevo texto crítico* 3.6 (1990): 95-104.

Clifford, James. *The Predicament of Culture: Twentieth-Century Ethnography, Literature, and Art.* Cambridge: Harvard UP, 1988. 269-86.

Foucault, Michel. *The Order of Things: An Archaeology of the Human Sciences.* New York: Vintage, 1973.

García Canclini, Néstor. *Culturas híbridas: estrategias para entrar y salir de la modernidad.* México: Grijalbo, 1990.

"Interview with Cornel West." Andrew Ross, ed. *Universal Abandon? The Politics of Postmodernism.* Minneapolis: U Minnesota P, 1988.

Joaquín Brunner, José. *Un espejo trizado: ensayos sobre cultura y políticas culturales.* Santiago: Flasco, 1988.

Minh-ha, Trinh T. "Of Other People: Beyond the 'Savage' Paradigm." Hal Foster, ed. *Discussions in Contemporary Culture.* New York: Dia Art Foundation, 1987. 138-41.

Mosquera, Gerardo. "The Marco Polo Syndrome: A Few Problems Surrounding Art and Eurocentrism." *The South Atlantic Quarterly* 93.2 (1993): 529-42.

Rajchman, John. "Postmodernism in a Nominalist Frame." *Flash Art* 137 (1987): 49-69.

Rama, Angel. *Transculturación en América Latina.* México: Siglo XXI, 1982.

Subercaseaux, Bernardo. "Nueva sensibilidad y horizonte 'post' en Chile." *Nuevo texto crítico* 3.6 (1990): 135-45.

Terán, Oscar. *Michel Foucault: el discurso del poder*. Buenos Aires: Folios Ediciones, 1983.

Vattimo, Gianni. *La sociedad transparente*. Barcelona: Paidós/ICE-UAB, 1990.

Yúdice, George. "El conflicto de posmodernidades." *Nuevo texto crítico* 4.7 (1991): 19-33.

IN COLOMBIA:

COMMUNICATION AND MODERNITY IN LATIN AMERICA
Jesús Martín-Barbero

The Ambiguous but Strategic Centrality of Communication

During the last years, in the wealthy countries of the First World, communication has become central to all activities, something like the center of the center. In the search for a new societal model, communication forms the core of what has come to be known as the "Information Society." This society sees information as a valuable natural resource and communication as *the paradigm for its own organization*: the information network serving as connecting circuitry for all of the domains and functions of social life; autorregulation, constant retroaction and transparency of communication enabling convertibility and translatability of all knowledge to the hegemonic code of information (Baudrillard and Lyotard).

Communication has become central also in another sense, paradoxically opposed to the positivistic aspects of the informational model: communication implies a search for and a defense of a type of a rationality different from the instrumental, that defined by Habermas as underlying the "praxis communicative." This rationality may be defined as that in which we still find those liberating aspects of modernity which permit us to question the process of modernization when reduced to its purely technical and economic aspects. Communicative reasoning appears at the center of social reflexion filling the void produced by the crisis in the paradigms of production and representation, and providing society with both the potential for resistance and an orientation which feeds new social movements ranging from the ethnic to the ecological to the feminist (Habermas, *El discurso*).

At the other end of the spectrum, those who question modernity as a social model or as a reserve for thinking and social orientation, nevertheless place communication in a key position. For the most daring of the postmodernist thinkers, such as Vattimo, communication constitutes a revealing social example of the collapse of modernity: the experience of declining values in the rootless life of the urban citizen whose life is both constructed and constantly mediated by the narratives of information and the web of images produced by the technological simulation of art and the enactment of politics as spectacle ("Ciencias").

Latin America has, in its own way, also experienced that centrality of communication since it has become a key dimension of technological and economic modernity. One of the few industries which attracted large investments and which developed enormously in the "lost decade" of the 1980s was the communication industry. As an example: the number of television stations in Latin America grew from 400 to close to 1500 between the 70s and the mid-80s; Brazil and Mexico acquired their own satellites which enabled radio and television stations in these countries to link up with international communication networks; information networks, parabolic antennas, cable TV and regional channels all were established. Beginning in the 1980s, information and communication became the bulwark of the new neo-liberal economic model (Zallo). We see this in the priority given to the privatization of Argentine Telephone Company and the complete privatization of Mexican public television (with the exception of one small channel rescued by a group of intellectuals who were led by Carlos Monsiváis), and the conflict generated by a proposal to privatize the Telecom Corporation in Colombia.

Why this emphasis on privatization, particularly in the communication industry? I believe that the answer lies in a strategy for economic and social reorganization. The political and economic space which communication occupies has become crucial to serving the ends of designing and restructuring society and its economy. The concept that state structures are incapable of understanding and dominating the full spectrum of technological changes in the communication industry has been spread throughout the information network.

In fact, this is what has been happening in Latin America in recent years. The development of the communication industry has been completely oriented to the logic of the marketplace. The introduction and development of new information technologies have been left entirely to market movement, while the State has withdrawn more and more from the regulation of this new industry to the point that any State intervention is viewed as interference. These developments negate the concept of "public space" as it has been understood until recently.[1] In this sense communication may be viewed as strategic: it redefines the relationship between the public and the private sectors in our society.

   In Colombia, the 80s witnessed the development of the communication industry. We have one of the most modern radio systems in Latin America and a well-developed television network, both in the technological and in the entrepreneurial aspects, as well as in its communicative and aesthetic competencies. We have available to us all of the technological paraphernalia of satellite hook-ups, parabolic antennas, cable networks and cellular phones, but at the same time Colombians are experiencing a profound crisis of communication between the many constituencies which form our society. This is a critical paradox: few countries have such a technologically advanced communication network while experiencing at the same time such a deep crisis of coexistence, a crisis of *communication* between the communities which together form our nation.

   This crisis of coexistence affects the possibilities available to us for redefining our national goals, and makes itself most evident, in a perverse but significant manner, in the sphere of communication. I have been preoccupied by the relationship between the media and fear.[2] In Colombia, more than any other Latin American country, the media thrive on fear. The fears of Colombia's citizens have given the media a significant place in our society—the media have been able to catalyze, particularly with radio and television, those fears which imprison us in our homes and cause us to mistrust each other. In our latest presidential campaign, television swallowed up all the communication and replaced the political street theater, in which Colombians are accustomed to participate, with a TV show which continues to be aired. In a country as fragmented as Colombia, television has become the place where our diverse communities "meet," although in a vicarious and perverse manner. At the same time, television has become the sacrificial goat, accused of being responsible for the violence that surrounds us, the moral decay and the cultural degradation (Martín-Barbero, "Violencia"). This is the central ambiguity of communication.

---

[1]This has been attested by the works gathered by Elizabeth Fox in *Medios de comunicación y política en América Latina*, and by Hugo Zemelman in *Cultura y política en América Latina*.

[2]See my "Comunicación y ciudad: entre medios y miedos."

Social and Cultural Manifestations of Modernity in Latin America

Taking the above as a point of departure, eloquent of the role which communication plays in both the obstructions and development of Latin American nations, it is possible to understand the transformations of the debate over modernity, and also to comprehend our crisis between the debt and the doubt, and between new conditions of dependency and new ways of overcoming this dependency.

Until recently, modernity was considered in Latin America as a mere prolongation of European modernity; although deformed, twisted and even paradoxical, it still has always being connected with *the* only possible definition of the word, developed out of the principles of Enlightenment and "literate culture" (Ramos and Gutiérrez Girardot). This definition grew out of the principles of the Enlightenment. However, some sociologists have proposed in recent years an examination of modernity from a different perspective (Brunner, *Los debates* and *Tradicionalismo*). According to this new perspective, Latin American modernity as a collective experience has less to do with the doctrines of the Enlightenment and the literate aesthetics than with increased access to public education and the expansion of culture-producing industries. From this perspective, modernity should be considered as the process by which the sources of cultural production are no longer the community, the church or the State, but the communication industry and its specialized apparatus instead. The traditional sources of cultural production have been replaced by the images and styles fueled by the dynamic of consumption which moves the market system; of course the "old" forms and traditional values still exist, but they have "mixed" with those propelled by market forces. Modernity is primarily the substitution of values and life styles which are no longer pictured in "exemplary lives" but rather in mirrors which give images proposed by market mechanisms and fashion.

Modernity has come to mean the secularization and internationalization of the symbolic worlds. But secularization today has not much to do with the irreligiosity of the nineteenth century nor does it mean hispanic anti-clericalism. Secularization in Latin America means the progressive autonomy of the cultural world in aspects ranging from sexuality to science, with respect to its subordination to the religious power sustained by the Catholic church. We are witnessing the revitalization of religious beliefs, and the expansion of Protestant, animist and oriental faiths. Nevertheless, this has not slowed the impetus for the autonomy of cultural expression, which is redefining its role in society and is beginning to play a decisive part in its orientation (González, "Etica").

Another characteristic of modernity is the process of segmenting cultural habitats and converting communities into audiences who are increasingly shaped by market influences. Post-modern thinkers call this a "liberation from differences," with a resulting crisis of definition of all categories phrasing totality concepts, whether it be nation, town, or culture. As Richeri affirms, we have entered into a dynamic of transnationalization which at the same time implies the dissolution of any common cultural horizon within a particular society (*L'universo*). The absence of a representational place for the society which may be shared on a large scale becomes "visible."

In a peculiar manner modernity in Latin America speaks of the interpenetration and complicity between orality—as the primary cultural experience of the majority of the people—and electronic visualization.[3] This complicity has shaped a "secondary orality" which has formed its grammar of expression through radio, television, movies and video and represents a dramatic break with the core of Enlightened modernity, that is, the culture of books. Majorities in our countries get to appropriate modernity's principles without leaving behind their oral culture and without going through the book's mode. This represents a scandal and a challenge for our cultural models.

Some of these processes started early in modernity's inception around the 1930s, or even before in some countries in the Southern Cone. It is only in the 1950s, however, that these processes gained social visibility via increased access to public education and the development of mass media and industries for cultural production. From that moment onward, professionalization of cultural producers and the segmentation of the consumers' domain becomes a collective experience; cultural production increasingly lies in the hands of the communication industry, and the world is more and more divided into consumer groups. The production of culture is no longer a shared experience or a global offer. The production of culture falling to a few specialized professionals, and the fragmentation of audiences makes it necessary to examine the media not only from a market perspective, but also from a cultural perspective. This implies that mass media and industrial cultural production should be considered a space for production and circulation of culture corresponding not only to technological innovations or movements of capital but also to *new forms of sensibility*, new modes of appropriation and *juissance*.

---

[3]On the cultural span of electronic visualization, see Anceschi et al., *Video-culturas de fin de siglo* and, on the complicity between electronic visualization and orality, my "Libros y medios: nuevos modos de leer."

These new sensibilities are parallel to the new forms of socialization which people confront today with the symbolic heterogeneity of the City and the impossibility of seizing it. These processes, which M. Maffesoli calls new forms for encountering (*El tiempo*)—those of exclusion, recognition and clashes—give social and cognitive significance to the events which occur on and through the mass media and the new communicative technologies. It is from this perspective that the mass media have begun to construct a new image of public space, to mediate in the production of a new imaginary which in some way integrates the disjointed urban experience of its citizens. Examined from another point of view, the fragmentation which people experience provides the media—especially TV—with an opportunity to create a somewhat global vision of the city and the society, which makes the world more comprehensible and to a certain point, "reasonable." For this motive, television dematerializes culture, strips it of its historic weight and proposes—in close association with video clips and video games—discontinuity as the dominant perceptive habit.

Any analysis of the relationship between communication and modernity in Latin America requires that we reexamine all theoretical baggage or ideological ballast which might impede our analysis of the cultural industries as sources of the disorganization and reorganization of the social experience (García Canclini, *Culturas*). At the heart of these issues we find deterritorializations and relocations caused by social migrations and by the fragmentation of urban experience. This is a new experience that might overthrow that painstakingly maintained division which put massification or industrialization of cultural commodities as opposed to social development, allowing the elite to embrace technological modernity with enthusiasm while at the same time to maintain a strong rejection of and nausea from the democratization and expansion of cultural power and creativity.

We must rethink the relationship between politics and culture, recognize the connection between cultural policies and the transformation of political culture and link these to the crises of political parties and labor unions. In other words, we must examine the crisis within the traditional forms of arranging consensus and settling disputes, because it would enable us to understand the communicative importance of political culture. Oscar Landi has repeatedly proposed that political culture is a mode of interpellation between social actors, a mode in which they constitute themselves as subjects (*Reconstrucciones* and "Videopolítica"). Thus, the communicative web of politics cannot be reduced only to the street theater nor to the staged TV spectacle, as it has to do with the convocation, and the netting of interpellation and discourses with which social actors constitute themselves. For that reason, the transformation of modernity in the arena of communication cannot be reduced to a mere matter of markets and technologies. Communication has become the decisive space in the redefinition of the public and in the construction of democracy.

New National Images and New Latin American Imaginary

Modernization as we experience it today involves a displacement of the mass media from the position which they occupied in the first wave of modernization (in the decades of the 1930s through the 1950s).[4] This first wave was heavily influenced by the populist styles of leaders such as Vargas in Brazil, Cárdenas in Mexico, and Perón in Argentina. In these first years of the process of modernization, the media played a decisive role in the formation and diffusion of a sense of a national identity. The concept of modernization which underlies this process of construction of national identities in the 1930s links an economic movement with a political goal. The economic movement toward the inclusion of Latin American economies into the international market is linked to the formation of a sense of national identity by means of the creation of a national culture, a "national feeling" in words of that period. This political goal is achievable only through *communication* between the urban masses and the State. The media, particularly radio, became the means by which the State spread its message which would convert the masses into a people and the people into a nation. The populist caudillos found in radio a medium which allowed a new means of communication and the emergence of a new political discourse which broke with the rhetorical tradition of sermons and parliamentary discourse. Oscar Landi, in his study of Perón's discourse, states that Perón is the first to call laborers and farm workers "citizens." This new discourse, which spread via the radio, was profoundly affected by "popular" language, particularly in its capacity to re-elaborate the rules of oral discourse.

As well, the media allowed those people living in the provinces and remote areas to participate in the experience of integration into a nation. In particular, the radio—and in some countries film—acts as a mediator between rural cultures and the new urban cultures. These media organs introduced elements of an oral culture, which was based on an expressive/symbolic rationality, into a modernity based upon instrumental rationality.

---

[4]For an analysis of the role of media in this earliest modernization, see my "Modernidad y massmediación en América Latina."

The processes we experience today in many respects are the inverse: the media are one of the most powerful agents of devaluation of national identity (Schward, "Nacional"). What is configured today through media is the emergence of a culture with no territorial memory—particularly in the perceptions of young people. This culture defies especially the images which educators and intellectuals have about concepts of national identity. How difficult it is for us, adults, not to project upon these new deterritorialized perceptions—such as those aroused by music and video—the basic dichotomy founding of the nation-states in the first wave of modernization! But the media has introduced today a different order of cultural organization which is not reducible to national/antinational terms. And this is so because the media has put into play at the same time the globalization and the fragmentation of culture.[5] The media, from the written press through radio to television, are the ones most interested in "differentiating" segments of society by region, by profession, by gender or by age. Radio programming, particularly on FM stations, provides a clear example: "old" programming aimed at large audiences has given way entirely to programming aimed at an ever more segmented and compartmentalized listening group.

The devaluation of a national ethos comes not only from the effects of the deterriorialization resulting from circuits of global interconnection, economy and culture, but also from an internal erosion producing "a liberation of differences," particularly between regions and generations. Viewed from the perspective of planetary culture, national culture seems provincial and full of the state ballast: viewed from the perspective of diverse local cultures, national culture is identified with centralist pressures for homogeneity and ritualistic rigidity. National culture's domain is therefore surpassed in both directions, radically redefined by the new concept of national boundaries. What meaning can geographic boundaries have in a world in which satellites and information networks can violate every minute at will what we understood as national sovereignty? Where is the concept of sovereignty in today's world at play, when satellites can map subsurface riches, and when important information escapes ritual State control and circulates through "informal" networks? The very concept of national boundaries has lost references and with this is lost the concept of nation which inspired our previous configuration of the cultural world. Obviously, geographical boundaries still exist, but they delineate other "worlds" and in a different way. Are not

---

[5]For a consideration on this matter, see A. Mattelart, *L'Internationale publicitaire*, and G. Richeri, *L'universo telematico: il lavoro e la cultura del prossimo domani*.

geographical boundaries probably more insurmountable than the "old" boundaries of class and race, or the new technological and generational barriers?

Despite the deterritorialization produced by the movement toward globalization in both the economic and the cultural spheres, and despite the erosion which pushes back the revitalization of the local and its fight for its rights and for its own images and narratives, the concept of nation still retains validity as a strategic place for resistance to domination and as a mediator for the long memory of its people, the same which makes possible dialogue between generations.[6] But this concept of nation cannot be mistaken with the various forms of intolerance and dogmatism which we have witnessed in several outbreaks of nationalism in Europe. It is precisely this movement toward the breaking down of boundaries which the Western world is experiencing that offers a potential for increasing particularisms—those which, although responding to historic injustices, do not abandon an enormous ambiguity.

What new meanings acquire the Latin American within this re-invention of images of national identity? It has been many years since the media have integrated a Latin American imaginary. It has been many years since the music industry and radio fashioned music, whether tango, ranchera, bolero or today's salsa, as a meeting place. This "place" allowed Latin Americans to come together to listen, to dance, to enjoy themselves together, to live together. However, the media, the cultural industries of radio, television and film, are working inside a new situation. We see the paradox that the integration *of* Latin American nations is now inextricably tied to their integration *into* a world economy ruled by the purest and harshest market logic and supported by a technological revolution which generates a new form of dependency.

It is in the name of Latin American integration that many of our countries justify the enormous social costs of this "opening": this economic and technological modernization threatens again to support the social project of modernity in our countries. In the field of communication more than in any other, we see the inescapable necessity and the "insurmountable" contradictions of integration. The mass media, new technology and information networks give impetus to a powerful movement toward surpassing barriers and dissolving borders. But the same new technologies also accelerate the integration of our people and our cultures into a global market.

---

[6]See Ernest Gellner, *Cultura, identidad y política. El nacionalismo y los nuevos cambios sociales,* and Eric J. Hobsbawm, *Nações e nacionalismo desde 1780.*

What kind of integration can market forces produce by themselves?[7] How does integration into a global communication network affect the everyday lives of our people? We have just begun to experience the hybridization of and resistance to this movement. However, we may already appreciate the enormous power which the cultural industries, particularly the audiovisual industries, wield in the strategic area of the production and reproduction of the images with which those peoples define themselves and present themselves to the rest of the world. If it is important that Latin American corporations such as Televisa or Redeglobo stake their territory in audiovisual global space, it is also disturbing that these corporations end up molding an image of these people for the sake of neutral, everyday more undifferentiated audiences, and also dissolving the differences into cheap and marketable exoticism (Getino *Introducción* and *Cine*).

The film industry has been caught between the withdrawal of the State from production—which has produced a radically abrupt decreasing of cinema production—and the diminishing number of spectators. From 1982 to 1988, the number of moviegoers in Argentina fell from 45 to 22 million, and from 123 to 61 million in Mexico. Movie making is seen today as a solely commercial project, worthwhile only if it is capable of "overcoming" national boundaries. As a cultural project, movie making is viable only when it is able to articulate local themes with the sensibility and the aesthetics of world culture.

With respect to television, we see a shift toward an internationalization of contents and the replacement of quality criteria with purely technical sophistication.[8] This is most "visible" in the two formats which occupy the largest space on Latin America television: commercial announcements and soap operas. Commercials occupy a privileged place beyond that which economic importance might imply. In their experimentation with images through computing technology a renewal of the forms or representation of modernity is apparent. Commercial images and video clips draw aesthetically closer every day and increasingly allow for a mediation between technological innovation and narrative transformation. In a similar fashion, soap operas, weighty with dense narrative schematisms and an accomplice for ideological inertias, also play a decisive role in the reproduc-

---

[7]See M. Castells and R. Laserna, "La nueva dependencia. Cambio tecnológico y reestructuración socioeconómica en Latinoamérica," and J. Sutz, "Ciencia, tecnología e integración latinoamericana: un paso más allá del lugar común."

[8]See Regina Festa and L.F. Santoro, "A tercera edade da TV: o local e o internacional."

tion devices of a Latin American imaginary (Martín-Barbero, "Telenovela"). In this, we witness both new processes for the construction of identity and a long-term experience which allows cultural industries to capture the ritualized dimensions of daily life in the repetitive structure of series. Understanding this imaginary is a task of anthropological scope, for what is at stake is not only the displacement of capital and technological innovations, but also a deep-seated transformation of the culture of the majorities.

Cali, Colombia; August 1992
Translated by Gail González

Works Cited

Anceschi, G., et al. *Videoculturas fin de siglo*. Madrid: Cátedra, 1990.

Baudrillard, J. "El éxtasis de la comunicación." In *La postmodernidad*. Barcelona: Kairós, 1985. 187-98.

Brunner, J. J. *Los debates sobre la modernidad y el futuro de América Latina*. Santiago: FLACSO, 1986.

—. *Tradicionalismo y modernidad en la cultura Latinoamericana*. Santiago: FLACSO, 1990.

Castells, M., and R. Laserna. "La nueva dependencia. Cambio tecnológico y reestructuración socioeconómica en Latinoamérica." *David y Goliath* (Buenos Aires) 55 (1989).

Festa, Regina and L.F. Santora. "A terceira idade da TV: o local e o internacional." In *Rede imaginária: televisão e democracia*. São Paulo: Companhia das Letras, 1991. 179-95.

Fox, Elizabeth, ed. *Medios de comunicación y política en América Latina: la lucha por la democracia*. México: G. Gili, 1989.

García Canclini, Néstor. *Culturas híbridas: estrategias para entrar y salir de la modernidad*. México: Grijalbo, 1990.

Gellner, Ernest. *Cultura, identidad y política. El nacionalismo y los nuevos cambios sociales*. Barcelona: Gedisa, 1989.

Getino, Octavio. *Introducción al espacio audiovisual latinoamericano*. Buenos Aires: Instituto Nacional de Cinematografía, 1990.

—. *Cine latinoamericano: economía y nuevas tecnologías*. Buenos Aires: Legasa, 1988.

González, Fernán E. "Etica pública, sociedad moderna y secularización." *Colombia, una casa para todos: debate ético*. Santa Fe de Bogotá: Programa por La Paz, Compañía de Jesús, 1991.

Gutiérrez Giradot, Rafael. *Modernismo: supuestos históricos y culturales*. México: Fondo de Cultura Económica, 1987.

Habermas, Jurgen. *El discurso filosófico de la modernidad*. Madrid: Taurus, 1989.

——. *Teoría de la acción comunicativa*. Madrid: Taurus, 1987.

Hobsbawm, Eric J. *Nações e Nacionalismo desde 1780*. São Paulo: Paz e Terra, 1991.

Landi, Oscar. *Reconstrucciones. Las nuevas formas de la cultura política*. Buenos Aires: Puntosur, 1988.

——. "Videopolítica y cultura." *DIA-LOGOS de la comunicación* (Lima) 29: 1991.

Lyotard, J. F. "La naturaleza del lazo social." *La condición postmoderna*. Madrid: Cátedra, 1984.

Maffesoli, M. *El tiempo de las tribus*. Barcelona: Icaria, 1990.

Martín-Barbero, Jesús. "Comunicación y ciudad: entre medios y miedos." *Imágenes y reflexiones de la cultura en Colombia*. Bogotá: Colcultura, 1990.

——. "Libros y medios: nuevos modos de leer." *Revista de El Espectador* (Bogotá) 474 (1992).

——. "Modernidad y massmediación en América Latina." *De los medios a las mediaciones: comunicación, cultura y hegemonía*. México: Gustavo Gili, 1987.

——. "Telenovela: melodrama e identidad." *Cortocircuito* (Lima) 15 (1991).

——. "Violencia televisada: sociedad y comunicación." *Revista de la Universidad Central* (Bogotá) 33: 1989.

Mattelart, A. *L'Internationale publicitaire*. Paris: La Decouverte, 1989.

Ramos, Julio. *Desencuentros de la modernidad en América Latina*. México: Fondo de Cultura Económica, 1989.

Richeri, G. "Crisis de la sociedad y crisis de la televisión." *Contratexto* (Lima) 4 (1989).

——. *L'universo telematico: il lavoro e la cultura del prossimo domani*. Bari: De Donato, 1982.

Schwarz, Roberto. "Nacional por substracción." *Punto de vista* (Buenos Aires) 28 (1987): 15-22.

Sutz, J. "Ciencia, tecnología e integración latinoamericana: un paso más allá del lugar común." *David y Goliath* (Buenos Aires) 56 (1990).

Vattimo, Gianni. "Ciencias humanas y sociedad de la comunicación." *La sociedad transparente*. Barcelona: Paidós, 1990. 89-110.

Zallo, R. *Economía de la comunicación y la cultura*. Madrid: Akal, 1988.

Zemelman Merino, Hugo, ed. *Cultura y política en América Latina*. México: Siglo XXI, Editorial de las Naciones Unidas, 1990.

IN MEXICO:

MEXICAN *OFICIO*: THE MISERIES AND SPLENDORS OF CULTURE
Roger Bartra

In order to hide its nakedness in times of scarcity, the jewels and treasures of Mexican "official culture" have been sent to New York, the northern metropolis.[1] Its proponents dream of flaunting their artistic splendors before the stunned eyes of savage millionaires, thus warming the cold heart of the United States. And, as always, they try to affirm its identity through a confrontation with Anglo-American culture and, in doing so, strengthen the waning legitimacy of the Mexican political system.

Mexican "official culture" is displaying thirty centuries of Mexican splendor to the world. I would like to take this opportunity to reflect on the way in which "official culture" is generated. The concept can be understood from two different angles. First, as an ethnologist I can demonstrate that there is a culture which emulates from the offices of the government, and which impregnates the exercise of authority. It is an ensemble of habits and values that identify the behaviour of Mexico's political and bureaucratic class; a swarm of college-graduates, professionals and leaders who share folklore and customs that are worthy only of being carefully catalogued in order to be put in museum storage. Painters have already begun this task: Covarrubias, in his celebrated painting, *The Bone*, captured the typical Mexican bureaucrat with extraordinary irony.

---

[1]This essay was originally presented at the "Mexico, Here and There" conference that was held at Columbia University in November 1990. This event constituted the sole attempt to a critical look at the implications of *Mexico: The Splendors of Thirty Centuries*, the blockbuster exhibition that opened at New York's Metropolitan Museum that fall. "Mexico, Here and There" was organized by Lucha Libre Productions, an independent, interdisciplinary organization dedicated to developing critical awareness of contemporary Mexican culture in New York.

First published by *Third Text. Third World Perspectives on Contemporary Art & Culture* 14 (1991): 5-15. Reprinted by permission of the author.

Second, we find that these same government offices issue a stamp of approval for artistic and literary creation, to restructure it in accordance with established canons. This peculiar reconstruction is also part of what I call "official culture": but let it be understood that I do not mean that the writers and artists themselves are the official spokespersons of governmental culture (although this is the case with a few of them). Nonetheless, there is a close relationship between the folklore of government offices and the form that the reconstruction of official culture takes: together they can be seen as the practice of a Mexican *oficio*.[2]

In as much as there is a Holy Office with prayers, psalms and songs that mark the canonical hours, there is also a Mexican *oficio* that marks out national periods in accordance with the official established canons. There is a Mexican *oficio* that recounts and chants our national splendors. That Mexican *oficio* is the "official culture" that imprints its *nihil obstat* on the works of time. That Mexican *oficio* decrees that Mexico has been resplendent for thirty centuries.

Matins

At the dawn of history, the Olmecs raise their enormous, strange heads to contemplate us. In the tradition of the old argument invoked by Roger Fry since the beginning of the century, those first Mexicans are there to remind us that modernity is born marked by primitivism. Those figures of primitive art are

---

[2]Translator's note: Crucial to Roger Bartra's essay are the terms *oficio* and *cultura oficial*, which are loaded with culturally specific meanings whose significance would not be evident in any attempt at direct translation. Both are polysemantic terms that Bartra uses to underscore the symbolically charged nature (and religious fervor) of state control over representations of national identity and culture. While *oficio* can mean craft, trade profession or metier, it also carries the ecclesiastical implication of referring to the Holy or Divine Office. In Mexico, *cultura oficial* (literally, official culture) is the culture sanctioned and promoted through a variety of governmental mechanisms that play a more substantial role in cultural management than similar institutions in the United States or Britain. *Cultura oficial*, then, comes to represent an idea of national identity. Although "mainstream culture" might be considered to be an English equivalent, I chose to avoid such a transfer of terminology because of an apparent distinction in racial valorization, i.e. Mexican official culture's emphasis on its indigenous and mestizo components.

there so that we, modern Mexicans, recognize ourselves in them and see in their otherness the hidden and buried part of our national self. It concerns an old and well known topic of art history, but in Mexico it has once again been made functional since mid-century by the frantic search for "Mexican-ness" that accompanied the modernization boom of the post-war period.

In keeping with this argument, the origin of contemporary Mexican art is to be found on the coast of the Gulf of Mexico and not in the Mediterranean or the Middle East. Contrary to appearances, it decrees that our roots lie more in the figures of Precolumbian codices than in the verses of the Old Testament. This is a cultural decision that can only be understood fully if history is read against the grain of time: it is from the *here and now* of the present—from the perspective of the current Mexican state—that the thirty centuries of Mexican art make sense. The reasoning of the State, in involving itself in culture, is naturalized. Geography becomes an immense living setting for history; the earth becomes the fertile mother in whose body grow the deep roots of national culture. Nature is the first element that gives unity and continuity to cultural history. It is a certain idea of nature in which volcanoes, fauna, forests, valleys, and lakes are no longer simply part of geography; rather, they metamorphose into the anatomy of the living body of culture. Because of this, José María Velasco and Doctor Atl[3] are considered indispensable elements of Mexican art; they are testimony and at the same time creatures of the palpitating landscape that defines the parameters of the nation-state.

I do not mean to say that a consciousness of origin and of landscape is simply an ideological formation created by the Mexican state to trick the dominated population. Cultural processes do not have a legitimating, cohesive and homogenizing effect simply because they are instruments of the ruling classes. Still, if "official culture" has an instrumental character, it cannot be explained as other than being a function of the complex process that nourishes it. Through that process an amalgam of myths about Mexican identity is created.

Unlike a Weberian interpretation of society, modern society had not ceased to generate myths. One of these myths is precisely that of a national character. In Mexico this myth has crystallized in what I call, jokingly, the axol-

---

[3]José María Velasco (1840-1912) painted idealized landscapes of the Mexican countryside. Dr. Atl (Gerardo Murillo, 1875-1964) was best known for his series of paintings of the El Paricutin volcano and for his aerial landscapes.

otl[4] canon. This canon orders and classifies the features of the Mexican character in accordance with a basic duality: the Mexican is an amphibian being who oscillates between the rural savagery of the melancholic Indians and the artificial and disturbing aggressiveness of the urban underclass. In my book, *The Cage of Melancholy*, I carry out an anatomical dissection on the amphibian myth that is Mexico's national identity. The result is that this operation might surprise many sociologists, because it shows that the rationality inherent in the unification of the modern States requires a mythological structure to maintain its legitimacy. There is no purely rational legitimacy that emanates from capitalist economic structures or the modern bureaucracy. The legitimacy of modern political systems generates a mythology capable of creating the "subject" of the capitalist state. This mythology develops around the notion of national culture and, more specifically, around the conception of a national character.

Laud

We can praise the first twenty-five centuries of Mexican splendor which represent that singular, primordial otherness without which national culture could not exist. But with laudatory words it is not possible to create a continuity which was broken by Conquest and colonization. The ancient artistic traditions were annihilated in a few years. Nonetheless, a cultural continuum is spoken of insistently, one which, over the abyss opened by the Conquest, extends a bridge between Precolumbian Mesoamerica and colonial and independent Mexico.

We recognize that 20th century Mexican artists have searched intensely through Precolumbian culture for formal and spiritual values. What they found enriched their own creations, but it's doubtful if they contributed to filling the immense void left by the destruction of ancient societies. "Official culture" has also made a leap of many centuries in search of a foundation for the modern state in ancient Mesoamerica.[5] In the same way, the critique of political authori-

---

[4]The axolotl is a Mexican salamander, an amphibian that lives and breeds without metamorphosing.

[5]The archeological excavation of the "Templo Mayor" in the middle of Mexico City is an example of the use of spectacle to connect the present with Precolumbian history.

tarianism has looked for the origins of presidentialism in the ancient Nahuatl *tlatoani*.[6]

Many would consider it useless to look to history for the formal or stylistic continuity of Prehispanic art in colonial and modern Mexico. The only continuity that really exists is hardly accepted outside ethnographic museums; the millions of marginalized indigenous people are the only maltreated bridge that remains: they are a symbolic reference of the past, but they are accustomed to being rejected as an active presence.[7] In his introductory essay in the *Mexico: Splendors of Thirty Centuries* exhibition catalogue Octavio Paz indicates how the problem of continuity has been resolved; throughout an incredible variety of forms we find the persistence of one sole *will*, the will to survive in and by means of form.[8] An attentive and loving look can perceive a continuity that is not manifested in style or ideas, but rather in something more profound: a sensibility. That will of form is nothing other than the transposition of the reason of the state onto the Mesoamerican past, an artistic past where the figure, the form, reveals the metamorphosis of a unitary will.

This game of transformations, of transfigurations, perfectly exemplifies an intellectual process that in theology is known as figural interpretation. It is frequently used by modern nationalism. Elsewhere, I have already discussed this phenomenon,[9] which goes beyond imaginative, metaphorical relations that artists establish between distant epochs and between different cultural spheres. We are faced with a delicate and complicated process that manages to establish in the collective consciousness a structural relation between two cultural dimensions that are distant from each other. This structural connection operates simultaneously on two levels, *mimesis* and *catharsis*. The mimetic element of the process finds similarity between the ancient cultural features of, for example, the Mexicas

---

[6]The *tlatoani*, or Nahuatl ruling figure, has traditionally been characterized as having been authoritarian.

[7]The political action of the National Institute of Indigenous Studies has been, for decades, an example of the rare combination of an official policy of exaltation of "Mexican roots" with the governmental practice of burying the indigenous people progressively more deeply in the mire of modern society.

[8]"Will for Form," *Mexico: Splendors of Thirty Centuries* (New York: The Metropolitan Museum of Art, 1990), 4.

[9]*La jaula de la melancolía* (México: Grijalbo, 1987).

or the Mayas and colonial or modern history. I am not going to expand much on this problem, but I do want to cite some of the themes that are usually found in the metahistorical link (*vinculación*): sacrifice, guilt, cyclical events, baroque exuberance, dualism, the cult of the virgin, etc. We find that current themes and conflicts are transposed onto a more or less imaginary past, so that there is a prefiguration of the scenes of modernity. This transposition onto an imaginary past is similar to that which occurs in the reconstruction that modern mythology has made of the *homo mexicanus*, an android whose anatomy must be known, since in it we find the keys to what I call the institutionalization of the national soul. Between the hunched Indian and the urban, underclass mestizo there extends a line that passes through the principal points of articulation of the Mexican soul: *melancholy—negligence—fatalism—inferiority—violence—sentimentalism—resentment—evasiveness*. This line marks the voyage that each Mexican must make to find himself, from the original natural Eden to the industrial apocalypse.

Prime

The spectacle that this cultural simulation offers permits us to signal the importance of another level, that of catharsis, in the connection between the dimension of the real and that of the imaginary. The scene of national culture is a space in which the feelings of a people can be released. This is where nationalism reaches its maximum efficiency, in securing an identification between politics and culture.

Nationalism is the transfiguration of supposed characteristics of national identity to the terrain of ideology. Nationalism is a political current that establishes a structural relation between the nature of culture and the peculiarities of the State. In our country the official expressions of nationalism tell us: if you are Mexican you should vote for the institutionalized revolution. Those who do not are traitors to their deepest essence, or they are not Mexican. Nationalism is, therefore, an ideology that disguises itself with culture to hide the intimate means of domination. But in order for this identification between politics and culture to be successful, it is necessary that a process of sedimentation must have been produced in the country, one that separates the elements that are generally considered national from those ingredients that are not specifically national. This is a complex process that cannot be generated artificially: that is to say, neither the state, nor the ruling classes can instrument this process from above. It must be a global process, in which multiple factors interact, among them the same formation of the nation-state. Based on this process the ruling class can establish its cultural hegemony through the use of a nationalist ideology. But this is not the only way in which a social class can establish its hegemony. I would say that the nationalist means is one of its most dangerous forms. It can lead to the institutionalization of a pernicious authoritarian nationalism, as it has in Mexico. And it is even more pernicious when nationalism provokes a collective catharsis, thanks to which it legitimates a way of engaging in politics as the *only* way of being Mexican.

Terce

We live in the age of the collapse of great ideological blocks; that being the case, cultural criticism is becoming increasingly important. There are a variety of ways to conceive cultural criticism. In Mexico it has been common to engage in criticism from an outdated rationalist perspective. This is to say, from the perspective of modernity: it is essential, it is said, that Mexican culture be "modernized" to adapt it to the requirements of mass culture and industrialization. This proposition quickly leads to a dilemma: do we recreate national culture in accordance with a "true" popular culture, or do we accept the transnational invasion of the new mass culture? But these alternatives rapidly reveal themselves as false, because national culture is precisely the amalgam of these two options, and therefore complementary. By this I mean that the modernization of Mexican culture has already occurred. What I call the exercise of "official culture" is precisely the result of the national culture's modernization, not an archaic and premodern vice that we must reactivate, or even destroy, to give way to modern culture.

What I criticize is precisely the modernity of national culture. It is its modernity that oppresses us, since from it has emanated an authoritarianism that characterizes the Mexican system. The current dilemma, therefore, is not about having to choose between the populist option and a transnational proposal: it is enough to turn on a Mexican television set to note that hegemonic culture has already managed to overcome this contradiction, in imposing a culture that is profoundly patriotic and aggressively aligned with the mass culture produced in the United States. When I look at these problems from the perspective of postmodernity, I suggest that the lines of fire have changed and the contradictions have been displaced into other territories. We can no longer critique Mexican culture in the name of modernity, of a modernity of liberal inspiration that raises the flag of "progress." It is necessary to criticize modernity from the position of *la desmodernidad.*[10]

Sext

There now emerges the sense that we should distinguish three phenomena: national identity, cultural politics and official political culture. In examining the relationships between these three aspects, we should see that they concern the connection between the formation of a myth (identity), its intersection with institutional life (cultural politics) and the ideology that attempts to explain and direct this process (official culture).

The myth of national identity is not a real ideological phenomenon serving as an instrument for the dominant class or for the government. In order for the myth to integrate into political culture in, shall we say, "natural" and lasting form, diverse conditions are necessary, ones that would take too long to explain here. Suffice to say that it concerns an overflow of historic opportunities that are transfiguring and transposing various elements leading toward the relative homogenization and coherence of political culture. The government's political culture, for its part, is an ideological expression which, among many other functions, utilizes cultural manifestations to legitimate the system. An example: the circulation of Mexican culture defines the space of that which is officially national. Nonetheless, official cultural policy only lightly modifies the constitution of Mexican political culture. The *fotonovelas*, private television, comic books, commercial music, detective fiction, plebeian best sellers and pornographic and romantic novels continue to exert enormous influence. Much as they might be denigrating "foreign" manifestation, they form an equally integral part of Mexican political culture. On the other hand, the myth of the "Mexican soul" has managed, with success, not only to survive the avalanche of "foreign" influences, but also to insert itself in a long-lasting way into political culture.

---

[10]*Desmodernidad* is a play on words based on the terms *desmadre* (disorder, or more literally, a condition of disorder brought about by the absence of mother), *madre* (mother) and *modernidad* (modernity). Bartra coins this neologism to express what he sees as the current state of disruption and transcendence of modernity by forces that may have once been American or foreign, but in the postmodern age are now Mexican. (Translator's note)

The "Mexican soul" has a stable place in political culture precisely because it appears as something non-Western. The myth of the Mexican self has contributed to the legitimation of the political system, but was established as a mythical form which was hardly coherent with the development of Western capitalism typical of the end of this century. In other words, the myth is efficient for legitimating the power of the PRI,[11] but inefficient for legitimating the rationality of the factory. The myth is enclosed in the cage of melancholy, not in the iron cage of which Max Weber wrote in reference to industrial society. Of course, if one wishes, the myth corresponds to the peculiarities of a backward, corrupt and dependent form of capitalism. From there emerge the contradictions that Mexican contemporary culture lives: the myth of national identity is becoming dysfunctional. But this "dysfunctionalism" comes in large part from its "popular" and "anticapitalist" origin. The myth contains a good dose of protest, of bitterness, of disorder, of resistance; this circumstance explains the popularity of the Mexican stereotype.

None

The idea of the dividing line, the wound or the border is an important ingredient in the configuration of national identity. In Mexico this should be understood, at least, in two ways. First as a tear or internal wound: Mexicanness split between the destroyed indigenous ancient world and the colonial, Christian modern world. In the second place, the great border that separates Mexico from the potentially hostile territory of Anglo-American culture. Without a doubt, the confrontation with the Other of the North has stimulated the definition of Mexican identity. But here we find a pious medieval and Christian idea: it was necessary to go to the land of the Moors, temptation and suffering were needed to reaffirm the faith. The border is a permanent threat. The border is a constant source of contamination and threats to Mexican nationality. The very existence of the border is that which permits, therefore, the tense maintenance of nationalist passions. It permits, shall we say, a permanent state of alert before the threats from outside. It is clear that this principally functions at a symbolic level, since the demographic reality of hundreds of thousands of Mexicans that come and go

---

[11]The PRI (Partido Revolucionario Institucional) is Mexico's ruling political party and has been (under different names) since the revolution.

across the border (more go than come) generates a sociocultural process of *mestizaje*[12] and symbiosis that no nationalist discourse can stop.

Although the dialectic of self and other has played an important role, it is necessary to recognize that the long border has also been a wide space of interaction. I do not think that, from the perspective of culture, we should be alarmed by what is happening at the border. What we are accustomed to call an "Americanization" of life at the border is not an especially damaging and dangerous process. As an anthropologist, I cannot conceive of a border territory between two cultures in which transcultural processes do not occur. Any attempt to impede them would be, at best, utopian. Some North Americans are also alarmed by the "Mexicanization" of border life: they have the same conservative and reactionary impulse that chauvinist Mexicans exhibit.

This does not mean that there are no problems at the border; rather, they are principally the political problems of a relationship between two states. One is a wealthy state run by imperialist leaders and the other is a poor state monopolized by authoritarian leaders. The mechanical transposition of political problems onto the territory of culture will only lead to the deformation of our perception of a situation that is extraordinarily complex.

All Mexicans and Latin Americans who have lived in the United States know that the Latin American does not end at the Rio Bravo: there is a profound penetration of the Latin continent in the Anglo-American sociocultural world. In the United States, the "Hispanic" community, economy, politics and culture are vast and exercise notable influence on American society. Mexican nationalism has traditionally refused to recognize this fact, since the "Mexicanization" of life in the United States is seen rather from another perspective: as the "Americanization" of Mexicans. As we are used to saying, some see the glass half empty, others, half full.

Vespers

At the dawn of a new era, which is leading us we know not where, Mexican culture lives tensions that are pulling it apart. The thirty centuries of splendors fall over the heads of Mexican writers and artists like a bewildering avalanche; but in its outline can be seen no more than an eternal present, folded back onto itself: the cultural context seems to have been constructed yesterday

---

[12]*Mestizaje* is the Latin American term for cultural and racial hybridization.

and to be at the point of falling apart. In the daily cultural landscape—a semblance of our urban surroundings—the past hardly exists and lives in the fragility of a dream that ends every morning when one wakes in a miserable and backward world. The creators are followed by a forbidding sensibility of refulgent will that hides in the dark side of the myth. They are obliged to express an identity that does not belong to them: they are compelled by an ancient originality they do not understand. All should create suppurating from the same wound and hurting from the same border or fracture. All should be countrymen of the same landscape and suffer its geography in the same way.

At the dawn of a gray financial battle, which for Mexico should open the doors of the mercantile paradise that is shared with the northern powers, "official culture" adapts the famous Napoleonic discourse to current times: *"soldiers of culture, from the height of these pyramids thirty centuries contemplate you!"* In the adaptation there are ten centuries less than those that contemplated Bonaparte in Egypt in 1798, but it was not prudent to invoke the barbarism of descendants much too close to the man of Tepexpan. . . . The triumphalist vision of Mexican cultural history seems to continue the old recipes of orientalism, which used to concentrate the entire history of non-Western countries in grand packages of resplendent exoticism. It is the cult of museum culture, which integrates in grand block sums, until it constructs monuments of pyramidal splendor, in which characteristics of individual creation are usually lost, flattened with the mass of symbols: jaguars, eagles, baroque angels, violently colored tropics, inflamed revolutionaries, suffering women. In the interstices of the grand granite symbols, there remain, often flattened, living intellectuals inhabiting a world whose new signs they have not yet learnt how to decodify. Therefore writers and artists run the risk of staying trapped in the loneliness of a dense jungle of national symbols, or involved in a war against words, in an effort to manoeuvre them like a flock toward the triumphal splendor of the signs of identity.

Compline

The canonical hours of national identity are complete. The circle of immanence closes, the service ends and satiates us. Nationalism has invented a Mexican that is the metaphor of permanent underdevelopment, the image of frustrated progress. This devalued self only makes sense inside the networks of official political power. It is a being that survives thanks to the State. The individual is seen as an unfinished and worm-like being, whose metamorphosis can only occur in the breast of the revolutionary state.

But the revolutionary state has reached its end and the Mexican service is becoming an office for the dead. It is not modernization that is bringing about its extinction, but rather postmodernity: that is to say, the tensions brought about by an excess of modernity, in a context of fragile modernization. Here I translate, and I hope not abusively, the literary notion of modernism to political theory: *modernity* is a revolt against the rigidity of the old oligarchical order, in search of political forms that are free but circumscribed and unified by symbolic structures and imaginary nationals. Therefore modernity is a specific form that civil society adopts, it is a structure of cultural mediation that legitimates the political system. *Modernization* is, in usual sociological terminology, the capitalist transformation of a society, based on industry, science, and secular institutions. Modernity is the *imaginary country* whose legitimating network traps civil society. Modernity is the *real state* of capitalist social and economic development.

In Mexico we have had an excess of modernity, to the point that its weight has become unbearable: national identity is excess, exorbitant nationalism, unmeasured revolution, extra symbolism. . . . We have borne hardly seventy years of institutionalized modernity, but it seems as if it has been thirty centuries! On the other hand, as was shown by the crisis of 1982, our modernization is fragile and a failure in many senses. The country is replete with modernity, but thirsty for modernization; that is the disagreeable paradox: behind the "splendors of thirty centuries" we discover the "miseries of thirsty centuries."

Postmodernity with all its bitterness has brought us, nonetheless, the hope of escaping these flattening metadiscourses. The experience of a fragmented Mexico—the Mexico of here and there—and the constant transgression of all borders, political and cultural, is one of the stimulating symptoms of the last years: it is a way of living that, far from shutting off the creative impulses of the Mexican intelligentsia, has opened new perspectives. One of the most refreshing effects of what Guillermo Gómez-Peña calls the "borderization" of the world[13] is the proof that it is possible, we say here, to be Mexican without subjecting oneself to a State or territory: this deterritorialization and denationalization of the intellectuals is beginning to define the profile of the postmodern experience. We do not know where this path will take us, but we hope that cultural life will not have, as its only future, a pedestal in the glass cases of museums.

Translated by Coco Fusco

---

[13]Guillermo Gómez-Peña, "Wacha Esa Border, Son," *La Jornada Semanal*, October 25, 1987.

IN BRAZIL:

LOUSY POETRY, WORSE SOCIETY

Iumna Maria Simon
Vinícius Dantas

Less than a hundred years ago Parnassianism dominated the Brazilian poetry scene.[1] This school promulgated the restraint and passivity which indulged the Franco-Greco-Latin aesthetic whims of our elites. An embodiment of the Belles Lettres concept, it was perfectly adapted to the pretensions of elegance and superiority of the half-austere, half-bohemian bourgeoisie. Since then, poetry's cultural expression has swung from one extreme to the other—from that ideal of gentility and propriety which was bestowed from the "ivory tower" to the immediacy of informal convention, based on spontaneous appearance (not exclusively literary), and fleshed out by everyday situations. The catalyst for this change was an attitude by the avant-garde that repudiated all traditional literary conventions, while internalizing what is generically known as a "crisis of representation." Thanks to modernist good sense, the concept of modernity here inaugurated, and soon brought to maturity among the poets of the 1930s generation, was successfully translated into a response to the demands of the Brazilian sociocultural context, multiplying the possibilities of poetic representation without losing its connection to the crisis of language. From negation to negation, reluctantly untangling itself from the bourgeois order and its esteem for poetry's literary value, contemporary poetic expression does not distance itself from everyday language and experience, neither does it aspire to formal idealization. As a response to the crisis of representation, poetry became rooted in the natural, less exacting soil of real-life consumer society, which explains why it shifted to more anti-literary forms and anti-conventional attitudes, assuming the anti-traditionalist rhythm of the marketplace. Could it be that its capacity for sensible and critical apprehension of reality has been so democratized that poetry has become a mode of collectively knowing and communicating? Or has it become an acritical and devalued form of expression?

---

[1]Published originally in *Novos estudos CEBRAP* (São Paulo) 12 (June 1985): 48-61, this article is the result of more extensive research (in progress) about postmodernist Brazilian poetry, from the 1930s to its current manifestations.

One way or the other, the avant-garde's trajectory, initiated by Modernism, undoubtedly established the standards of competence and invention that have resulted in a new, up-to-date literary tradition. Although its latest unfolding has not produced works of significant poetic quality, the quest has yielded elaborate, curious by-products that follow the internal logic of a literary process which parallels modernity's global context. Certainly, there is much originality in its dynamics and proposed solutions: Brazilian poetry has managed to be, over the course of the last century, a literary form attuned to its living, contemporary environment, both nationally and internationally. In other words, if the Brazilian modernist poetry is modernist in the full sense implied by such a general concept, its present symptoms betray the specter of post-modernity that is beginning to sow its destructive effects.

Recently, an anthology which gathered together poetry of the 1970s was published under the title *Young Poetry*. The title does not imply simply poetry written by young people, but rather poetry written with a youthful spirit, which criterion is elevated to editorial and critical value. The title and criterion both adequately characterize the regressive sense of Brazilian poetry during that decade. Driven by an unyielding anti-literary sentiment, the new product forged by contemporary poets is the poem of easy access and appeal, directed at a teen audience who identify with the everyday experiences it describes, the playful and carefree attitude it exhibits. The development is analogous, in the music industry, to contemporary music, which is now completely devoid of its early rebellious nonconformist impulse. The foundation for the poetry of the 1970s was a movement called "Marginal Poetry," which proclaimed a decisive break with the literary standards of the day—the formal and existential asceticism of the avant-garde—in the name of actual experience and behavior.[2] By the end of the decade, its growth and offshoots indicated how much the movement had already become mainstreamed (despite—or on account of— its so-called marginality), responding to the tastes of young consumers, who thus acquired their own poetic corresponding to that of the culture industry.[3] This new poetic form had the

---

[2]For a minimum bibliography on this poetry, see: H. B. Hollanda, *26 poetas hoje*, and *Impressões de viagem*; C.A.M. Pereira, *Retrato de época*; A. C. Brito, "Tudo da minha terra: bate-papo sobre poesia marginal." While not exhaustive, this list presents interesting criticism.

[3]The movement's growth, not yet fully analyzed, is documented in *Poesia jovem* and in *O que é poesia marginal?*, an instructive little book by Glauco Mattoso, a brief overview of the movement's history that shows the inadequacy of definitions and the extraordinary growth the movement experienced well

advantage of dispensing with literary tradition and training, which in a country such as Brazil, are always perceived as values of the dominant classes. In truth, however, such cultural literacy is rare; the culture adopted by such classes is increasingly the culture of the mass media (primarily in its television form). The initial characteristics associated with marginal poetry, its nonconformist, anti-literary bent, rapidly evaporated, and today poetic production has sunk to the level of homogenized, standardized consumer commodities, but obviously without a corresponding infrastructure. The "new sensitivity" gains, in such a way, a mode of expression appropriate to current lifestyles, behavior, and relationships, at a moment when subjective experience, precluded from subjective stylistic expression, must revert to the anonymity of collective experience in which the individual has disappeared.[4]

This is the most characteristic feature of new Brazilian poetry, unless one interprets it, as some critics have, as mere cultural imitation, superficial parroting, which contributes little to an objective, critical assessment. It is important to notice that the movement took shape in the latest years of the decade (since the political "abertura" in 1978), and that it is known for its distinct editorial style, as well as by the flow of the old "Marginal" poets, late avant-garde, to the area of pop music. Their work thereby gained a circulation and popularity unknown to most of the earlier poets.[5] On the other hand, this poetry is filled with clichés and irreverent nonconformist posturing, while refusing to embrace obscurantism in the midst of a society living under the crushing burden of conservatism and authoritarianism—as witness the process of democratization, the ill-fated campaign for direct presidential elections, and the current transitional phase to a civilian government elected by an electoral college. Evidently, the movement is confined to those few cultural elites who enjoy correspondence with the more developed socialist societies. And now it has been able to overflow to other bases, as it becomes disseminated and domesticated through such mass

---

beyond the control of the Rio de Janeiro groups who started it.

[4]We are basing this diagnosis on Fredric Jameson's suggestive insights about postmodernity's cultural symptoms in the context of the late capitalist "postindustrial society," which may not necessarily fit the Brazilian reality completely. See his "Postmodernism and consumer society."

[5]One needs only to mention that in 1940 one of our greatest poets had to cover all the expenses to publish an edition of his own collected poetry, in order, after he was accepted into the Brazilian Academy of Letters, to have a volume in print. Manuel Bandeira was then, at age 50, already recognized as one of the most important modernist poets in the nation (see M. Bandeira, *Itinerário de pasárgada* 119).

media of unprecedented reach, such as magazines, records, radio, and television. In face of the evidence, it becomes hard to produce a balanced judgment—are we against or in favor of it? Do we defend the process and critique the poetry, or defend the poetry and critique the process? Or should we believe that behind the movement's success (and its unforeseen scope), rather unusual for a genre such as poetry, there is an exceptional increase in the population's literacy level (something Brazilian intellectuals have always struggled for), with a corresponding proportional increase in its quality?[6] Whatever one's position, it is essential to realize that this poetic movement is a transformative agent that creates a literary sensibility and increasingly registers its presence. Although its profile is not fully delineated, the movement has become an indispensable index in any appraisal of the cultural changes that have taken place in Brazilian poetry. Besides, it is not something completely detached from the previous history of Brazilian poetry; it echoes and responds, in its own way, to the most important events of Brazilian poetry's modern evolution—it is in fact their culmination. As a movement, Marginal Poetry casts a new light upon the poetry produced in the previous decades; after all, Concrete Poetry, the avant-garde of the 1950s, as well as the nationalist left-wing poetry of the 1960s both fought steadfastly to establish a poetics based on accessibility; poetry was supposed to reach the distracted urban dweller, said some, poetry was supposed to raise the alienated consciousness of the exploited worker, said others—and yet both addressed a public of no more than 500 readers, composed for the most part of middle-class intellectuals. These poets were misunderstood, persecuted, boycotted, and went through hell. And now, as our greatest poet would say, "What next, Joe, what next?"

"Without a utopian perspective, the movement loses its raison d'être"—declared last year the theoretician and concrete poet Haroldo de Campos, without probing any further into the historico-cultural consequences of the present crisis.[7] By 1984, it is apparent that the esprit de corps and emulation of

---

[6]The Brazil of today is a virtual factory of best-sellers; works that before never reached more than 2,000 copies, and never went out of print, now have multiplied. At the same time, one witnesses the modernization of the editorial market, despite its eternal deficiencies of distribution. The market now operates in conjunction with other media—thus, it is not rare that a best-seller becomes a mini-series, a movie, a play, or a subject for journalists.

[7]See Haroldo de Campos's long reflection on the subject in "Poesia e modernidade," published in two partes: "Da morte da arte a constelação," and "O poema pós-utópico." An outline of the several phases of Poesia Concreta, until the crisis of the avant-garde, is described in our introductory remarks to the volume *Poesia concreta*.

the avant-garde are no longer meaningful ideals. Their role has been eclipsed, or if there is any intervention nowadays, it is no longer motivated by a sense of critical protest, nor will it be resisted by a public hostile to its proposals. The expectation of conflict, or the planning of long-term creative projects are things of the past: slogans and tactics are nowhere to be seen. This realization on the part of the most important thinker in the Brazilian avant-garde was late in coming. After all, it was recognized by a number of literary critics during the 1960s that the utopia of the avant-garde had lost its radicalism and negativity (not to mention other harsher critics, who suspect that any movements sprung after the first two decades of this century are simply opportunist repetitions of the radical avant-gardes that emerged around the time of World War I).[8] Although not quite as disillusioned, Haroldo de Campos' realization touches a vital point: the total absence, on the poetic horizon, of any vestige of hope for a socially transformative project or praxis; the kind of hope that animated the avant-garde's impulses toward an ideal future, endowing them with a totalizing sense of finality. In this new reality, the future promises nothing, and the idea of utopia has lost its place; albeit that for the old concrete poet, poetry persists as a dignifying and valid experience, an experience of "symbolic concretization" that can still challenge hopelessness and provide a last guideline for action. For a poet like Haroldo de Campos, rooted in a "classic" concept of modernity that provides him with the understanding of poetic language as autonomous structure, what acquires value as a positive ideal of hope is the creative present (its "nowness"), through which the poet sustains a dialogue with words and signs. Thus his additional comment—"This poetry of presentness, to my thinking, must not be a poetry of surrender, must not be an alibi to eclectic thought and easy solutions." As the demands of the avant-garde dissipate, it becomes necessary to affirm poetry as an independent value, as an ideal form of language—an ideal that rejects pastiche and redundancy. In this diagnosis of contemporary despair it is evident that the adversities of the present historico-cultural context force a poet grounded in a certain tradition of modernity to re-think and re-formulate his premises, without illusions, making it imperative to salvage what critical elements he can while maintaining caution in the face of this new poetic sensibility. Nevertheless, will avoiding the bastardization of poetry be enough to preserve poetic language as rectification and resistance in this post-utopian landscape? To what extent is poetry itself a trans-historical value, untouched or undefiled by the poverty of

---

[8]These positions, with slight variations, are taken by several critics in more than one text. Among the better known are: Octavio Paz, *Los hijos del limo*; Hans Magnus Enzensberger, *As apórias da vanguarda*; Michel Hamburger, *The Truth of Poetry*; Daniel Bell, *The Cultural Contradictions of Capitalism*; and T.W. Adorno, *Esses anos vinte*.

postmodern poetic sensibility? Are the norms a poet chooses a reaction to and a questioning of the concrete historico-cultural conditions, or are they given by an ideal of modernity in which the poet is immersed and which he must enact?

For poets of other generations, little interested in modernity as such and given to little reflection on the matter, the experience of post-utopia is the empirical reality, not necessarily uncomfortable, but rather a sensory datum which profoundly informs their poetic expression. In the Brazilian case, we could point to 1968 as the watershed year of this poetic bankruptcy, being connected with Tropicalia, and the best films of Júlio Bressane, Rogério Sganzerla, and the late Glauber Rocha, among other manifestations of all that lately was mislabeled as Counterculture. This process was triggered internally by the stiffening authoritarianism of the military dictators who ruled the country, the turbulent climate of armed struggle, and the crisis of political legitimacy. Step by step, however, the disillusionment became less associated with the immediate consequences of political repression, only to reveal its broader spectrum and resemblance to the complex global effects of the present stage of advanced consumer society. To this process of assimilation, neither opposition movements nor radical, avantgarde artistic production, were immune, absorbed as they were into the demands of the cultural industry's routine. The failure of the projects that aimed at social and political transformation, the psychology of cynicism and impotence, and the lack of perspective that, from the margins, were once attributed to local political factors suddenly became, as if by magic, the everyday reality of post-modernity in Brazil. As relationships with international capitalism grew in Brazil and the country became more vulnerable, accentuating thereby the strict correspondence, previously less rigid, between core and periphery, the effects were felt not only in the country's economy but also in its cultural life. With the failure of the ideological and political program inaugurated in the 1960s, it became easier to discern the complex and paradoxical mixture of riches and misery present in the country, although in aesthetic terms, critical reflection on this point has a ways to go. The nationalist and pro-development ideology that served as a point of reference for the Brazilian artist eroded in the face of unequal and inequitable modernization, whose social and political costs fell upon the working classes and the majority of those excluded from participation in consumer society. This state of affairs directly affected cultural production, since modernization had become intrusive and violent, accommodating itself to the perpetuation of social stagnation and widespread poverty that a modern consumer society now reproduced. Obviously such contradictions shaped the Brazilian artist who, while on the one hand was closer than ever to the forms and trends of the international artistic scene, was at the same time exiled in an underdeveloped limbo, excluded from the dominion of the modern; the best songs of Caetano Veloso capture this feeling well and the ambiguity of its bittersweet, courageous melancholy.

The Tropicalia generation endured the transition from populist democracy to military authoritarianism in perplexity and despair; the generation who started to write in the early 1970s lived in a political wasteland, saw the immobilization of projects of social change, witnessing hopelessly and without illusions the consequence of unchecked rampant modernization. Cultural and artistic discussions then were reshaped by the media and the culture industry, which were increasingly organized according to the rigidity and logic of the marketplace. Thus, the first wave of Marginal Poetry, up until 1979, was marked by the affirmation of an independent, alternative space, in which production and consumption did not fall into the straitjacket of commercial editorial guidelines, but emphasized instead the artisan aspects of the production, distribution and dissemination of poetry. What used to be simply the normal conditions of a financially impoverished art form, frequently self- or group-financed, became (perhaps because of its artisan quality and by being a youthful enterprise) an ambiguous trademark and "political response to the reigning adversities" (Hollanda and Brito 81)—an interpretation given credence by its tone. One is left to question whether the "political response" was expressed in the content and forms of the given poetry, if it discerned a new social experience translated into alternative forms of socio-cultural relations and values, or if, more simply, its artisan form hindered its political tenor. The Marginal Poet's image was likened to the street peddler who sold his goods in bars, movie and theater ticket lines; and who promoted recitals, readings, happenings and even political parades to sell his product and open new channels of distribution.

It is, however, important to keep in mind that this marginal condition only makes sense when seen in the context of the years of political repression and censorship, when the public arena was preempted. This historical contingency greatly fueled the modus operandi of the movement, fostering its nonconformist, irreverent, and rebellious attitude as the poetic keynote of the new behavioral and existential practices of an alienated youth, lending the form a greater symbolic value than its poetic content. Toward the close of the decade, with the end of censorship and the first signs of political "abertura," Marginal Poetry was finally accepted and published by powerful and established publishing houses, to acclaim rather than censure. Its mainstreaming signaled the end, paradoxically, to the animated debates surrounding alternative modes of publication, marketing and distribution. As the question of poetic value had always been less urgent than the aesthetics of reception (the conquest of the audience being more important than poetic content), the movement was left without a leg to stand on when the artisan value ceased to matter.

The agenda proposed by Brazilian Marginal Poetry was small—it confined itself to denouncing the authoritarianism of past avant-gardes, especially those connected with the intellectual tradition of João Cabral de Melo Neto, and with advocating a "strategic retreat" (Hollanda, *26 poetas* 8)[9] to the modernist poetry found in the 1920s. It is important, however, to say that what is called Marginal Poetry's *agenda* here is in reality an inference of critics who lent their services to the first groups of marginal poets, and were searching for a theoretical framework of literary politics within which to situate them.[10]

With its emancipation from the marketplace and the dominance of the publishing industry frustrated, it only remains to examine this poetry's *poetic form*, which can perhaps result in objective insights concerning the content of this poetry, illuminating the consequences of its rejection of literariness. What a serious critic detected in the current Brazilian literature, a "strong desire for re-subjectivization" (Merquior, "Comportamento" 168), fueled by the rehabilitation

---

[9]The proposal to return to the Modernism of 1922, with the aim of recovering its "richest contributions," that is, "the poetic integration of the colloquial as a factor of innovation and a rupture with lofty academic discourse" (H.B. Hollanda 8-9) that until now has served to characterize the "re-conquest" made by marginal poetry is, in itself, meaningless. Colloquialism was an irreversible conquest of the Modernist movement, permanently incorporated into the subsequent development of modern Brazilian literature, while varying, of course, the mode of incorporating and combining with erudite literary language. Even the classicizing tendencies of the poetry found in the Generation of '45, or the postmodern diction of Carlos Drummond de Andrade, which find parallels in all the fellow travellers of 1920s Modernism, from Mario de Andrade to Cassiano Ricardo, are stripped of pedantic syntax and vocabulary. The lofty, solemn tone did not preclude an indiscriminate linguistic opening to every available linguistic register. Besides, since the 1940s the linguistic reform brought by Modernism has systematized scientific prose and encouraged the integration of conversational language into the dramatic dialogue of Brazilian dramas and movies. And let us not forget that since 1972, with the celebration of the 50 year anniversary of the Semana de Arte Moderna by the Medici government, the elements of innovation and rupture have been formally admitted to the official pantheon.

[10]This precarious theoretical program, anti-avant-garde and re-modernist, was virtually plagiarized from the position defended earlier by José Guilherme Merquior in a 1968 essay, "Capinam e a nova lírica." However, all those elements that weighed in on the side of a curiously and explicitly conservative defense of the reflexive and classicizing diction of the "philosophical lyric" (interpreted as the pinnacle of post-modern evolution, and at the same time as an impasse to the new poetry) was appropriated to celebrate spontaneity, intuition, and casual indifference.

of personal intimacy, does not seem to compensate in our opinion for the intentional rejection and consequent loss of the "objective lyric" from João Cabral to Concrete Poetry. No doubt, re-subjectivization characterizes all Marginal Poetry, but the subjective experience is no longer the same, since it is now inscribed in a socio-historical situation where the anguish for identity, its subjective urgency, appears as symptomatic of anonymity, isolation, atomization, and loss of frame of reference. The re-subjectivization allows for the poetic subject to coincide with the empirical subject, but literary representation becomes relative when it comes that close to reality. Even so, there is room for elaboration, willful or not, since poetic representation entails the *formal* arrangement of its elements; the confessional and the autobiographical record, the irreverent chronicle of everyday life, the spontaneous registering of feeling, sensation and the random, are all poetic solutions that amount to an imposition of *informal, anti-literary stylization*. Its recurrent traces are easily recognizable: its colloquialism and unpretentious subject matter, its conversational tone and wit, its bringing of extravagant metaphor down to earth, the simplicity of syntax and vocabulary; all these are techniques amenable to simultaneity, collage, ellipsis, and brevity.

Such writing betrays residual influences of the avant-garde: a proclivity for clever effects, verbal games, puns. The only difference is that now the literal and informal dominate the raw material, which emerges as prosaic verse, halfmedley, half-pastiche, overwrought as the tone that informs it, a melange of old modernist clichés, mixed with the outworn rhetoric of pamphleteers, surrealists, and quasi-philosophers. The objective is to assimilate every disruptive strategy of modern poetic language into a fluent and flowing sensibility—naturalizing poetic perception by means of everyday speech. The effects of irony and parody so common to Modernist poetry which the colloquial-ironic tradition salvaged from changing poetic registers (from lofty, erudite diction to everyday speech) are here homogenized and undifferentiated within a single chord. The whole is a transparent, truncated image—chaotic yet simple—which attains to an undiscriminating, direct, and unmediated perception.

Devaluation of the literary was meant to showcase the subject's vitality and the testimony of experience, both of which had been considered off-limits to Brazilian poetry since the intellectual/poetic arguments of João Cabral. Of course the argument put the cart before the horse, since poetic technique is the translation of experience into a formal problem, its formed content having been apprehended in the world. Such attitudes fostered a return to pure lyricism, endowing the poem with neo-romantic expressiveness, through the use of informal, almost spontaneous language and an aversion to "technique" in versifying. In other words, such subjectivity was intended to replace the sterility of technical experimentation with the lived experience of real life. Seen in this light, marginal poetry would be empowered to stand as a witness to its time, to become a singular mode of poetic expression, which in the worst case scenario, should document the expressive conflicts lived by the youth, its urges to transgress, to rebel against the family, education, or class; and although such portrayals might be narrowly conceived and literarily awkward, such rendering would endow the implicit generalizations with documentary authority. From the point of view of content, what is surprising (and deceptive) about Marginal Poetry, is that the quest for the testimonial, the confessional, stylization intervenes and mediates the data of everyday life. In other words, experience is lost in stylized transcription. The poetic solution to the figuration of ambivalent feelings—chaos and passion, pleasure and horror, seduction and loneliness, compassion and wrath, personal vitality and general anonymity, is reducible to the expedient of devaluation: not even the ability to feel emotion has value as such, when the stylistic and literary project proposed by Marginal Poetry lacks the ability to so dignify it. The subjectivization needs then a mode of expression commensurate with the manifestation of individual impulses—devaluation of the literary provides both image and identity where this subjectivity is lacking. Those who take the time to leisurely leaf through the pages of this poetry, perusing poems and poets of various tendencies, groups, phases, and artistic communities, will see for themselves a poetry that is vague, generic, without uniqueness. This poetic expression of an objective phenomenon (historical?), stylistically apathetic and self-defeating, takes a certain hedonistic pleasure in the devaluation of sensibility itself.

To sum up: there is a collective sensibility in Marginal Poetry, with its standardized feelings, emotions, sensations, and reactions that presents itself without betraying a personal voice behind its multifaceted mask. The end result is the devaluation of the literary—with its confusion and mixture of discourses, routinizing of disruptive procedures, and naturalizing and consequent trivializing of the suggestive power that can be found in poetic imagery. Emanating from other social conditions of production, an analogous phenomenon was provocatively described recently by Frederic Jameson. Operating from a socio-historical perspective in his attempt to define the pastiche as a symptom of the transition from classical modernity to post-modernity, he noted:

> . . .the great modernisms derived . . . from the creation of a private, personal style as recognizable as one's own body. However, that means that the aesthetic of modernity was somehow organically linked with the concept of a single and private self, with unique personality and individuality, from whom one could expect the framing of a unique worldview, characterized by its own singular, unmistakable, style. (114)

According to Jameson, the pastiche, as a negation of such stylistic experience, is "a vacuous parody" (i.e. something that lacks the critical or satiric motivations of parody) or "neutral practice," since it is no longer possible to have individual styles at a time when the subject as personal identity no longer exists; in other words, the era of classical bourgeois individualism is over.

To more than one spokesperson of Marginal Poetry (back in the days when it still had a "style" and it was restricted to the groups who created it) the collective, anonymizing tendency described above was quite clear, and eventually it rendered impossible any system of values or poetic criteria, and ended in the complete banalization of effects. In 1975, Antonio Carlos de Brito would write: "A good portion of the marginal production seen in the poetic scene today suffers from the devaluation of artistic form and its technical requirements, which in turn leads to an undifferentiated hodgepodge in which it is hard to distinguish one author, one poem, or one vision from any other—everything resembles everything else" (Brito 43). In the same year, Heloísa Buarque de Hollanda added the following caveat to her "official" anthology of the movement: "The apparent ease with which poetry is written today is nevertheless dangerously misleading. A significant part of the so called marginal production already shows signs of becoming watered down and trendy, with the serious problematizing of the everyday and the mixing of styles losing their power to shape and transform, becoming instead a *mere index of subjectivity*, with greater symbolic, that is to say, poetic, power" (Hollanda, *26 poetas* 10).[11] We, on the other hand, see the problem with the new poetry as too little registering of the subjective and too much devaluing of the literary. In this sense, two exceptions to our criticism would be the poets who privileged the personal and autobiographical as the most reliable means of recording events, including political events. Francisco Alvim and Roberto Schwarz practiced a mode of narrating, less emphatic and more ironic, that described the evils of political repression, exile, bureaucratic life, and the family. To be sure, both of these established authors allowed themselves to be identified with the movement for strategic reasons. In Francisco Alvim's poems, the subjective-autobiographical recording of events acquires a pathetic revelatory power that can barely be contained in his succinct style. This unmistakable style, sometimes relapsing into the joke-poem or the indiscreet memoir

---

[11]In *Impressões de viagem*, H. B. Hollanda reconsiders this critical reservation with a mea culpa, in which she moves beyond her (bourgeois) incomprehension of marginal poetry's spontaneity (proof against all literary artifice) to assert euphorically that the poetry's language of refusal is a way of experiencing the banality of the commonplace as art. This represents a conformist acceptance of everyday life that in our opinion relapses into the aestheticization of the banal.

à clef, confirms the indissoluble connection between subjective narration and a personal style.

We thus arrive at a paradox: what is assumed to be the re-subjectivization of poetry, is instead just the general state of contemporary sensibility. After all, if universalization is the precondition for literary creation, why would the general expression of such sensibility here militate against the quality of the poetic work? Would not the collective and anonymous subject of such production entail the theoretical benefits that it is right to expect of poetry? Literary history offers good examples of such. All quasi-literature, as is well known, reflects the most characteristic traces of the sensibility found in its time, captured in every rendering of styles, mannerisms, fashions and taste. At other times, these characteristics not only are dominant but also preferentially cultivated by strict literary convention (for instance, the Baroque and Arcadianism). The avant-garde, on the other hand, always use this latter and traditional possibility as a strategy: distinctive individual characteristics are brought together in the name of affirming a certain ambiance of forms that seeks to impose itself as the conventional standard for its time. It serves us well to remember how this issue was addressed by one illustrious predecessor, João Cabral, who was faced with the same problem in the poetry of his generation. According to him, the challenge for the poetry of 1945 was the derivation of personal works from already existing works (the great Modernist tradition). The existing works had such idiosyncratic traits that the rising generation of poets—those of the Generation of '45—were hard pressed to produce work characterized by similar distinctness. Such a frustrating prospect was seen by Cabral as auspicious, however, since "the extent of the work determined by its own historical position can lead perfectly to the creation of a general Brazilian expression, constituted not by the simultaneous presence of a small number of dissonant and irreducible voices, but rather by a broad and general voice capable of integrating all dissonances into a harmonious chorus." If the crisis of modernity can be interpreted as a crisis of individual style, the choice of a collective, general style has allowed poets to affirm themselves individually. This was the goal methodically and objectively sought by the Concrete Poetry project. However, with marginal poetry the case is exactly reversed—there is no common linguistic project to be executed, no utopia envisioned as an end. The plurality of efforts, with so many diverse and divergent characteristics, becomes almost involuntarily the expression of a common datum, rendered by the informal and anti-literary style. The devaluation of the poetic thus comes to embody perfectly the content of this sensibility.

(One must mention, if only in passing, one of the most fascinating textual creations—poetry?—of this whole period: the *Jornal Dobrabil* of Glauco Mattoso. The journal takes advantage of this state of affairs in which the subject is nullified and style is undifferentiated, to articulate a perverse strategy. The author uses a journalistic format to create a disorienting anonymity, from which position he endows everything with the humorous but degraded status of poetic text, except that here the poetic experience is reduced to the level of excrement. This pastiche of every available technique, style, mannerism, proverb and citation, deformed or not by the discourse, and nearly always scatologically and pornographically perverted by context, creates a kind of elephantiasis of subjectivity, unpredictable and obsessive, with a mechanical gratuitousness that knows no bounds. The self-consciousness of this device for devaluing and rendering anonymous spins out of control, serving as a threatening and horrendous image of the kind of poetic sensibility here described, carried to the extreme of depersonalization.)[12]

To return to our argument: the secular poems of marginal poetry constitute a chaotic and banal portrait of everyday life that reflects the general secularization of a world equally chaotic and absurd. The only thing hard to discern here is whether the catch-all of such sensibility creates poems that are as trivial as the world that inspired them. To be sure, the ambiguity is the result of a deliberate style, a means of poetic figuration. If it makes room for either poetic devaluation or an apology for the undifferentiated order of a consumer society, this is owing to that same ambiguity. The foregoing invalidates the argument that such devaluation of the literary is the direct consequence of a lack of culture among our new literary elites, or is a product of mass education, or results from their lack of historical memory or of critical thinking, all factors with which the style has undeniable correspondences. As a matter of fact, there are poets who share the characteristic style of marginal poetry, but who exhibit exaggerated literary leanings, intimating specialized training. It is precisely because of such vanity that the poetry of Geraldo Carneiro, Afonso Henriques Neto and Eudoro Augusto is less interesting than the trivial anti-literary bent of other marginal poets.

Devaluation, however, is not only a risk, but it can become a threat, since the poem tends to accommodate the aberrant aspects of reality (in the same

---

[12]Glauco Mattoso summarizes his poetry in the following manner: "I start with the principle that I am a plagiarist, and respect the intellectual property of no one. This is my starting point. As a plagiarist, I mix my things and other people's. It matters little whether something is my idea or somebody else's. I sign my name underneath things that are not mine, and sign other people's names under things that are mine. So, from that position, I created a little newspaper. When I referred to crosswords or puzzles, I was speaking of leisure and pastime. That is how I see poetry: a way to pass the time and to busy myself. . . ." (Deposition in *Rebate de pares*, "Remate de males" 1).

fashion that it normalizes the workings of shock, estrangement and discontinuity in modern poetry) and to embrace them graciously, playfully and pleasurably. The banality of one coincides with the banality of the other, and such coincidence is taken as not only natural or positive, but enjoyed with cozy tranquillity. The fragmented world seduces and inhabits the core of such poetry, when its own language has already dispensed with technique as a means of validating experience and reflecting upon it. Thus, the poet affirms the collective substratum of his sensibility in the way he denounces and illuminates what he himself has suffered, what has affected his particular sensibility. That is why poetic revelation, though sometimes unusual or strange and always natural, cannot be critical, not even unsettling.[13] With some perplexity, one of the least anti-intellectual poets of the movement, one of its few theoreticians, wrote, at the expense of critical reasoning, about the risks of literary devaluation in a proverbial but poetically elusive quatrain:

> Is there not in the violence
> imitated by language
> something of violence
> per se? (Brito "As aparencias")

Compared to the North American confessional poetry (which peaked in the 1960s), of authors such as Sylvia Plath, Anne Sexton and Frank O'Hara,[14] the Brazilian Marginals seem to have watched the effects of modernization without suffering its corresponding internal traumatizing, without having their personal and social universe shaken—experiences so familiar in the everyday life of the developed advanced consumer societies. They have the luxury of transcribing the devaluation of sensibility from the stable point of view of middle-class dining rooms. To them, anonymity, fear, anguish, despair, homogenization are not gutwrenching experiences, nor threatening ones. In this poetry, the social foundation seems stable, while at the same time everything in view—and the foundation itself—become modernized. On the one hand, there is degradation and violence;

---

[13]"The fundamentally vital complexion of the new poetry—where even utopia seems to be absent—gives primacy to the transcribing of 'immediate life,' as an enormous poetic *graffiti*. Its apparently easy, good-natured, and 'uncommitted' language is not as critical as one might have guessed initially." H. B. Hollanda, "A poesia vai a luta" 59.

[14]A good summary of the new tendencies in North American poetry can be found in the *Harvard Guide to Contemporary American Writing*, by Daniel Hoffman, especially in its final chapters.

on the other, surprisingly, much pleasure, something carefree and guileless, and a compulsive happiness. Of course, ways of representing these and other ambiguities vary considerably, according to the demands of the issue being dealt with, of the intention and inflection. There are instances, many of them, in which the framework of the everyday cosmos consist of little delights, romances, flirtations, rides, vacations, fast-food places, night life and parties, always forgettable because always replaceable. All of it seems grounded in sameness and in a cozy boredom, since one can always find a quick diversion to amuse oneself with. Thus Chacal writes this famous "Fast and Low" verse:

> there's going to be a party
>> where I'm going to dance
>>> until my shoe begs me to stop
> that's when I'll stop, take off the shoe
>> and dance for the rest of my life.
>>>>> (Chacal 11)[15]

Even in the case of Ana Cristina César's poetry, the conflicts and divisions, the ambiguities of multiple, fleeting scenes, with their seductions, anxieties and desires, cannot be divorced from an artificial coquettishness, a chic affectation that masks the eve of great destructions with ellipses, silences, and style, always salvaging at the last moment an image of elegance that in the verse of another author and in another context might be called "little lady in flames." Such dubious sentiments are distilled in one or another verse, more in some authors than in others, many times playing out against the background of other explicit references to violence, urban life, popular life, police, etc. Thus, the poet's own sensibility approximates that of the deviant, the criminal, the impoverished debased by want ("the delirious poet/is the juvenile delinquent of the race," claims the most suburban and enraged of marginal poets). Such resemblance is also a social stereotype condoned by the drug scene; to gangs, the threat of police brutality, of physical destruction and despair, correspond with the problems and conditions created by the most wretched poverty. Such "populist sensibility" is not devoid of occasional platitudes and nationalist clichés, always effusive and impassioned. However, this is less a matter of political appropriation than it is an idealization that encompasses social reality by devaluing both poet and poetry; moreover, it is an emptying of all concrete social experience found in the sense of marginality. The postures assumed by the poet become attributed

---

[15]The ambiguity here should be noticed in the double meaning of the verb "to dance": the actual act of dancing and (in slang) the degradation of someone who delights in getting in trouble (the slang "to dance").

to the downtrodden: ignorance is condoned as anti-intellectualism, lack of social class and style is seen as petit-bourgeois transgression, and lack of prospects as a rejection of progress. The stylized devaluation of the literary imposes its class perspective, and interprets the other, the social, in its own image and likeness. The images of urban chaos, misery, loss give birth to genuine feelings, if dubious ones, since they are not grounded in the social experience of devaluation itself, but from the undeniably privileged position of the poet.

The tight, hermetic texture of modern poetic language, with its sensible but almost incomprehensible reasoning, gives way to a pragmatic literalism, that has no mystery or nuances. Multiple meanings, opacity, and uncertainties of expression find no place here—except in the form of joke, gloss and parody. This bold anti-literary attitude, to forge its immediate and spontaneous link with life, seeks to constitute itself as a kind of pragmatic form of communication. The language of such poetry, consumable as it is, is dissipated. Its simple, transparent, everyday revelations, in attracting the reader, promote a relationship of complicity that is based on personal affinity ("not the pretty little verse/but its way of being read by you," according to a marginal quasi-manifesto). This is a poetry that "climbs down from the tower of literary prestige and appears as a performance that in reestablishing the link between poetry and life, reestablishes the nexus between poetry and the public" (Hollanda, *26 poetas* 8). Evidently, the problem lies not in the fluency of such poetic communication, which is rare and always a legitimate concern, but in the implications of such anti-literary devaluation, through which it seeks to seal the communicative pact. Transparent, simple, literal, but chaotic, fragmentary and dispersed, the poem is demoted to a mode of sensibility, a therapeutic process that happens outside of the verbal medium. However, the poetic form is not dissipated; indeed, our point has been the importance of its stylization—to our thinking, it is this stylizing solution that in simulating literary devaluation, robs poetry of its power to denounce its socio-historical conditions from the vantage point of personal testimony. It is a problematic solution because the poem promises a personal and affective relationship that its subjective and stylistic anonymity cannot deliver. If, at the starting line, there was vitality in the subject, at the end of the race there is a generic reiteration of the state of contemporary sensibility. It is a defensive solution since the practice of devaluation smacks of privilege: not only is it enjoyed as a limited class pleasure, which obviously limits its critical impact, but it also represents a hedonistic version of the discriminatory dynamics of Brazilian modernization. The fundamental inequities of the whole process, which intensified during the 1970s under the authoritarian regime, are the socio-historical background for this poetic formula. However, modernization's contradictions and violence are not directly revealed in its poems, only its symptoms—those dubious feelings and sensations mentioned above. It is the very ideology of modernization itself—and its most blatant feature, the benefits of class privilege—which are reproduced. The poetry then cannot be valued as the formal experience that transcends the particulars of its socio-historical content. The coexistence of the devaluation of poetic form, with the poverty of a subjective register and the glorification of modernity, testify to the values of those who indulged in devaluation while enjoying access to the blessings of "progress" and consumption. Pleasure, joy, happiness are conducive to generalized devaluation—poetry's pleasure principle surrenders to the reality principle of everyday life, and banalization becomes its most literal and complacent illustration.

The new concept of poetry and poem that emerges from this situation is, however, the fruit of one of the most unbelievable acts of bravado in Brazilian poetry; thanks to its own particular stylistic standards, one of the areas most remote from the culture industry pushes this industry's ideals to their limits, promoting a pragmatic reconciliation and dialogue between public and poetry. By one of the ironies of history, this was the same old project hoped for in the 1950s formulated by Concrete Poetry as the "poem-product: the useful object" according to the quasi-mythical principles of constructive rationalism. What has happened then is a farcical replay of the debates and utopias of that time. Today, however, the farce brings us back to reality and removes us from the "perceptible universe of forms" of such attractive idealism. Concrete Poetry and the poetic avant-garde in general had in mind a transformative utopian dawn, guiding its strategies and pointing the way to a future global revolution, in which poetry would have a privileged function (which, since Futurism, has always entailed a good dose of mystification and ideology). Today, on the other hand, Brazilian poetry has as its horizon the banality of the commonplace, the unchanging, disagreeable, here and now. The scenario seems catastrophic, from the point of view of the recently created poetic languages, which are now reduced to a monotonous slang, incapable of openness to the multiple epistemes and languages which populate this horizon; nevertheless, when it comes to social responsibility they do not inspire ideals, nor promise what they cannot deliver—to change the world through poetic form.

The symptoms of the poetry we have delineated span the contemporary Brazilian poetic sensibility, and can be recognized by their anti-literary substance and disparagement of style. They are present even in many categories that are not historically identified with marginal poetry, such as certain strands of feminist, gay, porno, post-concrete, and late avant-garde poetry of more recent vintage. In this "post-utopian moment," as we have seen, poetry according to Haroldo de Campos must continue reigning as a cultural experience that is forever motivated by intertextuality (the trans-temporal dialogue with other poets and other languages); if that suggests the despair of an old avant-garde theorist when confronted with the pervasive literary devaluation, it is not possible on the other hand to imagine, in the post-utopian scenario described by him, that poetry will sail unharmed through the tempests of barbarism. Besides, the whole development we have described, from the "marginal" phenomenon onwards, indicates that what is being domesticated is the experience of a poetry that has been affected in its most intimate capacity to formulate and deliver to the world promises of rejuvenation. Without a doubt, it is imperative to endow the contemporary concept of poetry with a critical content, but would the Mallarmean formulation of absolute poetry be capable of guiding us in the midst of the needs of the present moment? At any rate, it is undeniable that the culturally devalued poetic experience of today demonstrates the objective condition of the contemporary sensibility; which is not very charming, but it has its interest and may come to possess a certain power as well.

Translated by Terryl Givens and H. B. Cavalcanti

Works Cited

Bandeira, M. *Itinerário de paságarda*. 3a ed. Rio de Janeiro: Editora do Autor, 1966.

Brito, A.C. "As aparências enganam." *Grupo escolar*. Rio de Janeiro: Coleção Frenesi, 1974.

—. "Tudo da minha terra: bate-papo sobre poesia marginal." *Almanaque 6* (1978): 38-48.

Campos, Haroldo de. "Poesia e modernidade." Two parts: "Da morte da arte a constelação." *Folhetim* 403 (10/7/84); and "O poema pós-utópico." *Folhetim* 404 (10/14/84).

Chacal. *Drops de abril*. São Paulo: Brasiliense, 1983. 11.

Hoffman, Daniel *Harvard Guide to Contemporary American Writing*. Cambridge: Belknap P of Harvard U, 1979.

Hollanda, Heloísa Buarque de. *Impressões de viagem*. São Paulo: Brasiliense, 1980.

—. "A poesia vai a luta." *Alguma poesia* 2 (April 1979): 59.

—. *26 poetas hoje*. Rio de Janeiro: Editora Labor do Brasil, 1976.

Hollanda, Heloísa Buarque de, and A. C. Brito. "Nosso verso de pé quebrado." *Argumento* 1.3 (1974): 81.

Hollanda, Heloísa Buarque de, and Carlos Alberto M. Pereira, eds. *Poesia jovem anos 70*. São Paulo: Abril Educaçao, 1982.

Jameson, Fredric. "Postmodernism and Consumer Society." *The Anti-Aesthetic: Essays on Postmodern Culture.* Hal Foster ed. Washington: Bay Press, 1983. 11-125.

Mattoso, Glauco. *O que é poesia marginal?* São Paulo: Brasiliense, 1981.

—. "Remate de males." *Rebate de pares.* Campinas: IEL/FUNCAMP: 1981.

Melo Neto, João Cabral de. "A geração de 45 - III." *Diário carioca,* 12/1/1952.

Merquior, Jose Guilherme. "Capinam e a nova lírica." *A astúcia da mimese.* Rio de Janeiro: José Olympio Editora/Conselho Estadual de Cultura de São Paulo: 1972. 179-87.

—. "Comportamento da Musa: a poesia desde 22." *O elixir do apocalipse.* Rio de Janeiro: Nova Fronteira, 1983.

Pereira, Carlos Alberto M. *Retrato de época.* Rio de Janeiro: Editora Funarte, 1981.

Simon, Iumna Maria, and Vinicius Dantas. Introduction. *Poesia concreta.* São Paulo: Abril Educação, 1982.

Interviews

IN BUENOS AIRES:

IN DEFENSE OF MODERNITY: ITS UTOPIAN IDEA, ITS REVOLUTIONARY MEMORY AND ITS CULTURAL CRITICISM. AN INTERVIEW WITH NICOLÁS CASULLO
Claudia Ferman

Nicolás Casullo: Postmodernity appears in Latin America in connection with political and ideological crises, and the end of the socialist political utopias; and so it turns out to be something quite traumatic. Moreover, the subject is completely adulterated by the media and appears linked to an image of Europe and the United States which is very much in keeping with the superficiality of things—it can be a fashion or a culinary style—all of which results in a certain resistance. On the other hand, as the matter is developing in the aesthetic realm and seems linked to a kind of aesthetic experience, there is a resistance to accepting it on the part of social and political sectors as well as social and political researchers. It is also rejected because the subject of postmodernity proposes the relationship with a cultural, aesthetic world which the social sciences are not accustomed to address, given that they are completely divorced from aesthetic questions. It could be said that, unlike the Frankfurt School, where what was known concerned aesthetics—a product of the German cultural tradition—the last thirty or forty years in the social sciences have been an arid wasteland, with hardly any connection with questions such as aesthetics or poetics. And so it is extremely difficult to recycle it and orient it toward the academy, toward the social sciences. (I am very critical of the social sciences, even though I am the director of an Institute of Social Sciences, because I think that it is an absolutely dead and outdated way of thinking.) In addition, there is a political and ideological rejection because the matter is combined with the idea that postmodernity could be a capitulation, the refusal to think anymore in terms of social change, about the end of utopias, about a world which has reached a kind of end point, an explosion of meanings: a kind of everything goes attitude. The social sciences are experiencing the creation of new social objects (the state, democracy), but when a profound question of cultural transformation suddenly appears, they cannot process it. Here in Argentina, the mass media have traditionally been analyzed in terms of the culture industry, and the thinking has only been connected with the question of imperialism.

63

Claudia Ferman: But the same thing also happens to the aesthetico-literary mind-set in academic circles: it is also incapable of processing other cultural transformations which are not related to books, to the specifically literary tradition.

NC: I agree. In the universities in which I am working, we experiment with ways of trying to articulate a position which is not simply the remnants of something aesthetic, like the novel, for example, but which is also not a kind of pop sociology of culture, or a kind of psychological analysis or an anachronistic communication analysis. In a certain sense, that is also the result of European and United States leftist groups which are normally very anachronistic, whereas in other places people work more in terms of thinking as a risk venture. We first situate ourselves on the edge of modernity. Here, in Argentina, if you work on postmodernity you are postmodern: our classes are catalogued as "postmodern" because we work on the theme of postmodernity. The first thing that we try to discuss is the dismissal of the modern—the idea of the end of the modern seems very easy and very suspect to us. In the sense that we think that modernity has always been a strange creature which has been producing those very people who tried to abolish and demolish it. Perhaps that is the secret of the modern: to engender languages, positions, situations or sensibilities and standards which consider it completely defunct, from Nietzsche onward. The first inclination was to decide whether we weren't being confronted with a new episode of this type: in the face of a very strong culture crisis which puts modernity in doubt or speaks of final demise of modernity, there appears a new language of the "avant-garde," or we could say a new discursivity at the center of the modern, which attempts to checkmate modernity. The other point is whether postmodernity continues to be a condition of the world, or rather, beyond those discursivities in aesthetics and in the theoretical domain. So that we start to follow the trail of the modern: for the last four or five years I have been working on everything which appears in Vienna, and that provided me with a very singular intersection of architecture, poetics and linguistics. I was analyzing those discourses or voices (solitary and not so solitary) which, although they have not explicitly said it, formulated a condition that today can be read as postmodern. In fact, if we analyze the whole Vienna phenomenon as well as other circumstances, it seems evident that this process has been going on for a long time. The time comes when aesthetics, acting in advance of other variables but also being the offspring of variables such as structuralism and poststructuralism, leads to the appearance of a postmodern predicament, but is also involved in a name game of modernity, and tries to give an account of the loss of meanings. For example, it can be asserted that certain aspects of Benjamin, interpreted in terms of our set of problems, prefigure the postmodern debate. And that's the way it is in relation to other authors. So, on the one hand, we work on modernity, in terms of a long-running crisis which, ostensibly, is reaching its climax. On the other hand, we work on certain elements of postmodernity which are already present in the social and cultural sectors, including behavior or youth studies. I don't believe that there is any theoretical debate in Buenos Aires, but there are certainly many postmodern elements, an infinite number in fact. In the urban area, and in the youth culture, it's a permanent fixture—although they aren't aware of it—but there are already thousands upon thousands of them who are living a kind of very strong postmodern existence in their behavior, relationships, values, in their relationship with popular culture, and, moreover, in their existential confrontation with the world. So we try to work on these manifestations of postmodernity in mass urban youth culture: in their relationship with the media, sex, with the values of modernity, and in their family relationships. It's not that we're discovering postmodern conditions or postmodern behavior patterns, but we certainly are uncovering new patterns of behavior, new values and normativities which put certain values of modernity in a crisis mode: the relation to the political—the disintegration of the political, the remoteness of the political—other kinds of rituals very different from those of the 60s. So in that world, which we could call urban youth culture, we are detecting certain elements of postmodernity, and at the same time we are also working on areas of what we might call poverty, in which there appears a postmodern presence, or we could say a crisis of values in what we could call the marginal in the modern. In that sense we are working a lot on certain comic book variables: the city of good and evil, the city of the losers. We work with certain comic book paradigms that point toward reality. That is, young characters, bands of youths, street gangs, their idols, the relationships they establish, their link with violence, their connection with a kind of utopian idea of community, their relationship to the idea of feeling like the ultimate losers in the consumer society, their link to the total loss of a sense of history. They are all contradictory elements which appear in the framework of an infinite number of typically modern and classic elements, but in which it becomes progressively more evident that we are entering a new rationality—or irrationality—where already the sociological and politicological arguments no longer serve any purpose, are already completely outmoded. And the analytical variables are invalid: fragmentation, segmentation. Fragmentation in relation to what, to something which wasn't fragmented? But from the standpoint of the new logic, there isn't any fragmentation, for modern youth there is no fragmentation: he is part of a world which is not linked by class, but by some rock group, or linked because he is involved in robbery, or because he lives in a certain way, or because he smokes marijuana, or because they all sleep together, or because the sexual relationship is based on rape. If you always analyze in relation to some type of ideal of modern society, well, certainly, there is a debasement of the social domain. In fact, there exists an extreme degradation of the social. And here another troublesome matter complicates the picture, and that's all the conceptualizing coming from the North which combines postindustrial society and postmodernism, which is not the same thing here. Here the question of autonomy and diversity takes on a whole new meaning. For example, in the North they are working in terms which champion an even greater amount of autonomy and diversity. Certainly, processes of individualization, of fragmentation and new avenues of autonomy are being continuously created there as well as here. But here diversity does not imply the difference among peers, but processes of social barbarization. It is not a question of a world which brings about the fusion of the modern within the postmodern, with an increasingly effective autonomy and hedonism in a kind of new world of narratives, but rather it is produced in terms of appalling social disintegrations, in which you can really demonstrate the same set of problems that are found in the North but with a different meaning.

CF: There is a North and a South, but there is also a problem of urban culture and of non-urban culture: it would seem that the urban centers of Latin America are connected to the North in a way that the non-urban centers are not. That could be a specific trait of Latin America, which might be delineating a "diversity of meanings" of those behavior patterns which are very similar but have different meanings (the non-distinct but different). This ties in with the limits of the youth movement, because it cannot be said that the presence of the young people spearheading the drive for historical change really starts in the 60s.

NC: Here the whole politics of the 60s involved young people. The difference is that the young people were involved in a larger, more encompassing social project, aligning themselves with politics of the resolution of history: today the youth groups exist as isolated entities, they're in it for themselves, they don't get involved in anything nor do they have any interest in getting involved, nor do they believe in any kind of larger discourse which concerns them, and their connection with politics is absolutely non-existent. Likewise, the intellectuals as well as the academic world of the 80s and 90s are undergoing a similar process. Those of us who today have an intellectual voice were youths in the 60s and 70s, and we have lived through the last thirty years in a particular way. That whole process through which the intellectual detaches from politics, who returns to the academy and then ends up working as a consultant or for some Argentinean political think tank, is a process which we see in Paris as well as in the US and Argentina. Here there are clear-cut cases: people who in the 60s and 70s were, we could say, "the revolutionary fringe," or the radical questioning the system, and who, for example, ended up as high profile, official advisors to Alfonsín,[1] writing his speeches and advising him. That is a trait that in Latin America is interpreted as the end of the utopias, as neoconservatism, as realism, pragmatism,

---

[1]President of Argentina (1983-89); leader of the Radical Civic Union Party.

and some call it the capitulation of ideas. But, undoubtedly, it's all leading to a particular role for the intellectual, and even to his disappearance. I believe that the Sartrean intellectual, the intellectual who transforms his life into a kind of *engagement* through which he must speak and discuss the whole social enterprise, disappeared, or is about to disappear. There is an enormous influence of the academic world and an extraordinary tendency toward specialization. For example, if they ask you about Eastern Europe, you can say with complete assurance: I don't know anything, I haven't read anything. Unlike the Sartrean intellectual who got involved in a whole range of problems which crossed his path: Vietnam, Algeria, China, or the child who is dying of hunger in Tibet (and that was exactly what prevented Sartre from continuing to write). I believe this is disappearing, that it's being forgotten: the consummate image of the European intellectual in opposition to society.

Some believe that postmodernity is the last surge of the wave which was born in '68. Or they divide the process into three parts: the existentialist period, the period of '68 and postmodernity; three waves which continue nurturing one another and which would create a trend toward greater autonomy and differentiation. This is an optimistic vision. The '68 period, and here I agree with Octavio Paz, is the last stage of the great utopias of 1789. Perhaps Paris symbolized it aesthetically: out they came, the anarchists, Breton's followers, the Utopians, the Leninists, the guerrillas. . . . It is the last ritualistic enactment of what we can say emerges with Babeuf, as an outcome of the first moment of the Revolution, and which culminates in what is called the '68 period, the Chinese cultural revolution, and all the things which can pass through the '68 period: from making love like the Sioux to Che Guevara, where you can stick Fourier, Marx, Saint Simon, Nietzsche and why not also Heidegger. I am more in favor of the idea that if indeed there is a cross-fertilization from one moment to the next, a rupture takes place: what appears after '68 is already something different. It no longer involves carrying out the mandate of the revolution, of the free world, of speaking out against parents, it's no longer a question of carrying out that long-standing mandate of 150 years of history, but it is something different. I believe that in '68 there is an end (and its dying days are the final years of the 70s); here in Latin America this is quite clear, but also in the rest of the world. The decade of the 80s sweeps all that away and in an accelerated, cybernetic and consumer-oriented fashion, it carries out its task in such a way that it leaves everybody in a state of alarm. In 1990 all that seems as somehow disintegrated, as if it had fallen into oblivion. In 1978, in Buenos Aires, many tributes were paid to the '68 period—I myself organized a dossier for *Babel* magazine—but it already seemed like ancient history, a postmortem testimonial. If you look at the present world, if you analyze the hegemonic discourses and you see the absolute lack of answers from all the leftist movements to the old problem in relation to what we could call "the new world order," if you see what is now being discussed, and how anachronistic have become those who were proposing the same things in the 70s, it does not seem possible that this outcome can be the product of only ten or twelve years. Although I am not saying that there has not remained a memory fragment or recognition factor of the ideas of the culture of redemption: "The-world-can-change."

CF: As Horacio González questioned me the other day, now what do we do with the emotionally-charged feelings of those years, how do we process and internalize these feelings to make them our own, what do we have to do to make them into a legacy, to recapture them? The least palatable attitude would be to repent and say: "Well, I made a mistake."

NC: In defense of modernity: its utopian idea, its revolutionary memory and its cultural criticism. But beyond the positions that can be taken by people like us who go around defending the modern, who understand by the modern that there still exists a meaning to history and it has to be recovered, and it has to be carried forward. We, then, are accused of being "Nostalgiaholics." This is a struggle, as the romantics would say, in which you already know that you are going to lose, but what you have to do is to continue it. We can't ignore the direction in which the world is moving. I would say that '68 is a file stored on a computer, and that right now what it can be used for is so that a researcher does a good piece of work, a good book about what '68 was all about and which will sell two thousand copies. And he is surely going to have all the information at his disposal, much more than we had in '68. We ourselves realize this transformation: in '70 I wasn't directing a research institute, nor was Horacio González. I wrote my first novel in '67 and, after '68, with its reduction of everything to politics, I said that I wasn't writing anymore, and that I was devoting myself to politics. I have spoken with Oscar Terán about this, and he also abandoned all philosophical study about that time. This means that we also, in our public and private lives, gave an account of everything which happened.

Today, in Buenos Aires, we are the only example of those who have formed a group which works on the problem of postmodernity. By recognizing that a tremendous split has taken place, that there are many dangerous elements in the postmodern conditions, we align ourselves with a kind of inheritance of German, anti-Illustration thinking. Using that as a point of departure, it's a matter of desperately recovering some signs, legacies, contributions and tenets of modernity, those which may once again re-enchant the highly disenchanted world of today: a world in which nothing makes a difference and in which the only thing remaining is the high degree of competency in our specialty for what reason no one knows. On the other hand, here there is another sector which is working on the idea of modernization. This is the latest political twist: the ratio-nalization of the social-democratic type which posits that the world is a dirty mess and everything is finished, but that it is necessary that in some way or another we arrive at a certain realism, a certain pragmatism. Then it's proposed like the serene, thoughtful, grown-up and contrite left of social democracy, or what passes here for social democracy, though that's not the way it's labeled. This was the case with Alfonsín, for example. It is the other posture: to bet again on a rationalization, to really believe that this cybernetic, teleinformatic world has gifts to make spirituality reawaken in man; to continue believing—although not in a Marxist fashion—that capitalism not only proposes irrationalities but also the means by which you can overcome them, if you appropriate them. A little like Marshall Berman's position: you have to return to Marx who criticized modernity, but by trying to complete modernity in a still superior way, since it proposed, thanks to technical innovation, that the world could be improved. But declarations like "the world is that way and everything is finished, what needs to be done is have a certain social sensibility for the adjustment programs," are accepting and ratifying the logic of late-capitalistic-cybernetics, the age-of-silicon. This variant which, here in Argentina, exists and has its journals, has an enormous fear of the irrationality of history. First, because it considers that '68 was the result of an enormous irrationality—in which we were all involved—and, second, because it fears that, beneath this parody of the democratic and the Europe of '92, what is really taking shape is a neofascist, brutal, blind, individualistic society of the masses—as I believe is undoubtedly taking shape. Beyond consumption, or being able to go to the Bahamas for five days, what is taking shape is a very dark thing, a kind of society of slaves of the globe, not traversed by any utopian or messianic discourse. Or if it has its own messianism, it has it in the dark sense of the word, that is, proposals which don't result in a political leader, but rather in a fortune-teller or in a ritual, in some kind of sect.

Then, on one side is our position of returning to a risky word—one which does not have any reason to be the explicit political word—and, therefore, to resort to certain legacies of modernity which worked on that cutting edge of risk (and there German culture is what yields the most: neither French nor English culture; those who worked eternally on chance, from Hölderlin to Heidegger, are the Germans, the only ones). To work on that in order not to abdicate. On the other side is the modernizing variant which says: I accept this world, they put a computer in front of me, and history is finished. And the violences will appear, and with the help of private police you go around dividing them up, going to exhibits, going to see a good play; because as the city of evil continues to increase in size, the city of good has more gifts, more goods so as to enjoy it in a kind of permanently satisfied desire.

This modernizing variant is associated with the politico-cultural techno-rationality of the academies, which talks about the new social subject, the relationship between state and society, the state and the new social subject, the new democracy, a whole flood of verbal diarrhea (financed by Ford and Rockefeller) to report on something which is disintegrating and crumbling to pieces in Latin America—although not in the central world, where evidently that has a certain logic and a certain consistency so as to carry it out. Here we are discussing that problematics about a world which is deteriorating: you can't cross a street in Rio de Janeiro without someone raping or attacking you; and it's within the context of such realities that we are discussing the State-Society relationship.

CF: Perhaps in Chicago you can't cross the street either.

NC: That's right. Or in the suburbs of Washington, D. C.: the United States is more savage when it comes to what is expelled and what is retained; in Europe there is still an older social-democratic heritage and there is a greater concern to at least see that those who lose out have greater protection.

On the contrary, other variables—following in the line of Heidegger—propose that this is a consummation, that here something ended and this is a sort of Apocalypse: this has to be completed in order to go on to something else.

CF: Talking about postmodernity in Latin America brings up the discussion of the theory of cultural and social communications in general terms. Because seen in the light of the 70s, the debate is a kind of "imported" discourse, which can turn out to be very irritating for a certain local community. This leads to the need of confronting an implicit debate: why to proceed with a category which has not been developed on this side of the ocean, and which has evolved within the analytical parameters which correspond to the "developed" world or, as they said in the 60s and 70s, to the center and not the periphery.

NC: In my opinion the term postmodernity is an invention, an operative fiction. It doesn't matter to me how exact the term is, it energizes me. Any debate which is predicated on a period definition is an invention. A novelist, or theorist, could have done it. If the term sheds light on a world of problematics for me, then it is worthwhile; if the object doesn't enlighten me at all, then, as Benjamin would say, to hell with the object. And if it does enlighten me, then it's worthwhile. I don't start thinking whether some trendy New Yorker or a German philosopher invented it, if it enlightens me enough to discuss what is going on here. It's the same as with any other concept—the terms "surplus value," or the "struggle between the bourgeoisie and the proletariat" also enlightened us, and these terms weren't developed here, nor among the Guaranis. . . , they were developed in Europe by a guy who was in a library in London. But he enlightened us and enabled us to understand the period, or not understand it. The adventure of knowledge is working on concepts, finding what is useful, what illuminates, what enables writing, what ignites the desire for the word.

CF: In this possible criticism there also is an implicit concept of Latin American difference and specificity in which one would be obligated to produce.

NC: I think that today we have difficulty in finding that certain problems which appear in the North are also found here. There are those who find that all of modernity has been an imposition for Latin America and that, beneath modernity, there is a kind of pure American being. That was exactly the great debate which took place in the international meeting on modernity and postmodernity which CLASCO organized in the area of culture. My proposition is just the reverse, and in that sense the work of Richard Morse helped me a lot: I believe that these problems not only concern us, but they also occur much more than that. If the crisis of the modern or the appearance of the postmodern in the West, as Habermas says, occurs when there is no concurrence between what we could call the advancement of the social and the economic and the culture which gives an account of it, that is, when the place from which one views oneself in the culture breaks up and there is no longer a total self-centering; if this is the way it is, then Latin America was eternally postmodern from the moment Christopher Columbus set foot here, that is, from its own inception, because here there was always a discourse which was not reflected in reality, and there was a reality which did not have any discourse which explained it. If postmodernity is that imbalance to be assumed in the face of modernity, where self-centering is no longer the natural or logical stance which, we could say, had defined the whole 19th century and part of the 20th, if what is already put in question is that modernity, then Latin America is postmodern because it permanently put modernity in question in different ways.

CF: The first thing Latin America did was, historically, to lay the economic and social foundation to produce modernity (that one which Europe tried to appropriate for itself, and conceive by and for itself), that modernity which Europe claims for itself and which we Latin Americans say that they transferred to us.

NC: The people who are saying that are products of Marxist modernity, which was also brought from Europe. This is an argument against illiteracy: Latin America emerges as a modern country at the dawn of modernity but it is conceived as distance, as Sarmiento would say. Richard Morse makes a study of peripheral cities: he takes Vienna, Buenos Aires, Rio de Janeiro and Saint Petersburg, and says that in reality they had certain postmodern elements before Paris, London and New York, and that they had that strange look which has a whole unpleasant postmodern aftertaste. We have very poorly executed modern elements throughout our history: the great waves of modernization have always coexisted with premodern elements. As I often tell certain Europeans who pass through here: if the problematics of democracy is proposed to you at this time, for us the problematics of democracy never jelled with modernity: we were modern but we did not have democracy. Or rather those hiatuses, those differences, that is what has produced a look of suspicion toward the modern, a critical view, a view from afar which has highly postmodern components, which can also be found in Vienna at the start of the century, but from another perspective. We constantly live being unable to give an account of the modern discursivity which comes from there, for which I believe that we are quite well equipped not only to work the term postmodernity, or whatever other more appropriate term (in any case I would express it as a "permanent crisis of the modern"), but also, we are in that sense more advanced than certain European countries, because our history has been the permanent crisis of the modern, the modern discourse which did not find its definitive shape.

Another trait which escapes the social scientists is that we are already the products of forty years of mass media. So it's not like discussing in the 60s when television had only been around for five years: television has been present for thirty years, this internationalized culture has been present for thirty years; and therefore there are already two complete generations involved in what we were analyzing twenty years ago and about whom we were hypothesizing. A delightful world where everything is compressed.

CF: The same television which you find in Lima or in Bogotá.

NC: Today, via satellite, the Bolivian peasants receive German, Japanese, English, US and Bolivian news programs in Spanish. You sit down—in rural areas or in whatever spot—and you see five news programs in an hour and a half. What do you get in an hour from seeing nothing less than an ultrasophisticated synthesis of the major news programs? They are still Bolivian peasants, but every day they receive a Japanese news broadcast.

CF: This alerts us to understand the ways in which cultural changes come about, and the message of these cultural transformations. It could be said before that changes were brought by travelers (i.e., Alberdi, Sarmiento), and it was understood that those voyages were the means by which the cultural movements would travel: "the influences." Today, besides the complex phenomenon of new methods of communication, we have a Latin American population located throughout the North (in the United States and Europe), recycling what is happening from a particular vantage point. That is, the case of a Cortázar, for example, who always wrote for Argentina and Latin America, but who lived in Paris, has become more widespread.

NC: What's happening is that now it's much more overwhelming than in the time of Cortázar. In '68 I was in Europe and I went to see Cortázar: we were the young novelists, so he paid attention to us; a month later the May Revolution broke out in France. But at that time we were still closer than we are now to the voyage of Sarmiento and Alberdi in terms of forms of cultural contact. All that is closer to the beginning of the century than what has happened in the last twenty years. At that time you could still say, as they did in Argentina, that 18 years of anti-Peronist propaganda on television had not done anything more than guarantee that Perón won bigger than ever in '73. This was a constantly recurring theme in mass media analyses. Now it is very difficult to say that, because what's being produced is something new: the problem of sovereignty disappeared, and not so much in terms of geographic boundaries but rather of cultural domains such as that of identity.

CF: What separates Cortázar's situation from the present is who is processing that "distant Latin American" gaze. Cortázar, who spoke in French and wrote in Spanish, and who was published in Mexico and Buenos Aires and then translated into French, had a middle class reading public which was large but limited to that cultural practice: reading. But now we have a reading public which is connected to discourses produced in other countries, and, at the same time, thanks to satellites and to the whole mass media, we have all the sectors, from the least to the most closely connected ones with the book, the whole gamut, in one simultaneous process of contacts. Although the forms of production and social evolution (Benítez-Rojo's "fleet machine") were generating extensive areas of influence, beyond a shadow of a doubt there exists at least a question of degree between those processes of "voyages of cultural waves."

NC: Eighty percent of the population of Brazil has no contact with the written word: not that they have little, they don't even have the absolute minimum; while 90 percent of the population has contact with the verbal element of the image. The scenarios are different. That's where I say that we lag behind in our work and we're not aware of this transculture which appears in an infinite number of forms. For example, the relationship with the book disappeared for the student. Umberto Eco says that in Italy this relationship with the book has also disappeared, since all of them are photocopies. Which does not mean that it has completely vanished: but it disappears to the extent that we had that relationship with the book. At the end of their university education, my students are going to have only 10 percent of the books that I had. But they are completely satisfied, there is no longing or nostalgia.

CF: When you speak of transculture, are you referring to the model of Angel Rama or are you trying to define the so-called "global culture"? Perhaps we should be talking about something like "intensely producing poles," or "poles of producing initiative" or "poles of aggressive cultural production."

NC: When I say transculture I am referring to the reaction of the social subject vis-à-vis a homogenized model. Sting came here and he filled a stadium with 150,000 people, which no one does in Argentina, not even Peronism. What this means is that, and this is the phenomenon which escapes the understanding of many people, beyond the structural and economic conditions, beyond the social disintegrations, the different histories, there is a cultural level which generates attitudes, values, behavior patterns, norms, and actions which is the same in every part of the mass urban sector. Here, in Argentina, the poorest young people are linked with English heavy rock music: since there isn't any heavy rock here, there is slow rock music, then they immediately latch on to the English rock. When these English groups come here, all the young people from the city of evil appear and go to see them. This is indicative of certain values in the sense that these rituals mold them into subjects. Moreover, since they don't go to the factories, to work, they don't have any other type of relationship, they don't know what a *chacarera*[2] is, and it turns out that what they have to do is have chains and smash everything, just the way they see it on T.V. Then postmodern phenomena emerge, because those guys keep on internalizing that. With any luck they get to the explosion of meaning: nothing has any meaning. It's exactly those who would have to contain all the meanings in order to change society, who are living the whole thing as if they were English punk rockers.

CF: Within the culture of opulence or the culture of absolute poverty.

NC: Certainly, but they have certain things in common because, of course, the kid who goes to see a rock group is not the kid who has a yacht like the yuppie kid from the upper middle class of the south of France, and he is not going to associate with that poor kid. That is, a kind of choreographed ritual is being generated, a kind of collective message created by the simulacrum: because they live the violence, but when the English are on stage, they simulate violence. When the wild football gangs from here see the English hooligans with their make-up and shaved heads, they feel a common bond: you have to invade the city and smash it to bits.

CF: Because the city doesn't belong to us, it has other owners.

NC: That's right. I don't know if the same will apply in La Paz, but it certainly is true in Buenos Aires, in Rosario and Córdoba: there is an urban culture which is already global. And when I say global I don't want to get into the version of the global village which Eco talked about; what I'm saying is that there are phenomena of marginalization which occur far removed from the economic situations, and they cover an extensive urban sector. There is a large mass of people who are probably not living in poverty, but who probably don't have any jobs, and there is a mass culture which in some way is trying to anesthetize it, to gain control over it. But the resemanticization that people do has always appeared. Evidently the mass media try to neutralize the disaster. But the neutralization is very ineffectual: really what is being perceived is the model which is behind the times: what the youth gets is, not that rape is punished, he perceives that rape exists; the end of the film is what is least interesting. The neutralization which the media want to achieve has the reverse effect, it is a kind of monstrous offspring of what is being projected. What is communicated is that if there is a beautiful girl and you can rape her, you rape her, and why are you going to

---

[2]*chacarera*: Argentine folk dance.

worry about ethical and moral questions if 90 percent of the film up to the 89th minute was that, and afterwards, in the last minute, they capture the rapist and the guy starts to cry. That does not keep the situation in Argentina from being fifteen thousand times worse than in Italy, in social and economic terms: here there are people who only eat once a day.

CF: In that construction of relationships and communications, Argentina occupies a place of enormous, almost autistic, isolation, with very little possibility of receiving information other than that which has already been highly processed.

NC: In terms of a catastrophe, Argentina finds itself in a situation very similar to that of Peru, for example. If you go by the debt figures, everything is more or less equal or worse for Argentina as for the rest of the Latin American countries. But on the cultural level, perhaps the reading has to be different, since the catastrophe is lived in a different manner. Like every urban culture, having absorbed a whole set of problems from Europe, and living here as we are through the collapse of what we could call a "project for a country," here a more complex, pessimistic thinking appears.

CF: How do you see the new national project which is being attempted?

NC: Very difficult. Now, I invert the terms: while this may be a catastrophe, I am going to live here. As a novelist, writer, as a great admirer of people who lived sublimely through the catastrophe, I would say to you that, while it continues like that, with no way out and no solution, I will stay in Argentina. If this reaches the point where it more or less improves, or rather, if this project turns out well—it turns out well for those who are left alive—then I'll leave. In order for it to turn out well, there really isn't much which is required: what's needed, finally, is for seven or eight million people to die of hunger, which really isn't a lot when you consider that in Brazil, the number goes as high as sixty million. I say it cynically, but that's the way it is: a certain stability, a completely privatized Argentina, a certain economic balance, and here there is a bourgeois culture of the worst kind (not one which creates academies). That it turns out well means the loss of the last hope, because nothing will happen any longer, you'll no longer know why to do or not to do something. Here there is still hope, exactly because of the profound crisis which we are going through, the meanings of wanting to discuss, and thinking that by having a teaching position you can overcome poverty, are still preserved. I lived in Mexico for many years, but I left because I was dying. I needed to become indignant again about everything, and the only place where I get infuriated is here—when I leave the country I don't even read the newspapers, and at the end of four months I start to wonder who I can fight with.

We are in the last stage of a situation which is still present here, although the apocalypse has already arrived: this is the apocalypse. But this is still worth being lived because, as Baudrillard would say, we have the chance to live the apocalypse. I think that this disintegration of the great hope which was the idea of this country is worth being lived. And in the disintegration there are valuable things: there are reactions, there are very strong forms of spirituality, there are very beautiful forms of the appearance of consciousness, it's a time of many poets. In fact, we are working on the revalorization of the poetic, of the poetic word vis-a-vis the scientific word, and the students react very positively. And the students react and say that the whole career must be reinvented, because here what matters is Baudelaire and not mass communication, and the career director doesn't know what to do. We're living through a time which is catastrophic, very similar to Germany between the wars which was the last great German period, if you consider that in the Germany between the wars there were Brecht, Benjamin, Bloch, Piscatore.

I no longer have any desire to go to Europe, unless it's as a tourist without having to get involved with anything more human than a stone. What I feel there is a tremendous spiritual void, and a kind of professionalism which does not interest me; what I love most about Europe has been lost: its possibility of producing something like '68. The Europeans sense this difference and they are absolutely captivated by this dislocation of ours, but like it or not, their world is suffocating them. Here that period ended in another way: it was smashed to bits, but the crisis and the collapse are so strong, the entry into this last wave of modernity is so difficult, that the machinery is still not in place, and, what's more, it's still difficult for it to enter, in the same way as in the rest of Latin America. Latin America can be a beautiful model, a beautiful example of how to enter the year 2000 in a different way. Although it can also be a model of the great catastrophe: the blacks invading the cities of Brazil and eating them alive.

Translated by Robert Sims

IN MEXICO CITY:

FROM SOUTHERN ACCULTURATION TO NORTH AMERICAN CULTURAL TRADE. AN INTERVIEW WITH ROGER BARTRA
Claudia Ferman

Claudia Ferman: There is a certain level of metaphorization in your book, *The Cage of Melancholy*, which has traditionally been foreign to the domain of critical discourse.

Roger Bartra: At present there is a break of the borders between literary discourse and literature, between literary discourse and anthropology, etc. I believe that in *The Cage of Melancholy* there is a clear breach of two substantial paradigms. One is precisely this one: the boundary between speech genres; the other dissolved boundary is that of North-South, which is most obvious when a study is made of the question of Mexican cultural identity. Mexican cultural identity has been manufactured so much in contrast to the Anglo, the American, in contrast and in opposition to the U.S., that my first hypothesis was to state: I do not accept the division between South-North, backwardness-development, etc. What I propose is that the construction of this archetype, this stereotype, obeys antiquated Western patterns and canonic concepts. Which is to say that in my book I contend that Mexican identity is, in the final analysis, a Western invention; which is a way—a little violent and within the framework of Mexican culture—of disrupting that boundary, of not accepting the initial rules of the game. Those rules signal that there exists a polarity, or a South-North duality, Mexican-Anglo, the soul-in-pain-from-backwardness confronting the spirits-of-development-of-the-Western-dynamism. I do not accept the polarity and I maintain that the specifically Mexican is also a creation of the West.

CF: By rejecting this polarity, doubt is also being cast on the position of those who say that Latin America must also gain access to modernity before it can talk about postmodernity.

RB: That is too narrow of a focus which can be found in many parts of Latin America: until we achieve the development stage, we are not going to be able to speak of democracy, nor of high culture, nor of postmodernity, and meanwhile we'll have to satisfy ourselves with the crumbs. What that means is that while that canonic notion of the Mexican, "the Mexican prototype," is a creature of the West, it also has an underdeveloping effect on culture. Which is tantamount to saying that I don't believe that the root causes of cultural impoverishment lie in economic backwardness, or that the day we reach the threshold of modernity we will be able to have a Nobel Prize winner, etc. No, I think that what hurts us is what I call "the canon of axolotl," this amphibious animal, which is one of the mechanisms that is engendering the cultural blockade. In this case, the animal bites its tail. And so I refuse to accept that boundary, or many others; that is, the traditional boundaries between East and West, although those dichotomies carry less weight within the total metaphoric interplay of my book for obvious reasons: the book centers on problems related to culture, and the importance of the North is crucial, whether you consider it Spain, a colonizing country, a more developed country, or, of course, the United States. Spain and Europe, the developed West, would be the North. I do not accept this division and what I am saying exactly is that we, the Mexicans, are Europeans, Westerners.

Traditionally, many Mexican intellectuals have tried to escape the Anglo-American domination by taking refuge in France, and even Spain, although in Spain the effort proves more difficult because of the traditions of comparison. That loomed as another alternative on which to base our cultural heritage of the South, which really meant relying on another North; but one which was civilized, and not the American barbarians. But all that is the stuff of fiction. In reality, there is a cultural conglomerate which I prefer to call the West.

On the other hand, the so-called Mexican essence is completely fragmented in reality, and it only exists in the imagination (which is no small matter, since it is undoubtedly more real than reality itself). This situation of fragmentation is unified by the stereotype—and the stereotype is this fusion of the peasant, the Indian, etc., that is, the internal South, the internal North, which would be the proletariat, the Faustian man, the modern bourgeois, technology, and so on. Both of them make up the canonic concept, this stereotype of the Mexican, this dual being who never stops being a peasant while always struggling to be a proletariat, or who never stops being a native and who is never completely "civilized," and who lives in this vicious circle, which I characterize by the metaphor of this little animal, the axolotl.

CF: How is this position viewed in Mexico?

RB: In Mexico, on the one hand I feel solitary and on the other, no. Since I have stopped accepting those kinds of boundaries, then one of the first things I have done is refuse to recognize the border with the North, and I function just as well in the United States as I do here. And I find that in the United States there are many people of Latin or Latin American extraction, who, even though they are still a minority, accept this transcultural situation. Once they live there, it is much easier for them because that's the reality which surrounds them. To a chicano intellectual—especially to those who are not caught up in that kind of nationalistic backwardness that some chicano groups have promoted—or simply, to a Mexican, or to the Latin Americans who are living in the United States and who do not acknowledge the borders and who function just as easily in this American society as they do in Latin American society, it seems natural to take advantage of American liberalism, of that egalitarian spirit which no doubt exists in the United States. Unfortunately, this remains hidden within the masses of impoverished Latinos who live in the United States; it is an extremely complex set of problems. It's more difficult on this side of the border because it's one thing to accept a transcultural situation when you're living in New York, and quite another to accept it if you're living in Mexico City, because people immediately already see you as a traitor: you have already sold out to the Anglo, to imperialism, you're adopting imported values which are not ours, and the whole litany of ideological towel-ringing. So here, yes, it is a bit more difficult; nevertheless, I think that the situation has started to change and, even though it's a little more difficult to say everything up front and convince people to accept it openly, I think it's being accepted in an implicit but progressively clearer way. The fact that they have not lynched me for writing and publishing *The Cage of Melancholy* is cause for optimism. They haven't lynched me; there have been some unpleasant situations, they've told me about some journalists, especially in the provinces, who expressed a great deal of indignation. But things have gone well for the book, and it's in its fourth edition. I think that fifteen or twenty years ago it would have been cause for scandal, or even complete and total isolation. Let's say that it competes with the official version. There is a book by Guillermo Bonfín called *Mexico the Profound* which is diametrically opposed to my book, and it is the official point of view, and also more or less the position of the left. This book claims that, beneath all the apparently visible urban and modern elements, there exists a more profound Mexico, which is the indigenous Mexico, and which is the true Mexico, its authentic soul, which continues to throb and which has to be reached. Let's say that this book confirms the premises of my book. Bonfín's book is published by the Department of Public Education, since, despite the fact that the official policy of this country is "Modernity," integration with the United States, etc., the official cultural policy tends to support that type of thing; those are the paradoxes of this country.

CF: This imposition of a nativist, aboriginal, original condition comes from way back, from the "invention of America" which Edmundo O'Gorman has already explained.

RB: O'Gorman has a book entitled *Destierro de sombras* (*The Exile of Shadows*) in which he analyses the Virgin of Guadalupe as a creation of an imaginary, that is, an invention. He does not use all those metaphors which are so dear to French sociology, to the history of the mind, etc., no, he does not use that vocabulary, but it amounts to the same thing. I think that it is a precursor. It's older, so he does not like to talk about the imaginary, but in fact that is what he is talking about. That is what is so valuable. A famous Italian folklorist, Giuseppe Cocchiara, had already said in the 40s, I think, before O'Gorman, that the savage was invented before being discovered. In fact, in Europe, before the Discovery, that is, before the Conquest of America, they already had a stereotype of the savage, without ever having any contact with indigenous people, as an idea of European otherness. In reality I believe that European culture is dedicated to inventing an America, and afterward we live in that invention.

CF: Which would make America, right from its inception, an integral part of the unity of the West.

RB: I am firmly convinced that we are part of that West, even from the Mexican, Peruvian or Andean countries' perspective, in which the indigenous element is taken for granted: we are as Western as the Portuguese or the French. Another thing which I am convinced of is that in Mexico there is a canon, which I call the canon of axolotl, that precludes what I would not call integration (because we're already integrated, that has already taken place), but rather a total recognition of it, and therefore a usage of the wealth of that West to our advantage. When we reject the West, we impoverish ourselves, and thus there is an underdeveloping effect; not because we are the colonized, but rather because we are willfully rejecting a rich cultural heritage, and that is truly suicidal. It's an underdeveloping effect if the local intellectuals are only measured by locally invented parameters, and not within the framework of this larger conglomerate which is the West. So a poet from Guanajuato competes only within a spectrum or a scale of Mexican values, and it all ends right there, because competing on a Western level implies selling out to imperialism, or whatever. In the end, that is an underdeveloping effect. It's like cutting off your wings before flying.

CF: From an objective standpoint, what is certain is the difference in aggressiveness between various centers for contact and dissemination: from Latin America it proves more difficult to get in contact with other points, but this has nothing to do with the nature of our culture, with its "different" condition. Vicente Leñero was telling me in an interview a little while ago: "We don't reach France because we are different; we can't be listened to in Europe because we are too Mexican, and who is going to understand what the Paseo de la Reforma is?"

RB: In Paris they listen to us about as little as someone from Copenhagen. There is a problem of an accumulation of power: it's certain that the power of the country is reflected in the cultural domain. If you're Guatemalan you have less of a chance to sell your book with a European publisher than if you are Argentinean or Mexican, or than if you're French. Yes, there are power flows at the national level which are reflected, but that should not be interpreted as significant cultural differences. A Guatemalan speaks the language of Cervantes and he should believe that in Madrid he is on a level playing field with the

Andalusian with respect to the difficulties involved. There are those perverse, terrible effects produced by the transfer of economic and socioeconomic power to literature, and you have to fight against that. But instead of struggling, we accept it, and so we accept the idea that we are from the Third World, that we are different, and that, unfortunately, they don't understand us, but here, among ourselves, yes, we understand each other. This is a mechanism of underdevelopment which has its root causes in culture, and which can be corrected; I am optimistic about that. You bear the weight of the poverty of your country, but that doesn't mean that you also have to carry the burden of cultural poverty.

CF: If we agree that the Mexican is an imaginary construct, and that you have to redefine the relationships between cultural spaces in order to avoid repeating the errors of the past in the conceptualization process, what can now be done with the concepts of the center and the periphery? That is, which ones are the centers, and which ones are the peripheries?

RB: Centers of colonial and cultural expansion exist: Paris or New York, for example, are cultural metropolises. But that should not be included within the framework of metropolis/periphery and, therefore, we the backward/they the civilized. Certainly, people living in a town in Texas or, in general, in the Midwest, are more backward than we are here in Mexico City, in relation to New York City. That is, New York is a conglomerate, a center of culture, as is Mexico City. I would not like to extend the implications beyond geographical limits; places where there are more painters, more magazines. . . . (he laughs).

CF: I think that we can talk about poles of more aggressive cultural production.

RB: When I visit Milwaukee, I feel like Mexico City is a metropolis. I have lived in Wisconsin, for example, which in general is a cultural desert except for Madison, which represents a small cultural enclave. Texas is rather horrible, but Austin is something different; finally, Colorado has Boulder, and there is that type of phenomena. And I apply the same criterion to Mexico: I do not see the whole of Mexico as peripheral to the United States. Besides, I think that we have reached such a degree of integration between Mexico and the U.S., that it's absolutely impossible to establish a border, especially from the cultural point of view. Mexico extends beyond the Río Bravo, but, by the same token, the U.S. extends all the way to Chiapas. Culturally there is a border zone which is thousands of kilometers wide. You have to accept that fact: that's the way it has happened and, consequently, when the border is so wide, it's no longer a line, it's no longer a border, it no longer separates, it already unifies. That's why I believe that in some places here, to use the worn out terminology of the development-oriented mentality, are more "developed" than many places in the U.S., and therefore that whole notion ceases to be an interesting referent, especially, I think, when it comes to discussing the shape of cultural identities linked to the formation of cultural alternatives.

CF: What theory has to replace this whole conceptual system?

RB: I think that one of the things which has also fallen by the wayside is the need to look for and find *the* theory which has to explain our position. A process of fragmentation has also taken place. The borders disappear, but the critical spaces also split apart since they are entering a period of great difficulty. From the fragment space where I am standing, the answer can be found in my previous book, *The Imaginary Networks of Political Power*. What I try to do in that book is to develop a theory which attempts to explain this type of operation, but it is not held up as *the* theory. That is, it's a kind of theoretical implosion, where the ideas are quite disconnected from each other, and which try to account for the problems which have interested me in these two books: the legitimacy of power in general, and of political power in particular. *The Cage of Melancholy* is a book which attempts to determine how power is legitimized in Mexico from a cultural perspective: since I have stopped believing that that legitimacy stems from any mechanical idea of the class struggle, from imposition, or from domination in its traditional Marxist sense, you have to search for those networks that legitimize the forms of power, and which give a specifically Mexican coloring to the make-up of power, by which power is accepted as such. I have long been searching for the explanation of the forms of legitimization of modern states, and, in *The Imaginary Networks of Political Power*, I have developed theories which, in my judgment, enable me to explain some of these phenomena. While that may be my obsession, I am also involved in escaping from the ideologico-theoretical macrosystems.

CF: This reaction to the macrotheories and to the theoretical compulsion which led people to interpret everything through them, has, I think, spawned a dangerous secondary effect: in the newspapers, magazines and more specialized publications, you can see how the same discourse replicates itself and how it continues to maintain, almost against its will, the same old categories which should have already been refuted and replaced. For example, the classifications of "center and periphery." What we need now is not a macrotheoretical answer, but a different approach which clearly maps out the new lines of thinking.

RB: Of course, but the obsolescence of certain theories does not mean that there aren't any poor countries, and what's more, imperialism still exists and armies still invade. The problem is the group of theories which can explain that. I have mainly concerned myself with the forms of legitimization of power, especially those of a cultural type, and here is where I find it particularly difficult to distinguish between centers and peripheries. Do forms of power exist which are specific to the periphery, to the Third World, to backwardness, whereas in the West there are more sophisticated forms? I find that the mechanisms of political and cultural mediation are essentially the same in what is called the metropolis, development, etc., and in the underdeveloped countries. What I mean is that the Americans and the developed industrialized world do not live in We-ber's iron cage, while we still live in the premodern cage of myths. The modern West develops myths every bit as powerful as those that premodernity supposed-ly generates, and power mechanisms cannot be classified along a continuum which stretches in one long series from the marvelous French Republic to the horrendous Qadhafi regime. I also believe that the key to the legitimization of many of the distinctive qualities of the states of Western Europe can be discov-ered in the Sahara, or in South America, or in Mexico.

CF: What explanation would you propose for this phenomenon?

RB: Why the same myths when they are separated by such great distanc-es? One of the explanations, which really doesn't satisfy me, is the structuralist one: according to them, there exists a kind of basic structure, a kind of essential language of the human spirit, which continues to appear wherever. Or an expla-nation of a Freudian type can be offered: there exists a power, an internal force which is always going to manifest itself. I am inclined to think about a kind of economy of solutions—the same in nature, the cosmos and in society: for similar problems there arises a set of solutions which are nearly the mathematically possible ones. And so, if the same or similar problem arises in Kuwait, in Pata-gonia or Japan, there are going to be similar answers, given that the components of the problem are similar, and this does not happen because there has been contact, or that the myth has been disseminated. That is one of the most complex problems of modern social sciences, because that's where the problem of accept-ing the incoherence of the social world is introduced. The nineteenth century ideas in which we are so deeply rooted, that say that in the final analysis there is an essential unity of man and societies, are starting to be put in doubt, in a way which can even result in tragic consequences. That is, it has been shown that there are conglomerates, islands, which function in a very different manner, and, nevertheless, find similar solutions. It is the problem posed by Goedel, which I mention in *The Cage of Melancholy*: you achieve an infinity of mathematical solutions provided that you don't leave your island, because if you leave, the problem is different. These are the questions posed by Wittgenstein: does silence lie beyond language? Perhaps not. And the problem is that the answer is no. We are still living caught between a fundamental heterogeneity of culture and the strong pulsations which are generated at certain poles to unify the whole.

CF: How are those pulsations? When we consider, for example, the homogeneity of the youth rebellions of '68, phenomena like rock music and the "chavos banda" in Mexico, that is, certain cultural practices which are very similar in the North, South, East and West, it becomes evident that a system of communication and cultural contact exists between them. This cultural contact cannot be framed in the same Manichean and mechanical terms as it has been in the past: cultural penetration, transculturation, etc. There's no doubt that the contacts exist, but the dynamics of that contact must be rethought in terms of the activity which is verified on both sides of the communication. For lack of an understanding of the dynamics of this phenomenon, the literature of "la Onda," for example, was criticized for cultural colonization, without understanding the complexity and the interest of that cultural production.

RB: Why that explosion of similar phenomena in different places takes place is not easily explained by dissemination, although dissemination exists, and it can be proven. The same point was discussed for a long time in relation to the explosion of Romanticism: what it was, who influenced who. That dissemination-ist analytical exercise can be interesting, and many literary critics have engaged in that: to look for the influence of this one over here and that one over there, or the history of literary motifs, sources, the return to the origin in order to finish up by constructing a map of influences. In the 60s an opposing and alternative structuralist type of explanation emerged: dissemination undoubtedly occurs, but what the question is about is close to the medieval theory of "prefiguration," that is, previous conditions of a structural type exist which inevitably are going to give rise to parallel corollaries. I think that the structuralist alternative has also found itself in serious difficulties to the extent that it has turned out to be impossible for it to prove that there exists an essential architecture of the human spirit on all sides. Heterogeneity, incoherence are also facts of life, as well as dissemi-nation and coherence. And that's where the new explanations, of the kind pro-posed by Lyotard, can prove interesting, not as an explanation of everything, but they can serve as a guide. That is, to consider the possibility that coherence and incoherence coexist, that you can simultaneously explain a phenomenon by American influence and by internal conditions, and find at the same time an outcome whose ultimate explanation does not derive from either one, and it remains embedded in its incoherence. I believe that's the case of the definition of national identity: in all the cases I know, there is an explanation of dissemina-tion—the center can be Romantic Germany, or France at the turn of the century, that expands their influence, and, on the other hand, there is search for national identity all over the world. You can document those influences and analyze how the Europeans invent national identity. At the same time, you can document the local origins: in Mexico, after the Mexican Revolution, there is a series of circu-lating internal elements which condition and require the creation of a national identity, and where none existed, it is invented. And that invention starts to develop, it enriches itself and starts to become tradition, etc. Where does the truth lie? I don't think that it can be found in either of the two theories, that is, you have to think that it involves an interconnected network which has an essen-tially imaginary character, and which has its own evolution. At the same time, this network has a fundamental internal incoherence, it is penetrated by an incoherence which you are not going to be able to resolve: you have to accept the fact that the explanations are going to encounter a border which cannot be crossed; or if you go to the other side, you have to change your explanation and discard the previous explanation. Monism is no longer possible. So you have to learn to live with the contradictions, but not the Hegelian or Marxist kind, in which you arrive at a synthesis, but rather with contradictions which are going to remain intact because they stem from the fundamental incoherence of the networks in which you are embedded. To my mind this is one of the most interesting messages of all these discussions about postmodernity. For an ostensibly quite extended period of time we are going to be forced to live within the boundaries of incoherence.

CF: That same search for identity, which is one of the cornerstones of nation building, appears in the new panspaces constituted by the continents and the cultures which produce, for example, the concept of a Latin American essence.

RB: The definition of Argentinean or Peruvian or Mexican national identity goes hand in hand with a kind of cultural Bolivarism: the idea that all those combined identities are going to constitute a supernationalism. Carlos Fuentes is one of the most interesting theorists of that vision of an Ibero-American cultural conglomerate, and that is the meaning which can be found in his *Valiente Mundo Nuevo*, whose title paraphrases the *Brave New World* of Huxley. Leopoldo Zea gives an original twist to the same thing: this sum total of nations resolved into a great supernation, and all that more or less envisioned in opposition to the Anglo-Saxon world. It is interesting to remark that that idea of portraying solitude as something uniquely ours has many variants. For example, in Argentina you have turned numerous things on the subject, just like we have. One of the most important books which explains the American character is called *The Lonely Crowd*, and once again solitude is important. But the Danes also believe that they are alone when they feel themselves to be Danish, as do the Russians. For that reason I link this question to melancholy: melancholy lies at the root of nationalism. Nationalism needs to have a melancholic vein, or it is not authentic nationalism (he laughs). And that's why the image of solitude is used so much in such different and apparently unrelated places.

CF: What could be the political implications of this vision of fragmentation for Latin America? At least with respect to the elimination of the North/South polarity.

RB: There can be implications for the right as well as for the left. The most obvious rightist implications are the integration with the North American market, which is usually called imperialism, the integration into the world economy, the loss of sovereignty, all that. The implications for the left: success in giving democratic political representation to the fragmented segments, that is, it is not a strong national state held above the interests of the fragmented groups which is going to represent the nation and all of us, as is the case, for example, in Mexico, which thus makes a mockery of the most basic democratic process. And to return to the idea that, by the same token, the fragmented group has to represent itself, for another segment cannot represent us, there must be a principle of democratic political representation, and not a superstate which replaces the process. Those are the progressivist implications. That's why I don't like the interpretation of postmodernity as another smoke screen of imperialism. It can and cannot be that. Postmodernity has an advanced side: I believe that for Lyotard it is basically a set of leftist problems although, for others, it is clearly not the case. Are we going to lose our national identity because they are going to drain away our national soul? Well, okay, but on the other hand, it's really in the fragmented enclaves where the ethnic groups, the intellectuals of this or that stripe, and the inhabitants of such and such town really live. Each one of those little pieces must achieve a form of representation, and the only plan of action presently available is representative democracy. That is, some people get together and say: these people are going to represent us, and it will not be a superstate in the name of the idiosyncrasy of the Mexican or the Argentinean, or the Chilean, which will defend me. Nor will there be the great cultural caudillos like Carlos Fuentes who will defend the Latinos vis-à-vis the Anglos, who are going to subsume all the fragmented richness of the writers, essayists, poets, etc., into one category.

CF: In this rejection of influences I find a deep-seated elitist attitude: in the name of a certain genuine essence "those colonized masses of people" are rebuffed in a gesture which, in reality, represents a simple rejection of anything of a mass nature.

RB: Sure, the mass phenomenon as the place where the damaging influences coming from the outside can be arrested—which happened with the chavos-banda and rock music. Obviously, rock music is a product of North American influence, that can't be any more evident. But if you live in a barrio, you can prove that rock music is the most powerful mechanism of identity of the local group, without its origin being of any importance. The groups of chavos meet and admire a rock band which sings in English, and they dress in the punk style, or any other way. What I mean is that all this is a tremendously powerful element of local identity which, moreover, can have a strong anti-American quality, its class consciousness—against the "hueros"[1] as we say here. So you're faced with the contradiction that those who identify with a rock group, which sing in English, and who dress up like the same people in New York or Chicago, they

---

[1]"Hueros": the blond, and metaphorically, the privileged classes.

evidently have a class struggle with the blond-haired guys, "los hueritos," whom they see as foreigners. Although those "hueritos" of their barrio probably are nationalistic and support the strengthening of the national culture and identify with the ideas of Carlos Fuentes, and anything else that you want. So you're going to have the rocker, apparently very Americanized, who represents the true defender of a fragment of identity, and the nationalist, in the role of a foreign interloper.

In 1973 or 74, I was living about 300 kilometers north of Mexico City. This area, which was populated by the Otomi Indians, is one of the most backward, impoverished and ignored regions of the country. In this very region, where the women still wore their traditional attire, almost every indigenous community had its own rock band. One of them, for example, used the English name of "Purple Seed," and the other ones used similar names. So here are these "chavos" (buddies) who wore "guaraches" (Indian sandals)—the punk style still hadn't caught on—and played rock; and who do you suppose they were opposing? They were opposing the newcomers, the National Indigenous Institute representatives, belonging to the PRI bureaucracy, who shuddered at the sight of all this. These representatives were tying to instill in the Otomis a sense of the Mexican national culture. What you could see was that the oppressed Otomis were defending themselves against the foreigners, who were the nationalists calling for the revival of indigenous culture. And what were they using to defend themselves? Rock, as an affirmation of their Otomi heritage, in direct opposition to the nationalists, who spoke to the Otomis about the Mexican national entity and about what it means, in abstract terms that they could not grasp. That's where you find that essential incoherence. This is an example of that incoherence and of that potentiality.

CF: How do you reposition yourself in relation to all this criticism of the traditional leftist concepts?

RB: I still adhere to the leftist position, I can't say that I come from the left and that I am no longer part of the leftist position. Of the old concepts, I believe that one of the few which survives is that of "the left," exactly because of its vagueness, the leftist stand of society. That has not disappeared and I continue to position myself clearly on that side. What has happened with Marxism—and that process has accelerated considerably as a result of the '89 revolutions—is that it has continued to be watered down and blended with society. This is a very healthy and good process, since it was a medieval castle, a true church which was armed against any outside influence and, therefore, it completely deteriorated. What's happening to Marxism is the same thing which has happened to the great political and theoretical traditions of the left: they are like very narrow rivers which end up flowing into the sea. For example, Rousseanian thought, the French Age of Enlightenment: today no one is going to be an ardent supporter of the French Enlightenment, but what doubt is there that it did exist, that it was extraordinarily important and that it has entered the flow of that immense space which is the left, which still exists, and which is going to yield a great deal.

Fortunately, the moment has arrived for Marxism to disappear, to dissolve as it were. In fact, it is dissolving into an ocean of the left, but at the same time it's gaining a lot and so is everybody else. The limits are difficult to establish: borders are lost—just like the great traditions of the French Enlightenment were lost after the Revolution—they start to lose one meaning while acquiring another: that's what has happened to Marxism. So I, who for a long time was deeply involved, and militated within the framework of Marxism for many years, I feel that the very course of Marxism itself has led me to this point. I believe that this whole transformation of the past several years, the 1989 Revolution, which, I believe, is a good way to call it, was produced by the internal forces of that world. The Right and liberalism operated according to the traditional thesis that the socialist world was totalitarian and that nothing was happening, there couldn't be a single reform nor could anything change. In 1989, several changes and reforms in various nerve centers of the socialist world have changed the face of the world, and today there are no more blocs. With no more than that, this is already an extraordinary revolution. Did that happen because of the dynamism in Washington? No. In Western Europe? No again. It was in Moscow, in the backward, barbarian and totalitarian countries. This doesn't mean that I get all excited about it, because, in reality, socialism was already rotten to the core; but that's where the change comes from. So that the old idea of the poem of Cavafy that the barbarians bring about the changes turn out to be true. At the time when Europe was planning its unification and was proposing the European Economic Community, hoping to generate one of the most extensive spaces of civilization, well, all of a sudden, it finds itself caught up in the whirlpool of events because of what has happened in Northern Europe, and which wasn't included in its plans. And the whole map of the world has changed: history, which was organized into two blocs, now started to move and we don't know where it will all lead.

CF: How do you see these processes of economic integration between Mexico and the U.S., or between the countries of the Southern Cone, like Argentina, Uruguay, Brazil and Chile?

RB: The problem is whether or not all this economic integration has any corollary in the cultural domain. The non-acceptance of the cultural frontier does not seem to be the other side of the integration coin in the Common Market. I think that the dependency relationship (as it had been traditionally viewed) when reexamined, it becomes apparent that it really does not generate underdevelopment but development. I believe that we were mistaken when we thought in terms of the sociology of dependency which said that this process was the development of underdevelopment. I believe that the solid classical theses, Marxist as well as neoclassic, were right: when capital invades a backward country, it develops it. Development signifies poverty, but it is the same poverty which is also found in New York. It's the worn out discussion of Marx about colonialism in India. For example, what is going to happen now in Central Europe? There is going to be a new form of poverty, but we could say that it's going to be a different kind of poverty. Just as the Mexican form of poverty before the Revolution is different from that of today, which is a capitalist, bourgeois poverty with radios, etc.; poverty but with economic development. We have to evaluate integration from other points of view, but I don't think that it serves any purpose to say that it is going to underdevelop us even more. It's not going to underdevelop us more. A deeper penetration of American capital into Mexico is going to develop Mexico economically. I think that it's time to introduce criteria of a qualitative type. It's not that it's going to slow us down more, no, it's going to develop us, but the question is, what kind of development do we want? There are elements of a qualitative nature which must be analyzed. That is the strength of those guys like Salinas and Fujimori.[2] That modernity they introduce is certainly going to change things, produce development, and is going to introduce the country to the world of capitalism. It's not going to produce more poverty, nor is it going to solve the problem of poverty. I remember a trip which I took to India and to Nepal (that was fifteen years ago). In Nepal you saw widespread poverty, a rural poverty. Nepal had more or less just opened up half-way to the outside world, but we're talking about a very isolated country which had not even been a colonial country, because no colonial power had taken any interest in subjugating Nepal: it had never been politically dependent, or been a colony. From there you jumped to New Delhi, and so you found capitalist poverty, masses of people suffering from the worst kind of hunger, something completely different, but evidently it was a great power alongside Nepal which is a completely agrarian country. So you could see that Nepal was heading in that direction: after a little time passed, in Katmandú you were already going to see those phenomena of people dead or dying of hunger in the streets that you see in India, and which are not the product of backwardness, but rather of development. These things occur because India is a great power in Asia, like Brazil is in Latin America. So that is going to happen, but does it make sense to try and stop it? With these new rules of the game, we have to learn to fight like Westerners and not like Indians who descend from the mountains to the sound of drum beats, if we don't want to keep on losing out forever. We're going to see how the underdogs

---

[2]At the present time, presidents of Mexico and Peru, respectively.

defend themselves within the framework of the West; we must not forget that there they also have a long history of struggles.

Translated by Robert Sims

Works Cited

Bartra, Roger. *The Cage of Melancholy: Identity and Metamorphosis in the Mexican Character*. Christopher J. Hall, trans. New Brunswick, N.J.: Rutgers University Press, 1992.

——. *The Imaginary Networks of Political Power*. New Brunswick, N.J.: Rutgers University Press, 1992.

——. *La jaula de la melancolía*. México: Grijalbo, 1987.

——. *Las redes imaginarias del poder político*. México: Ediciones Era: Instituto de Investigaciones Sociales, UNAM, 1981.

Bonfil Batalla, Guillermo. *México profundo: una civilización negada*. México: Grijalbo; Consejo Nacional para la Cultura y las Artes, 1990.

Fuentes, Carlos. *Valiente mundo nuevo: épica, utopía y mito en la novela hispanoamericana*. México: Fondo de Cultura Económica, 1990.

Huxley, Aldous. *Brave New World*. New York: Harper & Row Publishers, 1946.

O'Gorman, Edmundo. *Destierro de sombras: luz en el origen de la imagen y culto de Nuestra Señora de Guadalupe del Tepeyac*. México: Universidad Nacional Autónoma de México, 1986.

——. *La invención de América. El universalismo de la cultura de Occidente*. México: Fondo de Cultura Económica, 1958.

Riesman, David. *The Lonely Crowd: A Study of the Changing American Character*. New Haven: Yale University Press, 1960, 1950.

WORDS FROM UNCERTAINTY. AN INTERVIEW WITH JORGE JUANES
Claudia Ferman

Claudia Ferman: In the interview published by *Casa del tiempo*,[1] you state that "from its inception modernity has had its counterpart, its protest or its rejection"—which is the case of "the romanticisms," in those which the response or the rejection of modernity appears in artistic terms. In that sense a certain continuity might exist between Romanticism, the avant-garde movements of the 20th century and the postmodern movements. The difference with postmodernity is that this protest no longer manifests itself in artistic terms: the answer ceases to be an artistic problem and becomes a global, social, philosophical and generalized problem. But one can trace that opposition, that debate back to the same inception of modernity.

Jorge Juanes: I refer the question about postmodernity back to the question about modernity, and the question about modernity to the question about Western culture and civilization. In my opinion, what has to be investigated is precisely what Western culture and civilization mean, what sense they have, what they are based on, what their values are. I believe that today that is the center of the questioning of theoretical thinking, and that is what I am trying to do. I believe that this culture, this civilization emerge, from the start, within an obvious, clear and manifest contradiction, and this can be seen in the same controversy which accompanies the birth of philosophy in Greece. That is, as a confrontation between what I would call the tragic position, in a very broad sense, similar to that of Nietzsche in *The Birth of Tragedy*, and what could be called the rationalist position. Let's not forget that the birth of philosophy has its inception in the denial of tragicity. The repudiation of tragicity is the repudiation of mystery, of the body, well, it's the rejection of everything that in some way impedes pure, pristine, unpolluted, finished, argumentative, representative thought, etc. There is a division at the birth of the West: when philosophy arises, the initial thesis that maintained that the known forms part of the unknown is opposed by the contrary principle: the unknown forms part of the known. That is, the known is presented as an a priori, and if something is not yet known, it is not difficult to find it out since in some way we already have the domain where this (or where

---

[1]Magali Tercero, "¿Existe el postmodernismo?" *Casa del tiempo* 8.81 (1989): 3-20.

everything) fits. I think that when the question of the idea of truth is really established, starting precisely from the hypostasis of the idea of reason, the difference is really born, or, in other words, what we can call the West. The idea of the Universal Man, the universal, the creation of universals, and the relationship of the universals before the "other" were already present in this. This relationship was always a universal: what is right will be the hegemonic, what advances, and what will continue to constitute World History on a global scale. All this originates in Greece, and, 2,000 years later, it's already a global truth, it's an established, real truth. Then, when this is carried out, when everything is already Westernized and these principles are really established, when the Universal Man already starts to exist, or he is already an indisputable reality, that's when the profound questioning of the meaning of the West manifests itself in an urgent manner: this is the moment that we are presently living. If all this is true, it is also true that the West is a culture which doesn't manifest itself in a monolithic way. I believe that the West carries its own answer in itself: the West has always produced its own response. This polemic explains in some way the dynamics of this culture, it accounts for its exclusions as well as its inclusions of otherness. That is, while on the one hand through the system of reason, the will to dominate, this is an anthropophagic, excluding culture, on the other hand, through what we can call the tragic will, this is an inclusive culture. This causes it to be a culture which moves in a paradoxical manner, excluding, including, eliminating and receiving. What I am really trying to do is retrace, rescue and reveal all that other part which sometimes people wish to ignore: today the idea of the West has been enshrined as an equivalent of the idea of pure reason in absolute terms, conveniently forgetting these nonconformist elements. In modernity, the non-conformist element is what I call the romanticisms, which would be part of the larger sphere which I would label tragicity. What are the romanticisms? At the time when the Enlightenment arises, at the moment when Descartes postulates the non-participation of the senses and body in the formulation of an exact, pure thought, precisely at that time, the call arises for the vindication of all that wishes to be expelled, thus creating two irreconcilable movements, two absolutely unyielding perspectives, which have given rise to modernity. For example, when modernity appears on the scene and tries to establish between men and the world the mediation of scientific, exact discursivity, or the physico-mathematical discursivity, the same Enlightenment realizes that no man struggles because it is clear to him that two and two are four. That is, the Enlightenment, in its indifference does not succeed in capturing the attention of the masses, nor does it succeed in attracting large numbers of people to its intellectual project, and the same Enlightenment is faced with the task of creating a mythology. German idealism, Hegel, will be the agent which creates the mythology of Reason: a conception with which men would transform themselves into subjects and for whom everything would be objects, something to dominate. The myth of Reason would consist of the triumph of the Spirit over Matter, drawing all that confronts with Reason or the Spirit, to the parameter, to the black hole of Reason. Afterwards this would be completed in Marx by the idea of socialism. I believe that the fall of socialism is the failure of the only modern myth that Reason has created; this myth has just collapsed and Reason does not have another myth right now. However, along with this myth of Reason another myth will arise in Romanticism, if you want an alternative, which is the myth of the return to nature, of the reconciliation with nature, and, as a result, the loss of the self. That is, there is something before and after Man, to which Man owes his existence, and does not stem from Man, it is Man who owes his existence to it. This is what will give rise to another idea of the self, to another idea concerning social relationships, and it will be what will make up the very core of Romanticism. Because of that it seems to me that postmodernity contains a good deal of banality: postmodernity considers modernity as something solid, so it would be the very agent which would inaugurate the transgression of modernity, the "post." Or rather, postmodernity does not base itself on the transgression which from the very start of modernity has been taking place, it does not establish a solid relationship with all the responses which modernity has been receiving. Postmodernity claims to be *the* answer *per se* which modernity receives: with the leadership of a group of French philosophers—to which we have already become accustomed—the start of a new era of thinking, a new way of being is proposed. I believe that at that point the possibility of tracking this incredibly subversive tradition emerging from Western culture is lost, which has manifested itself above all in the let's call them displaced, marginal ideas, and in the sphere of art. The sphere of art, from the very beginning, creates products, relationships of men with nature and between themselves, forms of seeing, of feeling, of touching and of living, which are specific and which cannot be explained from the parameters of reason (it's not in vain that Plato wants to expel the poets and the tragedians). The best proof of it are all the attempts which have been made to explain art outside the realm of art: sociological, economic, political attempts which sought to explain art as an expression of conditioning of a social and economic type. In reality art expresses itself, has its own history, follows its own path, has its own forms, its own parameters of its make-up, and a particular form of affirmation. In that sense, I am proposing that we abandon this monolithic vision of Western culture, that we stop reproaching a supposedly absolute culture, and that instead we question that which has really given rise to anthropophagy, barbarity, to the destruction of everything which has crossed its path, and which, in my opinion, has a lot do with the will of reason and the idea of truth. *I believe that the idea of truth is the disease which caused the most deaths, in comparison with which*

AIDS, cancer, tuberculosis or the diseases yet to come are nothing but child's play.

CF: According to this concept, the existence of this debate would be located at the very start of Western civilization, much farther away than modernity. How do you distinguish the specificity of this debate today?

JJ: The West keeps thinking about everything that it builds: the practical movement in the make-up of Western civilization is perpetually accompanied by the meditation on the meaning of that act. For the moderns—and here I am referring to the person who would finally complete this experience theoretically, that is Hegel—Western culture presents itself as a kind of odyssey. If it appears that this culture was always guided by Reason, it was guided, as Hegel says, beneath the *horizon of the Cunning of Reason*, that is, men attained Reason without really knowing it. Modernity's claim is that it certainly already knows what reason exactly and completely is. It's like the culmination of the odyssey, from which you can cast a backward glance and can reconstruct that history and see how full of detours it is, how many times it has taken the wrong road, has lost its way by taking paths which have not led anywhere. Even so, after all these experiences, a reading of an experience of experiences can be made, which would be the experience of Reason opening new pathways. Thanks to the self-knowledge of Reason, Reason continues to establish the dates, the names and the stages of the odyssey. Modernity traces a new demarcation toward the past and toward the future, from which it says what has been and what will have to be, but it does it with a power which Reason had never had, because modernity is born when Reason is associated with the idea of certainty. What modernity wants is a line of thinking of which there is no doubt: modernity doubts everything in order to arrive at non-doubt, indubitability, exactitude, absolute transparency. Each one of these philosophers who takes part in this argument will claim that he has attained absolute transparency: Kant, Hegel, Marx, Sartre, etc. (although there will also be an argument about what absolute transparency means). This is part of the matter. Another question which I consider decisive is also found in Hegel, but I believe that this philosopher does not draw the necessary conclusions. Hegel says that the decisive point to explain modernity, apart from this self-awareness and the liberation of Reason, consists of the rise of individuality for its own sake, for the first time in history. This means that the final principle on which anything can be founded is individual freedom, in an unconditional way. That is, autonomy, the irreducibility of each person, is the principle which cannot be violated in the building of any relationship. This principle not only alludes to possessive individualism—to egocentricity, egotism and narcissism, as some have wanted to affirm—but also to the fact that the person is in principle free, feeling, thinking, in all his acts. He must never relinquish this accomplishment before anyone, which is individual freedom. And this is extremely important; it is one of the greatest advantages which we enjoy: everything isn't apocalypses now. What has transpired? Why does everyday life suddenly change into the privileged space of all social experience, including art? One definite characteristic of modernity that is not necessarily implied in the logic of absolute rationalism consists of the attempt at unconditional emancipation of individual freedom. We can say that, at least since the Renaissance and in a more straightforward way starting with the 18th century, the conviction arises in the conscience of the moderns that life belongs to each person in an absolute way: his way of thinking, feeling, believing. As Hegel would say, freedom now resides in the self of each individual. From that comes the clarion call from the Enlightenment: think for yourself, be what you are, affirm your existence; a call to arms which, it must be pointed out, contains an undeniably subversive message. Well then, it seems to me that even with all the difficulties which one may find, the political institutionalism of the modern world, in terms of the order of civilian society as well as the order of the State, of the judicial but also moral structure, the order of everyday as well as private life, has had to start responding progressively to the demands of individual liberty, a fact that in some countries makes its presence felt in an earnest and effective manner. Without a doubt, tolerance, the democratization of life, freedom of speech and of election are today common practices which, in case they don't occur in some other place, as still happens in autocratic or totalitarian societies, are at least demanded and are included in the fundamental life agenda of every citizen. In the U.S., or in the Europe of the Common Market, to give one example, the antagonisms tend to diminish. Of course, the situation still has troublesome aspects: the indulgence of the individual self, superficiality, consumerism, emotional disengagement, passionless hedonism, apathy, indifference. This appears in art: even though it incorporates as never before immediate, risky, circumstantial and ephemeral experiences, avoiding any idea of meaning at all costs (in which artistic representation was nothing more than a pretext to smuggle in a certain idea or a particular conception of the world). On the other hand, it neglects the technical structures and the rigor which allowed it to distance itself and distinguish itself from the ordinary forms of life. It appears that contemporary artists are ready to efface any distance between art and life, a fact which, contrary to what one might think, does not cease to be disturbing as long as art has been—that's the way I view it—a focal point of resistance against the mediate and immediate intrusions of social life. But I insist, today everything is quotidian in nature. Quotidianness fascinated by spectacle and at grips with any attempt at complexity. There is no doubt that the postmodern works are not nearly as subversive as they could be. I acknowledge that the spontaneity defended by the postmoderns, in which existence concentrates on the gratuitous succession of irreducible moments, rejects the possibility of thinking in longer terms, a future, and that it bases time on personal life. Certainly, this mounts a needed attack against the idea of history, which permits freedom to remain open, to evolve, never closed by any limited theory. The postmoderns certainly do not claim to link freedom, their freedom, to the promise of absolute projects. The so-called postmodern art embodies this individualistic expression, but the present works are not as subversive as they could be.

Well then, this availability which we have concerning ourselves, this irreducibility that no one ever had before, and this freedom of infinite choice in which the only limit is oneself has continued to shape modern societies, and has continued to be a driving force, although it has been a very slow and tortuous process (and sometimes negated by the same course of events, since it is a very subversive principle). What are its implications? The institutional, political, legal, and even the moral structures of the modern world have become more and more plastic, and have continued to respond to this principle. What I mean is that this principle of individual freedom has progressively created an institution which resembles it. This has led to the opening of channels for the creation of an open personality, sanctioned, authorized and even driven by law, especially in the more developed societies. What has happened, then, is that a preponderant role has been granted to the totality of all individuals and, consequently, the possibilities of choice and of the voices which express opinions have multiplied. I believe that this has a lot to do with what erroneously and with absolutely inadequate concepts has been designated as postmodernism. "Postmodernity" is a word which is symptomatic of something much more complex and profound; what happens is that experiences more radical than those which postmodernity advances have been disregarded. It has even included in its program ways of thinking and thinkers which have nothing to do with it, because it has not been able to establish exactly what it is thinking. What it is thinking is what I want to say: *that daily life, the everyday life of men and women, this everyday life, has gained an irreversible role.* Obviously, postmodernity possesses an antirationalist will. In what sense? If we agree—as it seems that everyone agrees—that it arises in the field of architecture, against international architecture, its willingness to respond to this universality can be recognized. This movement rises up against an architecture which does not start with concrete and empirical man but with universal man, and therefore it is an architecture which builds its structures within absolutely artificial parameters, while it dispenses with the idea of nature and context. That is, it is a geometrico-abstract architecture, constructed in the offices of architects located in the great capitals of the central countries, from where architecture of any space, any territoriality is constructed. It doesn't matter if it's cold or it's hot, if the mountains exist or the sea exists, if it's green or otherwise, those guys always build the same thing, the same little box which has transformed the shape of the whole modern urban landscape into a homogeneous, universal experience, which responds to identical, common denominators, and has depersonalized any organic, contextualized and local possibility in which corporeality and physicality might participate. Postmodernity is thus an experience which breaks with all this universality identified with certain abstract, quantitative, perfectly definable and univocal principles, and which are moreover reduced to a set of formulas. That's one part of it. On the other hand, it is a crisis of the idea of truth, or rather, of those ways of thinking in which the philosopher possesses the truth, so that he can talk about everything, and from that basis he can totalize. *This totalizing way of thinking is bankrupt, the totalizing practices are bankrupt, the discourses of unitary meaning, and of all that which is called dialectic reasoning, the all-embracing, all-knowing reasoning, is in the process of falling apart; a very fortunate development I would say. In some way, the West has had the strength, the spirit to engender within itself its own gravedigger (a gravedigger who probably changes once again into the buried person).* I think that this idea of postmodernity, with which even its forgers are presently not satisfied, embodies the symptom of new things, and we can't simply shrug our shoulders and say: ah hell, one more style. When modernity comes into being, art (Romanticism, Symbolism, and later on all the modern artistic experience) turns its back on modernity, against modernity. And this explosion which we are witnessing, from the artistic and social point of view, opens up new horizons. I would even say that there isn't any modern art, that saying modern art is a linguistic misnomer that we have to overcome: it is a question of projecting the dominant language on to a group of displaced practices, which are then designated by a language which does not relate to them. Just like the idea of the avant-garde, which is a military idea created by the Jesuits and which relates to battle, to defeating the other side, to the idea that somebody knows while the rest are left in the dark, to the idea of truth; and it is used for art: it's inconceivable that one can consider art from the perspective of the avant-garde. What is true is that art continues a tradition which has always been active in the West, and also in the East, which is not that art is an exceptional, extraordinary, initiatory experience which requires a time which is not the time of daily life, that requires refuge, solitude, self-absorption, techniques, etc., which are not created in daily, immediate life but which have to be forged almost entirely in solitude, and already in the case of modernity, very much in solitude. Modern art is going to strive to differentiate itself from daily life, since in the eyes of this experience it would be an alienated life where the world of anonymity and the masses dominates. In this way, art is going to undergo a magnificent development but, at the same time, it will have a very private, closed character, especially in its fundamental experiences, which are very rigorous with respect to its shaping, its structuring of the artistic form. At a given moment, this is going to lead to experimenting with the language itself; that is, painting is going to be metapainting; the novel, metanovel; poetry, metapoetry. That is, artistic language is going to attempt to nurture itself: writing will live for itself without any consideration given to meaning—it does not allude to good or evil, it refers to itself, it is self-sufficient, it consumes itself. All the artistic poetics will pass through this experience of an autistic language. This gives rise to marvelous works, to grandiose things, but it also leads to exhaustion. When the post-war period comes with the reconstruction of a new form of daily life, of new ways of living, of relating to one another, of feeling—in which the U.S. undoubtedly leads the pack—new signs, signals, new forms of listening, new forms of musicality, new plastic and graphic forms are created which art is not registering because art continues to exist in the esoteric and the ivory tower, which in turn leads to extreme experiences. These forms of art exhaust themselves in closed experiences like those of Mondrian; and then comes the explosion from below. All those signs rebel, they want to be heard, they want to form part of the artistic experience, and a radical reshaping takes place in which pop art appears. The pop art of Andy Warhol is not as banal nor or as stupid as has been thought. It's precisely the explosion of this whole new world of signs, which arose in the experience of common man, which is going to nurture the artistic experience once again. I believe that this has a lot to do with what is going on in art today, although we don't know exactly where all this is leading. It is also going on in literature, painting, music and theater. Sure there are still people who continue to believe that all this is pure shit, that what has to be done is just the opposite: close yourself off even more, transform artistic experience into an absolutely hermetic one. For example, Grotowski, the dramatist, who contends that in theater you have to forget about representing anything, since this is a society which doesn't deserve representation. Then the theatrical experience is transformed into a life experience in a closed circuit, into a kind of sect which attempts to construct within its confines an untransferable, unmassifiable and absolutely closed form of living. That is, it's a question of resurrecting the polemic of whether art has to blend into life, or whether art continues to be the stimulus for the possibility of transgression in life.

CF: What is there beyond the West, or what are the limits of the West?

JJ: The West has imposed its limits, but it has also been capable of surpassing its limits; for example, starting with art. The West, in the field of the plastic arts, painting—which is what I know best—creates a plastic form of construction which responds to perspective. This principle maintains itself in an unshakable way, it arises with Giotto and stands above all the changes which take place in the movements in painting. Later come the Renaissance, the Quattrocento, the Baroque, Rococo, Romanticism, Symbolism, Naturalism, Impressionism, including Cézanne, and in spite of all the differences that these movements present among themselves, that pictorial order remains undisturbed. It is a paradigmatic order which can be considered as Western plasticity's ID card—the way in which it manifests itself. Already in the 19th century this order starts to show signs of exhaustion and then the absolutization of parts of that order appears, for example, as the use of atmosphere in the case of Turner, or the problem of banishing the beautiful and the bursting forth of agony in the case of Goya, or the problem of the absolutization of vision in the case of Impressionism, or the general eclecticisms in all Romantic as well as symbolic painting; that is, it is an order which no longer gives anything more of itself. There is a limit here: the West, in this area, has reached a limit and it doesn't know how to go beyond it. What happens then? Well, Western art breaks its limits by appropriating other experiences in an exceptionally creative way—which is the case with Picasso—that is, by appropriating forms of structuring and of plasticity taken from non-Western art: African, Pre-Hispanic and Oriental art. It appropriates them without any qualm and starts to explore them within its own dynamics. And this leads to the shattering of its limits, that is, it again enables the Western plastic arts to continue to evolve in an impressive way, as we have seen in the 20th century, like a kind of wild, infinite delirium which has created names as perhaps no other century has. The case of the plastic arts allows us to clearly see how a limit is reached and how one can crash the limit. I believe that the same thing has happened in the case of literature; Borges would be a good example: it's not a coincidence that at the end of his life he is studying Japanese. And if Borges had continued to live twenty years more, he would have studied Chinese and Sanskrit, because his project starts exactly from the premise that modern man is in principle a cosmopolitan man, and that cosmopolitan experience, which is the experience of going beyond the boundaries of Western culture, can nurture his creations. In that sense, Borges did not even deny being a Latin American or Argentinean writer, or merely a writer in Spanish: for him this matter was always a limit, an accident, but not the most fundamental concern. Or, in the case of theater, starting with Artaud it is no longer a theater of representation, it's a theater of the body, seduced by the Oriental theater, by the norms and disciplines of the Oriental actor. This has enriched the whole Western scene. This also applies to Eugenio Barba, Peter Brook, and many others.

When you get right down to it, you could say that the West has been unfaithful to what could be called its identification papers and, as this experience is then internalized, a loss of identity occurs followed by a kind of intercommunication and fusion with what is different from the West, a very interesting and characteristic phenomenon of the 20th century.

CF: From this side of the ocean, how do we belong to the West?

JJ: I believe that we belong in a complete way. You are referring directly to Latin America because what is located on this other side is what has been the advance guard of modernity—the U.S.—whose experience is now being imitated by Europe itself. *Because in reality the West is a soul, and souls are those which transmigrate, the bodies remain fixed but the souls transmigrate. The souls can occupy any territory, they can be in Latin America, the U.S., Japan, China, and what predominates is a metaphysical horizon. And it's possible that metaphysical horizon may find more robust bodies in other places than the bodies which gave life to them.* And that helps to explain the progressive displacement of Europe from the center, which is the event of the 20th century. I believe that the political event of the 20th century isn't the construction of socialism, nor all these things which have been said, no, I believe that it is really the displacement of Europe as a hegemonic center of universal history. That is, during twenty centuries Europe has been the axis of universal history, and in the 20th century it is displaced. Now Europe again wants to be the axis of universal history and it is doing everything it can to carry along another twenty centuries, and if it isn't stopped, Europe may just achieve it. But at the moment there is a transmigration. That transmigration is happening in the US and in Latin America. For example, it is very interesting to analyze the question of new Hispanic art. When the priests arrive here, the first thing they do is to worry about the world of images and about making a kind of translation of the pre-Hispanic beliefs into Christianity, starting from a kind of metamorphosis of the Christian images in terms of aesthetics. So that immediately they set up a school and "teach" the indigenous people to paint: they give them some pictures and the indigenous people copy them. Everything is a copy: it's the West, in this case, Spain, which establishes the models and possibilities of creating feelings and also of understanding. But starting at some point, there is a change and you can see that the models are taken over in quite a radical and more profound way than what has been believed. A real assumption then takes place and also a perpetual concern with being in contact with that culture, including posing the problem of creativity within the framework of that culture. I believe that this can be seen in the 17th, 18th, 19th centuries and even at the present time. But it does not stop being a singular experience, because that part of Europe which is coming here is also singular. It isn't a Europe like an abstract, generic bloc which is coming, but rather it is the Spanish world which in its turn is an eccentric world within the same Western culture. Therefore, the question is not to try to make some kind of exclusivism and to return to a Latin American autism, which I believe has not led anywhere and has hampered all the possibilities of thinking and creating. I don't believe that is the way, I don't believe that we need to have complexes, nor do you have to consider the thinkers who are not born right here, in this specific country, as foreigners, strangers, as not our own, etc. All this tires me out a little, it seems to me to be a little demagogic and populist, and I feel that it is some kind of complex which it has not been possible to remove.

CF: What new cultural practices do you recognize in this movement?

JJ: We are witnessing a rebellion of the masses (and here history certainly starts to tip the scales a little in favor of Ortega y Gasset), but curiously enough it is a rebellion in differentiation. You have to talk not of the mass, but of the masses, since it is a kind of rebellion of the downtrodden, completely social in nature, but in a very differentiated and particular manner thanks to the question of individual freedom and the irreducibility of the individual. That is, there are pleasures for all, there are multiple choices, there are multiple supplies and demands. In this sense, the existence of one principle which dominates the rest, of one pleasure which overshadows the rest, of a body of ideas which eclipses the rest, has eroded away. It's also certain that there exists a tolerance toward everything, a total indiscrimination, and an indisputable superficiality: a banalization. There is a coexistence of the things that are valid and things which are completely worthless: what we could say is the cultural industry, the products where, from a certain political, economic or ideological perspective, all the semiotic, scriptural and plastic practices are inferred; and that other part which adheres more to transgressive and subversive aims. Everything appears confused, everything seems mixed up, it's real promiscuity. It's difficult to move around in that promiscuity, for there are many things which seduce you. But if you ask me, I believe that of all this which comes from what would perhaps be the most relevant point for me, I would have no trouble in answering that with the demise of the myth of Reason a reassessment of life takes place. Because, according to the parameters of Reason, Reason conceives itself and establishes its primary purpose. But this purposiveness doesn't actually occur: everything must gravitate toward that purposiveness but it is never attained and always remains deferred—there is always some reason that intervenes so that it is not attained. What results is that real time turns out to be the time of history, a kind of infinite, eternal time which would transcend finite and concrete time between birth and death. So that upon the demise of this form of experiencing in terms of history, that infinite time also collapses, that future time which never arrives and which surpasses concrete life also collapses, and in lieu of this a reassessment of concrete life takes place. That is, there is no longer any time but that which flows between life and death, and that is the time in which one plays out one's destiny. It is that experience which counts, not the experience which I am going to live, because positing plenitude in a time which I am not going to live is tantamount to disqualifying me, it's like considering that my life is finally nothing more than a mediation in order to get to a full life in which I am not going to be a player. I believe that one of the valid principles of these postmodern times is precisely the awareness that people have that there is no other life than this one, there are no other experiences than those that one is living, everything is being played out in that present moment in which one is acting, loving, having relationships of friendship and hatred, and that there is a short time, which is not the extended time of history, in which one must define his life. In artistic terms this has given rise in American literature to a literature in which the characters are allowed to live in that circumstantial, instantaneous relationship in which the acts that they are carrying out only have meaning in the moment they are being carried out. These acts are not, as happened in the old literature, a moment in which what seemed circumstantial turns out to be the representation of something more transcendental where meaning manifests itself, the infinite time of meaning and of destiny. I believe that the recuperation of spontaneity, of chance, of circumstantiality and of the moment is something which has given a fresh look to contemporary art, more naturalness, self-confidence, antisolemnity, and which has dispelled many rigidities and pretensions. That seems to me to be the most recoverable virtue. Of course, virtue also contains the defect; I keep thinking—here it would seem that I am contradicting myself, but that's not the case—that art is an initiatory experience, an aureatic experience, that really needs an irreducible space, a distance. I continue to think that, although that distance may not be an absolute distance—as existed not many years ago, above all in the last experiments of the avant-garde movements of the 20th century which asked for an absolute distancing and which were of a sterile, esoteric nature—the problem continues to be the problem of distance (I am not using the term distance here in the sense that Bertolt Brecht proposes, so that perhaps it's better from now on to use the term "gap"). This gap separates daily, habitual experience in the world of work, political and civilian life, from the world of art. Many aspects of modern art are no more than pyrotechnical games that have no solidity and fall like autumn leaves: when the wind blows a little, they fall and vanish, yesterday's innovations become today's outmoded relics. I believe that there is a kind of superficiality in that. A good example is 1968, when Marcuse suddenly let himself get all wound up in the American thing, he almost became a hippie, and he started to say that art had to submit to life and life had to be estheticized, and that it's in immediate life that the aesthetic experience was really being created. I remember very well how Adorno slapped him on the wrist, and reminded him of this problem of form. I believe that Adorno was right; otherwise, everything dissolves and then everything becomes integrated, and what had remained unintegrated up to now, what had resisted, which is art, will end up succumbing, and along with it, with any possibility of radical resistance.

CF: You said that you referred the question of postmodernity to the question about modernity. How do you answer that question about modernity?

JJ: Theoretically, modernity rapidly acquires full status soon: it starts to sow its seeds with Descartes, the fruits of this seed grow during the Enlightenment, and mature in a way which I would venture to say was unsurpassable with Hegel. Why unsurpassable with Hegel? Because modernity's horizon is founded on a series of limited parameters, a limit which can be conceived until the end, and which Hegel conceives. In reality, the only thing that Marx supposedly does is to conceive the way of constructing that horizon in practical terms, but is in agreement with Hegel. This is what occurs in theory, but the practice has been much more complex and much slower. We could say that thought advances—modernity advances at the level of thought and is tortuously and slowly constructed at the level of events. When Hegel completes his theoretical grounding, Europe is still living in the shadow of the past and breaking with that shadow of the past will lead it into multiple wars and conflicts, still mediated by forms which we could say do not really correspond to modernity although it may already be present. That is, in my opinion, within the realm of events, modernity is something which starts with the post-war period, with the end of World War II. That is where ideas like "market," "scientificity," "reason," "individual freedom," "human rights," etc., start to become common currency and really start to order the relationships between nation-states, political as well as general relationships. But, moreover, in the field of material production and reproduction, in the field of social reproduction in economic terms, in technical terms, until the post-war period really the world was still moving within the realm of arcane forms of knowledge and productive realization. It is really with computerization, programmers, this whole world which we are witnessing, that what has been produced is a true innovation. I would say that practically no innovation had taken place in history like the one that's taking place now, that history moved with an exasperating slowness until the early 40s, and starting around 1945 is when it has already entered a dizzying pace, and in a way which puts everything in question. That change is nothing more than the real, true and practical constitution of modernity. For that reason I think that all these terms of postmodernity, dismodernity, etc., fail to comprehend modernity in profound terms. My proposal is: let's envisage modernity, and let's consider whether we are not really just witnessing the inception of modernity, whether we are really as "post" as we believe. People let themselves be taken in by a kind of cultural journalism which today is the dominant form where intellectuals are characters who appear in newspaper supplements, and in which those who write books no longer exist. It seems that what has to be done is write little articles in the newspapers and this makes you famous for at least a couple of minutes.

CF: Your position would then be related to that of Habermas: a modernity whose unfulfilled promise still can be attained?

JJ: I absolutely disagree with Habermas. I believe that the theory is already fine tuned and perfectly refined by big thinkers with Hegel; the problem which one sees in the 19th and 20th centuries is precisely the practical realization of that universal history within the parameters of modernity. All the barbarity which takes place and arises starting at least with the French Revolution up to the present time is a barbarity provoked by the construction of modernity. Thus all the barbarity cannot be attributed to vestiges of the past or to backwardness; it's not a question of backwardness but of progress. What has happened is not a result of an inconclusive modernity but of the attempt of modernity to reach a conclusion. Habermas does nothing more than reactivate the myth of reason, now starting with the idea of dialogic intercommunication and rationality, which is a way of reinstating the Hegelian project in terms of the modern jargon of communication. What Habermas intends is to continue maintaining a utopia for the purpose of existence of reason which would still have not been attained, and as long as it is not attained, it would   be an inconclusive project. This conceptualization can be verified in a   concrete way if we consider the fact that today people already conduct their lives, as the Enlightenment wished, in accordance with a kind of discursivity and relationship with the other, with the world, nature and with things, which is mediated by a scientific structure of representation. This structure has been incorporated by the schools, the universities, and it's according to what the majority of people guide their behavior: from the theoretical and scientific dimension to the legal structure based on clearly rational terms of argumentation and on a political configuration which is structured starting with problems of a technical nature, as, for example, the European Economic Community. In the EEC, the policy of all the representatives is homogeneous because it is not the policy of anyone but the policy that the market imposes, which is a policy of technical adjustments that all have to make, because it is the same impersonal legality of the market which is forcing them to carry out the changes. But this is nothing more than reflex actions; my position is that what has to be questioned is everything that oppresses and everything that leads to oppression; and what has to be freed up is everything which liberates and questions every oppressive structure. I believe that the make-up of this present world is ambiguous, and, therefore, it generates within itself the oppressive structures of the present and the future, but it also engenders the structures of liberation. All the theoretical cogitation must be directed to make this distinction, because if the distinction is not made, then we lose the possibility of transgression, insurgency, and of keeping the banner of freedom raised. Thinking has lagged way behind the times. I was saying a paradoxical thing: with Hegel, in a very sophisticated, refined and profound way—and with all those who come after him, because he condenses a whole tradition and completes it—and also with Marx, thinking still manifests itself with an exceptional lucidity. Then comes the other transgressive tendency which has really brilliant people in Nietzsche and Heidegger. We still see at the start of the 20th century a tremendous dimension in terms of thinking. But at a certain point, almost all the intellectuals fall prey to the myth of reason, which is the idea of socialism, and all thinking revolves around the construction of this mythology. When the innovations keep popping up and unknown things keep happening, these are not thought through, they are not even recorded; and suddenly, when the whole grandiose myth of reason falls apart, we find that we don't understand anything of what is happening. And we throw the blame on history. I see Octavio Paz saying: history is risky, it is to blame for never leading one to where it would seem to lead. It's not the fault of history, my friend, it's the fault of those of us who are not thinking, it's our fault that things always take us by surprise, because we hold on to sterile ways of thinking, we have not been agile enough, nor have we had the talent or the autonomy to consider what is happening to us. It now turns out that we no longer have to think—good has already triumphed and there now exists something called democracy, which is the new fetish, and it will last for another hundred years until it falls apart, and then they are going to say that history is full of surprises. Fine, it is full of surprises for the person who is asleep, who becomes bewildered. *I believe that Latin America in that sense has failed completely, and that what is now going on has to do in a large part with the failure of Latin American thought or of the Latin American intellectuals. Latin America is in the hands of ideologues and writers, but there is an absolute displacement of the thinkers and of thinking.* And this is very, very serious, and I believe that more than creating an autonomous way of thinking, a philosophy of the Latin American being, what simply has to be done is to regain this freedom, this irreducibility, this autonomy, this originality of being capable of thinking for oneself, which has been lost for many, many years with these myths, because it would seem that all the myths of the West end up germinating in the fantasies of the Third World. The tasks are exciting, and far from being crushed, we have to rise up to the challenge. *One has to get involved in many places, in all the possible places, even though we may fail. I prefer to fail because of my own limitations and because I don't succeed in thinking what I believe must be thought, to failing because of the convenience of relying on a dependable instrument that responds to everything, but which in the final analysis doesn't respond to anything.* I am navigating in a kind of realm of uncertainty; or rather everything that I am saying are words emanating from uncertainty; so this could be entitled: *words from the realm of uncertainty.*

Translated by Robert Sims

Voices in the North

ON THE CARIBBEAN:

THE REPEATING ISLAND: THE CARIBBEAN AND THE POST-MODERN PERSPECTIVE
Antonio Benítez-Rojo

In recent decades we have begun to see a clearer outline to the profile of a group of American nations whose colonial experiences and languages have been different, but which share certain undeniable features.[1] I mean the countries usually called "Caribbean" or "of the Caribbean basin." This designation might serve a foreign purpose—the great powers' need to recodify the world's territory better to know, to dominate it—as well as a local one, self-referential, directed toward fixing the furtive image of collective Being. Whatever its motive, this urge to systematize the region's political, economic, social, and anthropological dynamics is a very recent thing. For it is certain that the Caribbean basin, although it includes the first American lands to be explored, conquered, and colonized by Europe, is still, especially in the discourse of the social sciences, one of the least known regions of the modern world.

The main obstacles to any global study of the Caribbean's societies, insular or continental, are exactly those things that scholars usually adduce to define the area: its fragmentation; its instability; its reciprocal isolation; its uprootedness; its cultural heterogeneity; its lack of historiography and historical continuity; its contingency and impermanence; its syncretism, etc. This unexpected mix of obstacles and properties is not, of course, mere happenstance. What happens is that postindustrial society—to use a newfangled term—navigates the Caribbean with judgments and intentions that are like those of Columbus; that is, it lands scientists, investors, and technologists—the new (dis)coverers—who come to apply the dogmas and methods that had served them well where they came from, and who can't see that these refer only to realities back home. So they get into the habit of defining the Caribbean in terms of its resistance to the different methodologies summoned to investigate it. This is not to say that the definitions we read here and there of pan-Caribbean society are false or useless.

---

[1]Reprinted from Antonio Benítez-Rojo, "Introduction." *The Repeating Island: The Caribbean and the Postmodern Perspective* (Durham: Duke University Press, 1992). 1-29.

I would say, to the contrary, that they are potentially as productive as the first reading of a book, in which, as Barthes said, the reader inevitably reads himself. I think, nevertheless, that the time has come for postindustrial society to start rereading the Caribbean, that is, to do the kind of reading in which every text begins to reveal its own textuality.

This second reading is not going to be easy at all. The Caribbean space, remember, is saturated with messages—"language games," Lyotard would call them—sent out in five European languages (Spanish, English, French, Dutch, and Portuguese), not counting aboriginal languages which, together with the different local dialects (Surinamtongo, Papiamento, *Créole*, etc.), complicate enormously any communication from one extreme of the ambit to another. Further, the spectrum of Caribbean codes is so varied and dense that it holds the region suspended in a soup of signs. It has been said many times that the Caribbean is the union of the diverse, and maybe that is true. In any case, my own rereading has taken me along different paths, and I can no longer arrive at such admirably precise reductions.

In this (today's) rereading, I propose, for example, to start with something concrete and easily demonstrated, a geographical fact: that the Antilles are an island bridge connecting, in "another way," North and South America. This geographical accident gives the entire area, including its continental foci, the character of an archipelago, that is, a discontinuous conjunction (of what?): unstable condensations, turbulences, whirlpools, clumps of bubbles, frayed seaweed, sunken galleons, crashing breakers, flying fish, seagull squawks, downpours, nighttime phosphorescences, eddies and pools, uncertain voyages of signification; in short, a field of observation quite in tune with the objectives of Chaos. I have capitalized this word to indicate that I'm not referring to chaos as conventionally defined, but rather to the new scientific perspective, so called, that has now begun to revolutionize the world of scientific research, that is, *Chaos* to mean that, within the (dis)order that swarms around what we already know of as Nature, it is possible to observe dynamic states or regularities that repeat themselves globally. I think that this recent interest of the scientific disciplines, which owes a lot to mathematical speculation and to holography, brings along with it a philosophical attitude (a new way of reading the concepts of chance and necessity, of particularity and universality) which little by little is sure to permeate other fields of knowledge.

Quite recently, for example, economics and certain branches of the humanities have begun to be examined under this brand-new paradigm, constituting perhaps the most inquisitive and encompassing step that postmodernity has taken up until now. In truth, the field in which Chaos may be observed is extremely vast, for it includes all phenomena that depend on the passage of time; Chaos looks toward everything that repeats, reproduces, grows, decays, unfolds, flows, spins, vibrates, seethes; it is as interested in the evolution of the solar system as in the stock market's crashes, as involved in cardiac arrhythmia as in the novel or in myth. Thus Chaos provides a space in which the pure sciences connect with the social sciences, and both of them connect with art and the cultural tradition. Of course, any such diagrammatic connections must suppose very different languages and a communication that is hardly ever direct, but for the reader who is attuned to Chaos, there will be an opening upon unexpected corridors allowing passage from one point to another in the labyrinth. In this book I have tried to analyze certain aspects of the Caribbean while under the influence of this attitude, whose end is not to find results, but processes, dynamics, and rhythms that show themselves within the marginal, the regional, the incoherent, the heterogeneous, or, if you like, the unpredictable that coexists with us in our everyday world.

To experience this exploration has been instructive as well as surprising to me, since within the sociocultural fluidity that the Caribbean archipelago presents, within its historiographic turbulence and its ethnological and linguistic clamor, within its generalized instability of vertigo and hurricane, one can sense the features of an island that "repeats" itself, unfolding and bifurcating until it reaches all the seas and lands of the earth, while at the same time it inspires multidisciplinary maps of unexpected designs. I have emphasized the word *repeats* because I want to give the term the almost paradoxical sense with which it appears in the discourse of Chaos, where every repetition is a practice that necessarily entails a difference and a step toward nothingness (according to the principle of entropy proposed by thermodynamics in the last century); however, in the midst of this irreversible change, Nature can produce a figure as complex, as highly organized, and as intense as the one that the human eye catches when it sees a quivering hummingbird drinking from a flower.

Which one, then, would be the repeating island, Jamaica, Aruba, Puerto Rico, Miami, Haiti, Recife? Certainly none of the ones that we know. That original, that island at the center, is as impossible to reach as the hypothetical Antillas that reappeared time and again, always fleetingly, in the cosmographers' charts. This is again because the Caribbean is not a common archipelago, but a meta-archipelago (an exalted quality that Hellas possessed, and the great Malay archipelago as well), and as a meta-archipelago it has the virtue of having neither a boundary nor a center. Thus the Caribbean flows outward past the limits of its own sea with a vengeance, and its *ultima Thule* may be found on the outskirts of Bombay, near the low and murmuring shores of Gambia, in a Cantonese tavern of circa 1850, at a Balinese temple, in an old Bristol pub, in a commercial warehouse in Bordeaux at the time of Colbert, in a windmill beside the Zuider Zee, at a cafe in a barrio of Manhattan, in the existential *saudade* of an old Portuguese lyric. But what is it that repeats? Tropisms, in series; movements in

approximate direction. Let's say the unforeseen relation between a dance movement and the baroque spiral of a colonial railing. But this theme will be discussed later, although the Caribbean really is that and much more; it is the last
of the great meta-archipelagoes. If someone needed a visual explanation, a graphic picture of what the Caribbean is, I would refer him to the spiral chaos of the
Milky Way, the unpredictable flux of transformative plasma that spins calmly in
our globe's firmament, that sketches in an "other" shape that keeps changing,
with some objects born to light while others disappear into the womb of darkness; change, transit, return, fluxes of sidereal matter.

There is nothing marvelous in this, or even enviable, as will be seen. A
few paragraphs back, when I proposed a rereading of the Caribbean, I suggested
as a point of departure the unargued fact that the Antilles are an island bridge
connecting, "in a certain way," South and North America, that is, a machine of
spume that links the narrative of the search for El Dorado with the narrative of
the finding of El Dorado; or if you like, the discourse of myth with the discourse
of history; or even, the discourse of resistance with the language of power. I
made a point of the phrase "in a certain way" because if we were to take the
Central American ligament as our connection between continents, the result
would be much less fruitful and would not suit the purposes of this article. That
connection gains objective importance only on maps concerned with our current
situation seen as geography, geopolitics, military strategy, and finance. These are
maps of the pragmatic type which we all know and carry within us, and which
therefore give us a first reading of the world. The words "a certain way" are the
signs of my intention to give meaning to this text as an object of rereading, of
a "certain kind of" reading. In my reading, the link that really counts is the one
made by the Caribbean machine, whose flux, whose noise, whose presence cov-
ers the map of world history's contingencies, through the great changes in economic discourse to the vast collisions of races and cultures that humankind has
seen.

From Columbus's Machine to the Sugar-making Machine

Let's be realistic: the Atlantic is the Atlantic (with all its port cities)
because it was once engendered by the copulation of Europe—that insatiable
solar bull—with the Caribbean archipelago; the Atlantic is today the Atlantic (the
navel of capitalism) because Europe, in its mercantilist laboratory, conceived the
project of inseminating the Caribbean womb with the blood of Africa; the Atlantic is today the Atlantic (NATO, World Bank, New York Stock Exchange, European Economic Community, etc.) because it was the painfully delivered child of
the Caribbean, whose vagina was stretched between continental clamps, between

the *encomienda* of Indians and the slaveholding plantation, between the servitude of the coolie and the discrimination toward the *criollo*, between commercial monopoly and piracy, between the runaway slave settlement and the governor's palace; all Europe pulling on the forceps to help at the birth of the Atlantic: Columbus, Cabral, Cortés, de Soto, Hawkins, Drake, Hein, Rodney, Surcouf. . . . After the blood and salt water spurts, quickly sew up torn flesh and apply the antiseptic tinctures, the gauze and surgical plaster; then the febrile wait through the forming of a scar: suppurating, always suppurating.

Its having given birth, however, to an ocean of such universal prestige is not the only reason that the Caribbean is a meta-archipelago. There are other reasons of equal weight. For example, it is possible to defend successfully the hypothesis that without deliveries from the Caribbean womb Western capital accumulation would not have been sufficient to effect a move, within a little more than two centuries, from the so-called Mercantilist Revolution to the Industrial Revolution. In fact, the history of the Caribbean is one of the main strands in the history of capitalism, and vice versa. This conclusion may be called polemical, and perhaps it is. This is surely not the place to argue the issue, but there's always room for some observations.

The machine that Christopher Columbus hammered into shape in Hispaniola was a kind of *bricolage,* something like a medieval vacuum cleaner. The flow of Nature in the island was interrupted by the suction of an iron mouth, taken thence through a transatlantic tube to be deposited and redistributed in Spain. When I speak of Nature in the island, I do so in integral terms: Indians and their handicrafts, nuggets of gold and samples of other minerals, native species of plants and animals, and also some words like *tabaco, canoa, hamaca,* etc. All this struck the Spanish court as meager and tepid (especially the words), so that nobody—except Columbus—had any illusions about the New World. A machine of the same model (think of a forge with its sparkling clangor and combustion), with an extra bolt here and a bellows over there, was installed in Puerto Rico, in Jamaica, in Cuba, and in a few miserable settlements on terra firma. At the time of the great conquests—the fall of the upland civilizations of the Aztecs, the Incas, and the Chibchas—Columbus's machine was quickly remodeled and, carried on Indians' backs over the sierras, set into motion in a half dozen new places. It is possible to fix the date when this machine began working. It happened in the spring of 1523, when Cortés, manipulating the levers and pedals, smelted down a part of the treasure of Tenochtitlán and selected a smattering of deluxe objects to be sent through the transatlantic tube. But this prototype was so defective that the transporting machine—the tubing—got irreparably broken some ten leagues from Cape San Vicente, in Portugal. French privateers captured two of the three inadequate caravels that carried the treasure to Spain, and the Emperor Charles V lost his whole share (20 percent) of that year's Mexican revenue. This couldn't be allowed to happen again. The machine had to be perfected.

I think I ought to clarify at this point that when I speak of a machine I am starting from Deleuze and Guattari's concept. I am talking about the machine of machines, the machine machine machine machine; which is to say that every machine is a conjunction of machines coupled together, and each one of these interrupts the flow of the previous one; it will be said rightly that one can picture any machine alternatively in terms of flow and interruption. Such a notion, as we will see, is fundamental to our rereading of the Caribbean, for it will permit us to pass on to an even more important one.

In any case, in the years that followed the Cape San Vicente disaster the Spaniards introduced major technological changes and surprising elaborations in their American machine. This was so much the case that, by around 1565, Columbus's small and rudimentary machine had evolved into the Grandest Machine on Earth. This is absolutely certain. It's proven by statistics: in the first century of Spanish colonization this machine yielded more than one-third of all the gold produced in the whole world during those years. The machine produced not only gold but also silver, emeralds, diamonds, topaz, pearls, and more. The quantity of molten silver that fell in droplets from that enormous shelf was such that the haughtiest families of Potosí, after dining, tossed their silver service out the window along with the leftover food. These fabulous deliveries of precious metals were the result of various innovations, for example: guaranteeing the availability of the necessary cheap manpower in the mines through a system known as the *mita;* using wind energy and marine currents to speed up the flow of oceanic transportation; implanting a costly system of security and control from the River Plate estuary to the Guadalquivir. But, above all, establishing the system called *la flota,* the fleet. Without the fleet system the Spaniards would not have been able to hoard within the walls of Seville any more gold or silver than they could fit into their pockets.

We know who thought up this extraordinary machine: Pedro Menéndez de Avilés, a cruel Asturian of genius. If this man, or someone else, had not invented the fleet system, the Caribbean would still be there, but it might not be a meta-archipelago.

Menéndez de Avilés's machine was complex in the extreme and quite beyond the reach of any nation but Spain. It was a machine made up of a naval machine, a military machine, a bureaucratic machine, a commercial machine, an extractive machine, a political machine, a legal machine, a religious machine, that is, an entire huge assemblage of machines which there is no point in continuing to name. The only thing that matters here is that it was a Caribbean machine; a machine installed in the Caribbean Sea and coupled to the Atlantic and the Pacific. The perfected model of this machine was set in motion in 1565, although it had been tested in a trial run a bit earlier. In 1562 Pedro Menéndez de Avilés, commanding forty-nine sailing ships, set off from Spain with the dream of stanching the leaks of gold and silver caused by shipwrecks and pirate or privateer attacks. His plan was this: all navigation between the West Indies and Seville (the only port that allowed transatlantic trade) would be undertaken in convoys consisting of cargo ships, warships, and light craft for reconnaissance and dispatch; the cargoes of gold and silver were to be boarded only on given dates and in only a few Caribbean ports (Cartagena, Nombre de Dios, San Juan de Ulúa, and some other secondary ones); forts would be built and garrisons stationed not only at these ports but also at those defending the entrances to the Caribbean (San Juan de Puerto Rico, Santo Domingo, Santiago de Cuba, the eastern coast of Florida, and, especially, Havana); all of these ports would be bases for squadrons of coast guard and patrol ships, whose mission would be to sweep the waters and coastal keys clean of pirates, privateers, and smugglers, while at the same time providing rescue service to convoys in trouble. (The plan was approved. Its lineaments were so solid that 375 years later, during the Second World War, the Allies adopted it to defend against attack from German submarines, cruisers, and planes.)

Generally the name *flota* (fleet) is given to the convoys that twice a year entered the Caribbean to come back to Seville with the great riches of America. But this is not entirely correct. The fleet system was itself a machine of ports, anchorages, sea walls, lookouts, fortresses, garrisons, militias, shipyards, storehouses, depots, offices, workshops, hospitals, inns, taverns, plazas, churches, palaces, streets, and roads that led to the mining ports of the Pacific along a sleeve of mule trains laid out over the Isthmus of Panama. It was a powerful machine of machines knowingly articulated to suit the Caribbean's geography, and its machines were geared to be able to take greatest advantage of the energy of the Gulf Stream and the region's trade winds. The fleet system created all of the cities of the Spanish Caribbean and it made them, for better or for worse, what they are today, Havana in particular. It was there that both fleets (those of Cartagena and Veracruz) joined to form an imposing convoy of more than a hundred ships to begin the return voyage together. In 1565 Pedro Menéndez de Avilés, after slaughtering, with indifferent calm, nearly five hundred Huguenots who had settled in Florida, finished his network of fortified cities with the founding of St. Augustine, today the oldest city in the United States.

As we speak in our astonishment of the inexhaustible richness of the Mexican and Peruvian mines, we should think of them as machines joined to other machines; we should see them in terms of production (flow and interruption). Such mining machines, by themselves, would not have been much help in accumulating European capital. Without the Caribbean machine (from Columbus's prototype to the working model of Menéndez de Avilés), Europeans would have been in the absurd position of the gambler who hits the jackpot at the slot machine but who has no hat in which to catch his winnings.

We can speak, nevertheless, of a Caribbean machine as important or more so than the fleet machine. This machine, this extraordinary machine, exists today, that is, it repeats itself continuously. It's called: the plantation. Its prototypes were born in the Near East, just after the time of the Crusades, and moved toward the West. In the fifteenth century the Portuguese installed their own model in the Cape Verde Islands and on Madeira, with astonishing success. There were certain entrepreneurs—like the Jew Cristóbal de Ponte and the *Sharif* of Berbery—who tried to construct machines of this family in the Canaries and on the Moroccan coast, but the venture was too big for any single man. It turned out that an entire kingdom, a mercantilist monarchy, would be needed to get the big machine going with its gears, its wheels, and its mills. I want to insist that Europeans finally controlled the construction, maintenance, technology, and proliferation of the plantation machines, especially those that produced sugar. (This family of machines almost always makes cane sugar, coffee, cacao, cotton, indigo, tea, bananas, pineapples, fibers, and other goods whose cultivation is impossible or too expensive in the temperate zones; furthermore, it usually produces the Plantation, capitalized to indicate not just the presence of plantations but also the type of society that results from their use and abuse.)

So much has already been written about all of this that it is not worth the effort even to sketch out the incredible and dolorous history of this machine. Still, something must be said, just a few things. For one: the singular feature of this machine is that it produced no fewer than ten million African slaves and thousands of coolies (from India, China, and Malaysia). All this, however, is not all: the plantation machines turned out mercantile capitalism, industrial capitalism (see Eric Williams, *Capitalism and Slavery*), African underdevelopment (see Walter Rodney, *How Europe Underdeveloped Africa*), Caribbean population (see Ramiro Guerra, *Sugar and Society in the Caribbean);* they produced imperialism, wars, colonial blocs, rebellions, repressions, sugar islands, runaway slave settlements, air and naval bases, revolutions of all sorts, and even a "free associated state" next to an unfree socialist state.

You will say that this catalog is unnecessary, that the whole subject is already too well known. But how is one to establish finally that the Caribbean is not just a multiethnic sea or a group of islands divided by different languages and by the categories Greater and Lesser Antilles, Windward Islands, and Leeward Islands? In short, how do we establish that the Caribbean is an important historico-economic sea and, further, a cultural meta-archipelago without center and without limits, a chaos within which there is an island that proliferates endlessly, each copy a different one, founding and refounding ethnological materials like a cloud will do with its vapor? If this is now understood, then there is no need to keep on depending on the old history books. Let's talk then of the Caribbean that we can see, touch, smell, hear, taste; the Caribbean of the senses, the Caribbean of sentiment and pre-sentiment.

From the Apocalypse to Chaos

I can isolate with frightening exactitude—like the hero of Sartre's novel—the moment at which I reached the age of reason. It was a stunning October afternoon, years ago, when the atomization of the meta-archipelago under the dread umbrella of nuclear catastrophe seemed imminent. The children of Havana, at least in my neighborhood, had been evacuated; a grave silence fell over the streets and the sea. While the state bureaucracy searched for news off the short-wave or hid behind official speeches and communiques, two old black women passed "in a certain kind of way" beneath my balcony. I cannot describe this "certain kind of way"; I will say only that there was a kind of ancient and golden powder between their gnarled legs, a scent of basil and mint in their dress, a symbolic, ritual wisdom in their gesture and their gay chatter. I knew then at once that there would be no apocalypse. The swords and the archangels and the beasts and the trumpets and the breaking of the last seal were not going to come, for the simple reason that the Caribbean is not an apocalyptic world; it is not a phallic world in pursuit of the vertical desires of ejaculation and castration. The notion of the apocalypse is not important within the culture of the Caribbean. The choices of all or nothing, for or against, honor or blood have little to do with the culture of the Caribbean. These are ideological propositions articulated in Europe which the Caribbean shares only in declamatory terms, or, better, in terms of a first reading. In Chicago a beaten soul says: "I can't take it any more," and gives himself up to drugs or to the most desperate violence. In Havana, he would say: "The thing to do is not die," or perhaps: "Here I am, fucked but happy."

The so-called October crisis or missile crisis was not won by J.F.K. or by N.K. or much less by F.C. (statesmen always wind up abbreviated in these great events that they themselves created); it was won by the culture of the Caribbean, together with the loss that any win implies. If this had happened, let's say, in Berlin, children there would now be discovering hand tools and learning to make fire with sticks. The plantation of atomic projectiles sown in Cuba was a Russian machine, a machine of the steppes, historically terrestrial. It was a machine that carried the culture of the horse and of yogurt, the cossack and the mouzhik, the birch and the rye, the ancient caravans and the Siberian railroad; a culture where the land is everything and the sea a forgotten memory. But the culture of the Caribbean, at least in its most distinctive aspect, is not terrestrial but aquatic, a sinuous culture where time unfolds irregularly and resists being captured by the cycles of clock and calendar. The Caribbean is the natural and indispensable realm of marine currents, of waves, of folds and double-folds, of fluidity and sinuosity. It is, in the final analysis, a culture of the metaarchipelago: a chaos that returns, a detour without a purpose, a continual flow of paradoxes; it is a feed back machine with asymmetrical workings, like the sea, the wind, the clouds, the uncanny novel, the food chain, the music of Malaya, Gödel's theorem and fractal mathematics. It will be said that in that case Hellas does not meet our canon for meta-archipelagoes. But yes, it meets it. What's happened is that Western thought has kept on thinking of itself as the diachronic repetition on an ancient polemic. I am referring to the repressive and fallacious machine made up of the binary opposition Aristotle *versus* Plato. Greek thought has been subjected to such sleight of hand that Plato's version of Socrates has been accepted as the limit of the tolerable, while the glowing constellation of ideas that made up the Greek heaven by way of the Pre-Socratics, the Sophists, and the Gnostics has been ignored or distorted. This magnificent firmament has been reduced almost as if we were to erase every star in the sky but Castor and Pollux. Certainly, Greek thought was much more than this philosophical duel between Plato and Aristotle. It's just that certain not entirely symmetrical ideas scandalized the faith of the Middle Ages, modern rationalism, and the functionalist positivism of our time, and it's not necessary to pursue this matter, because we're speaking here of the Caribbean. Let's say good-bye to Hellas, applauding the idea of a forgotten sage, Thales of Miletus: water is the beginning of all things.

Then how can we describe the culture of the Caribbean in any way other than by calling it a feedback machine? Nobody has to rack his brains to come up with an answer; it's in the public domain. If I were to have to put it in one word I would say: performance. But performance not only in terms of scenic interpretation but also in terms of the execution of a ritual, that is, that "certain way" in which the two Negro women who conjured away the apocalypse were walking. In this "certain kind of way" there is expressed the mystic or magical (if you like) loam of the civilizations that contributed to the formation of Caribbean culture. Of course there have been some things written about this too, although I think that there's a lot of cloth left to be cut. For example, when we speak of the genesis of Caribbean culture we are given two alternatives: either we are told that the complex syncretism of Caribbean cultural expressions—what I shall call here *supersyncretism* to distinguish it from similar forms—arose out of the collision of European, African, and Asian components within the Plantation, or that this syncretism flows along working with ethnological machines that are quite distant in space and remote in time, that is, machines "of a certain kind" that one would have to look for in the subsoils of all of the continents. But, I ask, why not take both alternatives as valid, and not just those but others as well?

Why pursue a Euclidian coherence that the world—and the Caribbean above all—is very far from having?

Certainly, in order to reread the Caribbean we have to visit the sources from which the widely various elements that contributed to the formation of its culture flowed. This unforeseen journey tempts us because as soon as we succeed in establishing and identifying as separate any of the signifiers that make up the supersyncretic manifestation that we're studying, there comes a moment of erratic displacement of its signifiers toward other spatio-temporal points, be they in Europe, Africa, Asia, or America, or in all these continents at once. When these points of departure are nonetheless reached, a new chaotic flight of signifiers will occur, and so on ad infinitum.

Let's take as an example a syncretic object that has been well studied, let's say, the cult of the Virgen de la Caridad del Cobre (still followed by many Cubans). If we were to analyze this cult—presuming that it hasn't been done before—we would necessarily come upon a date (1605) and a place (el Cobre, near Santiago de Cuba); that is, within the spatio-temporal frame where the cult was first articulated upon three sources of meaning: one of aboriginal origin (the Taino deity Atabey or Atabex), another native to Europe (the Virgin of *Illescas),* and finally, another from Africa (the Yoruba *orisha* Oshun). For many anthropologists the history of this cult would begin or end here, and of course they would give reasons to explain this arbitrary break in the chain of signifiers. They would say, perhaps, that the people who today inhabit the Antilles are "new," and therefore their earlier situation, their tradition of being "a certain kind of way," should not count; they would say that with the disappearance of the Antillean aborigine during the first century of colonization these islands were left unconnected to the Indoamerican mechanisms, thus providing a "new" space for "new" men to create a "new" society and, with it, a "new" culture that can no longer be taken as an extension of those that brought the "new" inhabitants. Thus the Virgen de la Caridad del Cobre would turn out to be exclusively Cuban, and as the patron saint of Cuba she would appear in a kind of panoply along with the flag, the coat of arms, the statues of the founders, the map of the island, the royal palms, and the national anthem; she would be, in short, an attribute of Cuba's civic religion and nothing more.

Fine; I share this systemic focus, although only within the perspective offered by a first reading in which—as we know—the reader reads himself. But it happens to be the case that after several close readings of the Virgen and her cult it is possible for a Cuban reader to be seduced by the materials that he has been reading, and he should feel a reduced dose of the nationalism that he has projected on to the Virgen. This will happen only if his ego abandons for an instant his desire to feel Cuban only, a feeling that has offered him the mirage of a safe place under the cover of a nationality that connects him to the land and to the fathers of the country. If this momentary wavering should occur, the reader would cease to inscribe himself within the space of the Cuban and would set out venturing along the roads of limitless chaos that any advanced rereading offers. This being so, he would have to leap outside of the statist, statistical Cuba after searching for the wandering signifiers that inform the cult of the Virgen de la Caridad del Cobre. For a moment, just for a moment, the Virgen and the reader will cease to be Cuban.

The first surprise or perplexity that the triptych Atabey-Nuestra Señora-Oshun presents us is that it is not "original" but rather "originating." In fact, Atabey, the Taino deity, is a syncretic object in itself, one whose signifiers deliver to us another signifier that is somewhat unforeseen: Orehu, mother of waters to the Arawaks of the Guianas. This voyage of signification is a heady one for more than one reason. In the first place it involves the grand epic of the Arawaks; the departure from the Amazon basin, the ascension of the Orinoco, the arrival at the Caribbean coast, the meticulous settlement of each island until arriving at Cuba, the still obscure encounter with the Mayans of Yucatan, the ritual game of the ball of resin, the "other" connection between both subcontinental masses (such was the forgotten feat of these people). In the second place, it involves also the no less grand epic of the Caribs: the Arawak islands as objects of Carib desire; construction of large canoes, preparations for war, raids on the coastal islands, Trinidad, Tobago, Margarita, ravishing the women, victory feasts. Then the invasion stage, Grenada, St. Vincent, St. Lucia, Martinique, Dominica, Guadeloupe, the killing of the Arawaks, the glorious cannibalism of men and of words, *carib, calib, cannibal,* and *Caliban;* finally, the Sea of the Caribs, from Guyana to the Virgin Islands, the sea that isolated the Arawaks *(Tainos)* from the Greater Antilles, that cut the connection with the South American coast but not the continuity of cultural flow: Atabey-Orehu, the flux of signifiers that crossed the spatio-temporal barrier of the Caribbean to continue linking Cuba with the Orinoco and Amazon basins; Atabey-Orehu, progenitor of the supreme being of the Tainos, mother of the Taino lakes and rivers, protector of feminine ebbs and flows, of the great mysteries of the blood that women experience, and there, at the other end of the Antillean arc, the Great Mother of Waters, the immediacy of the matriarchy, the beginning of the cultivation of the yucca, the ritual orgy, incest, the sacrifice of the virgin male, blood and earth.

There is something enormously old and powerful in this, I know; a contradictory vertigo which there is no reason to interrupt, and so we reach the point at which the image of Our Lady venerated in el Cobre is, also, a syncretic object, produced by two quite distinct images of the Virgin Mary, which were to wind up in the hands of the chiefs of Cueiba and Macaca, and which were adored simultaneously as Atabey and as Nuestra Señora (this last in the form of an amulet). Imagine for a moment these chiefs' perplexity when they saw, for the first time, what no Taino had seen before: the image, in color, of the Mother of the Supreme Being, the lone progenitor of Yucahu Bagua Maorocoti, who now turned out to be, in addition, the mother of the god of those bearded, yucca-colored men; she who, according to them, protected them from death and injury in war. *Ave María,* these Indians would learn to say as they worshipped their Atabey, who at one time had been Orehu, and before that the Great Arawak Mother. *Ave María,* Francisco Sánchez de Moya, a sixteenth-century Spanish captain, would surely say when he received the commission and the order to make the crossing to Cuba to start copper foundries in the mines of El Prado. *Ave María,* he would say once again when he wrapped the image of Nuestra Señora de Illescas, of whom he was a devotee, among his shirts to protect him from the dangerous storms and shipwrecks of the hazardous passage to the Indies. *Ave María,* he would repeat on the day he placed it upon the humble altar in the solitary hermitage of Santiago del Prado, the merest hut for the poor Indians and Negroes who worked the copper mines.

But the image, that of Nuestra Señora de Illescas, brought to Cuba by the good captain, had a long history behind it. It is itself another syncretic object. The chain of signifiers now takes us across the Renaissance to the Middle Ages. It leads us to Byzantium, the unique, the magnificent, where among all kinds of heresies and pagan practices the cult of the Virgin Mary was born (a cult unforeseen by the Doctors of the Church). There in Byzantium, among the splendors of its icons and mosaics, a likeness of the Virgin Mary and her Child may have been plundered by some crusading and voracious knight, or acquired by a seller of relics, or copied on the retina of some pious pilgrim. At any rate the suspicious cult of the Virgin Mary filtered surreptitiously into Europe. Surely it would not have gone very far on its own, but this happened at the beginning of the twelfth century, the legendary epoch of the troubadours and of *fin amour,* when Woman ceased to be Eve, the dirty and damned seducer of Adam and ally of the Serpent. She was washed, perfumed, and sumptuously dressed to suit the scope of her new image: the Lady. Then, the cult of Our Lady spread like fire through gunpowder, and one fine day it arrived at Illescas, a few miles away from Toledo.

Ave María, the slaves at the El Prado mines repeated aloud, and quickly, in an undertone that the priest could not hear, they added: *Oshun Yeye.* For that miraculous altar image was for them one of the most conspicuous *orishas* of the Yoruba pantheon: Oshun Yeye Moro, the perfumed whore; Oshun Kayode, the gay dancer; Oshun Aña, the lover of the drum; Oshun Akuara, she who mixes love potions; Oshun Ede, the *grande dame;* Oshun Fumike, she who gives children to sterile women; Oshun Funke, the wise one; Oshun Kole-Kole, the wicked sorceress.

Oshun, as a syncretic object, is as dizzying as her honeyed dance and yellow bandanas. She is traditionally the Lady of the Rivers, but some of her avatars relate her to the bays and the seashores. Her most prized objects are amber, coral, and yellow metals; her favorite foods are honey, squash, and sweets that contain eggs. Sometimes she shows herself to be gentle and ministering, above all in women's matters and those of love; at other times she shows herself to be insensitive, capricious, and voluble, and she can even become nasty and treacherous; in these darker apparitions we also see her as an old carrion-eating witch and as the *orisha* of death.

This multiple aspect of Oshun makes us think at once of the contradictions of Aphrodite. Both goddesses, one as much as the other, are at once "luminous" and "dark"; they reign over a place where men find both pleasure and death, love and hate, voluptuousity and betrayal. Both goddesses came from the sea and inhabit the marine, fluvial, and vaginal tides; both seduce gods and men, and both protect cosmetics and prostitution.

The correspondences between the Greek and Yoruba pantheons have been noted, but they have not been explained. How to explain, to give another example, the unusual parallel of Hermes and Elegua? Both are "the travelers," the "messengers of the gods," the "keepers of the gates," "lords of the thresholds"; both were adored in the form of phallic stone figures, both protect crossroads, highways, and commerce, and both can show themselves in the figure of a man with a cane who rests his body's weight on one foot alone. Both sponsor the start of any activity, make transactions smooth, and are the only ones to pass through the terrible spaces that mediate the Supreme Being and the gods, the gods and the dead, the living and the dead. Both, finally, appear as naughty, mendacious children, or as tricky and lascivious old men; both are the "givers of discourse" and they preside over the word, over mysteries, transformations, processes, and changes; they are the alpha and omega of things. For this reason, certain Yoruba ceremonies begin and end with Elegua's dance.

In the same way, Africa and Aphrodite have more in common than the Greek root that unites their names; there is a flow of marine foam that connects two civilizations "in another way," from within the turbulence of chaos, two civilizations doubly separated by geography and history. The cult of the Virgen de la Caridad del Cobre can be read as a Cuban cult, but it can also be re-read—one reading does not negate the other—as a meta-archipelagic text, a meeting or confluence of marine flowings that connects the Niger with the Mississippi, the China Sea with the Orinoco, the Parthenon with a fried food stand in an alley in Paramaribo.

The peoples of the sea, or better, the Peoples of the Sea proliferate incessantly while differentiating themselves from one another, traveling together toward the infinite. Certain dynamics of their culture also repeat and sail through the seas of time without reaching anywhere. If I were to put this in two words, they would be: performance and rhythm. And nonetheless, I would have to add something more: the notion that we have called "in a certain kind of way," something remote that reproduces itself and that carries the desire to sublimate apocalypse and violence; something obscure that comes from the performance and that one makes his own in a very special way; concretely, it takes away the space that separates the onlooker from the participant.

From Rhythm to Polyrhythm

Nature is the flux of an unknowable feedback machine that society interrupts constantly with the most varied and noisy rhythms. Each rhythm is itself a flux cut through by other rhythms, and we can pursue fluxes upon rhythms endlessly. Well then, the culture of the Peoples of the Sea is a flux interrupted by rhythms which attempt to silence the noises with which their own social formation interrupts the discourse of Nature. If this definition should seem abstruse, we could simplify it by saying that the cultural discourse of the Peoples of the Sea attempts, through real or symbolic sacrifice, to neutralize violence and to refer society to the transhistorical codes of Nature. Of course, as the codes of Nature are neither limited nor fixed, nor even intelligible, the culture of the Peoples of the Sea expresses the desire to sublimate social violence through referring itself to a space that can only be intuited through the poetic, since it always puts forth an area of chaos. In this paradoxical space, in which one has the illusion of experiencing a totality, there appear to be no repressions or contradictions; there is no desire other than that of maintaining oneself within the limits of this zone for the longest possible time, in free orbit, beyond imprisonment or liberty.

All machines have their master codes, and the codebook to the cultural machine of the Peoples of the Sea is made up of a network of subcodes holding together cosmogonies, mythic bestiaries, remote pharmacopoeias, oracles, profound ceremonies, and the mysteries and alchemies of antiquity. One of these subcodes may lead us into the labyrinth of Minos, another to the Tower of Babel, another to the Arawak version of the Flood, another to the secrets of Eleusis, another to the garden of the unicorn, others to the sacred books of India and China and to the divining *cauris* of West Africa. The keys to this vast hermetic labyrinth refer us to "another" wisdom that lies forgotten in the foundation of the postindustrial world, since at one time it was the only form of knowledge there. Clearly, I don't have an interest at this point in saying that all peoples are or at one time were Peoples of the Sea. What I do care to establish is that the people of the Caribbean still are this in part, and everything seems to indicate that they will continue to be so for some time, even within the interplay of dynamics that carry models of knowledge proper to modernity and postmodernity. In the Caribbean, epistemological transparency has not displaced the dregs and sediments of the cosmological arcana, the spatterings of sacrificial blood—as we shall see in the chapter on the work of Fernando Ortiz—but rather, unlike what happens in the West, scientific knowledge and traditional knowledge coexist as differences within the same system.

Then what kind of performance is observed before or beyond the chaos of Caribbean culture? The ritual of supersyncretic beliefs? Dance? Music? By themselves, none of these in particular. The regularities that the culture of the Caribbean shows begin from its intention to reread (rewrite) the march of Nature in terms of rhythms "of a certain kind." I'll give an example right away: Let's suppose that we beat upon a drum with a single blow and set its skin to vibrating. Let's suppose that this sound stretches until it forms something like a salami. Well, here comes the interruptive action of the Caribbean machine; it starts slicing pieces of sound in an unforeseen, improbable, and finally impossible way.

To anyone interested in the way machines function, I ought to say that the Caribbean machine is not a Deleuze and Guattari model of the kind we saw some pages back (the machine machine machine). The specifications of that model are clear and final: here is a flow machine; we hook up an interrupting machine, to which another interrupting machine is then connected, making the previous interruptor appear to be in motion. We're dealing with a system of relative machines, given that, according to how it's seen, the same machine may be one of flow or of interruption. The Caribbean machine, on the other hand, is something more: it is a technological-poetic machine, or, if you like, a metamachine of differences whose poetic mechanism cannot be diagrammed in conventional dimensions, and whose user's manual is found dispersed in a state of plasma within the chaos of its own network of codes and subcodes. It is a machine very different from those we've been discussing up to now. In any event, the notion of polyrhythm (rhythms cut through by other rhythms, which are cut by still other rhythms)—if it takes us to the point at which the central rhythm is displaced by other rhythms in such a way as to make it fix a center no longer, then to transcend into a state of flux—may fairly define the type of performance that characterizes the Caribbean cultural machine. A moment will be reached in which it will no longer be clear whether the salami of sound is cut by the rhythms or these are cut by the salami or it is cut in its slices or these are cut by slices of rhythm. This is by way of saying that rhythm, in the codes of the Caribbean, precedes music, including percussion itself. It is something that was *already there,* amid the noise; something very ancient and dark to which the drummer's hand and the drumhead connect on a given moment; a kind of scapegoat, offered in sacrifice, which can be glimpsed in the air when one lets himself be carried away by a battery of *batá* drums (secret drums to whose beats the *orishas,* the living and the dead, all dance).

It would, however, be a mistake to think that the Caribbean rhythm connects only to percussion. The Caribbean rhythm is in fact a metarhythm which can be arrived at through any system of signs, whether it be dance, music, language, text, or body language, etc. Let's say that one begins to walk and all of a sudden he realizes that he is walking "well," that is, not just with his feet, but also with other parts of his body, which nonetheless adjusts admirably to the rhythm of his steps. It is quite possible that the walker in this circumstance might experience a mild and happy sensation of well-being. All right, there's nothing particularly special about this yet, nothing that we could call "Caribbean"; we've simply taken up the conventional notion of polyrhythm, which presupposed a central rhythm (the rhythm of footsteps). It's possible, though, that a person might feel that he wants to walk not with his feet alone, and to this end he imbues the muscles of his neck, back, abdomen, arms, in short all his muscles, with their own rhythm, different from the rhythm of his footsteps, which no longer dominate. If this should come to pass—which finally would be only a transitory performance—he would be walking like the anti-apocalyptic old women. What has happened is that the center of the rhythmic ensemble formed by the footsteps has been displaced, and now it runs from muscle to muscle, stopping here and there and illuminating in intermittent succession, like a firefly, each rhythmic focus of the body.

Of course the process that I just described is no more than a didactic example, and therefore somewhat mediocre. I haven't even mentioned one of the most important dynamics working toward the decentering of the polyrhythmic system. I'm talking about the very complex phenomenon usually called improvisation. Without it one could never arrive at the optimal rhythm for each particular muscle; one has to give them their freedom to look around at their own risk. Thus, before a person can walk "in a certain kind of way," his entire body must pass through an improvisational stage.

This theme is nowhere near exhausted, but we have to keep moving. I know that there must be doubts and questions at this point, and I'll try to anticipate a few. Someone might ask, for example, what the use is of walking "in a certain kind of way." In fact, there's not much use in it; not even dancing "in a certain kind of way" is of much use if the scale of values that we use corresponds only with a technological machine coupled to an industrial machine coupled to a commercial machine. A jazz improvisation (jazz being a kind of music that dwells within the Caribbean orbit), which achieves a decentering of the canon by which a piece has been interpreted previously, is hardly useful either. The improvisation can be taped by a record company, but the product is a recording, not the improvisation, which is linked indissolubly with a space and time that cannot be reproduced. Of course the company in question will try to persuade us that it is not selling us a phantom. And this company or another will try to convince us that if we acquire certain audio components we'll be able to hear the phantom improvisation better than the improvisation itself. Which is not necessarily false, of course. The deception lies in giving out that "listening" is the only sense touched by improvisation. In fact, improvisation, if it has reached a level that I've been calling "a certain kind of way," has penetrated all of the percipient spaces of those present, and it is precisely this shifting "totality" that leads them to perceive the impossible unity, the absent locus, the center that has taken off and yet is still there, dominating and dominated by the soloist's performance. It is this "totality" that leads those present to another "totality": that of rhythm-flux, but not that of rhythms and fluxes that belong to industrial production, to computers, to psychoanalysis, to synchronicity and diachronicity. The only useful thing about dancing or playing an instrument "in a certain kind of way" lies in the attempt to move an audience into a realm where the tensions that lead to confrontation are inoperative.

The case here is that we are speaking about traditional culture and its impact on Caribbean beings, not about technological knowledge or capitalist consuming practices, and in cultural terms to do something "in a certain kind of way" is always an important matter, since it is an attempt to sublimate violence. Further, it seems that it will keep on being important independently of the power relations of a political, economic, and even cultural nature that exist between the Caribbean and the West. Contrary to the opinions of many, I see no solid reasons to think that the culture of the Peoples of the Sea is negatively affected by the cultural "consumerism" of the industrial societies. When a people's culture conserves ancient dynamics that play "in a certain kind of way," these resist being displaced by external territorializing forms and they propose to coexist with them through syncretic processes. But aren't such processes perhaps a denaturing phenomenon? False. They are enriching, since they contribute to the widening of the play of differences. To begin with, there is no pure cultural form, not even the religious ones. Culture is a discourse, a language, and as such it has no beginning or end and is always in transformation, since it is always looking for the way to signify what it cannot manage to signify. It is true that in comparison with other important discourses—political, economic, social—cultural discourse is the one that most resists change. Its intrinsic desire, one might say, is one of conservation, as it is linked to the ancestral desire of human groups to differentiate themselves as much as possible from one another. Thus we may speak of cultural forms that are more or less regional, national, subcontinental, and even continental. But this in no way denies the heterogeneity of such forms.

A syncretic artifact is not a synthesis, but rather a signifier made of differences. What happens is that, in the melting pot of societies that the world provides, syncretic processes realize themselves through an economy in whose modality of exchange the signifier of *there*—of the Other—is consumed ("read") according to local codes that are already in existence; that is, codes from *here*. Therefore we can agree on the well-known phrase that China did not become Buddhist but rather Buddhism became Chinese. In the case of the Caribbean, it is easy to see that what we call traditional culture refers to an interplay of super-syncretic signifiers whose principal "centers" are localized in preindustrial Europe, in the sub-Saharan regions of Africa, and in certain island and coastal zones of southern Asia. What happens when there arrives, or there is imposed commercially, a "foreign" signifier, let's say the big band music of the forties or the rock music of the past thirty years? Well, among other things, the mambo, the cha-cha-cha, the bossa nova, the bolero, salsa, and reggae happen; that is to say, Caribbean music did not become Anglo-Saxon but rather the latter became Caribbean within a play of differences. Certainly there were changes (different musical instruments, different tunes, different arrangements), but the rhythm and the way of expressing oneself "in a certain kind of way" kept on being Caribbean. In reality, it could be said that, in the Caribbean, the "foreign" interacts with the "traditional" like a ray of light with a prism; that is, they produce phenomena of reflection, refraction, and decomposition. But the light keeps on being light; furthermore, the eye's camera comes out the winner, since spectacular optical performances unfold which almost always induce pleasure, or at least curiosity.

Thus the only thing that walking, dancing, playing an instrument, singing, or writing "in a certain kind of way" are good for is to displace the participants toward a poetic territory marked by an aesthetic of pleasure, or better, an aesthetic whose desire is nonviolence. This voyage "in a certain kind of way," from which one always returns—as in dreams—with the uncertainty of not having lived the past but an immemorial present, can be embarked upon by any kind of performer; it's enough that he should connect to the traditional rhythm that floats within him and without him, within and without those present. The easiest vehicle to take is improvisation, doing something all of a sudden, without thinking about it, without giving reason the chance to resist being abducted through more self-reflexive forms of aesthetic experience, irony for example. Yes, I know, it will be said that a poetic voyage is within reach of any of the earth's inhabitants. But of course, achieving the poetic is not exclusive to any human group; what is characteristic of the Caribbean peoples is that, in fundamental aspect, their aesthetic experience occurs within the framework of rituals and representations of a collective, ahistorical, and improvisatory nature. Later on, in the chapter devoted to Alejo Carpentier and Wilson Harris, we shall see the differences that there can be between those voyages in pursuit of the furtive *locus* of "Caribbeanness."

In any event, we can say that the Caribbean performance, including the ordinary act of walking, does not reflect back on the performer alone but rather it also directs itself toward a public in search of a carnivalesque catharsis that proposes to divert excesses of violence and that in the final analysis was *already there.* Perhaps that is why the most natural forms of Caribbean cultural expression are dance and popular music; that is why Caribbean people excel more in the spectator sports (boxing, baseball, basketball, cricket, gymnastics, track and field, etc.) than in the more subdued, austere sports where space for the performer is less visible (swimming), or is constrained by the nature of the rules of the sport itself, or perhaps the silence required of the audience (shooting, fencing, riding, diving, tennis, etc.).

Although boxing is a sport that many people detest, think for a moment about the capacity to symbolize ritual action that boxing offers: the contenders dancing on the mat, their bouncing off the ropes, the elegant jab and sidestep, the flourish of the bolo punch and the uppercut, the implicit rhythm in all weaving, the boxers' improvised theatrical gestures (faces, challenges, disdainful smiles), the choosing to be villain in one round and gentleman in the next, the performances of the supporting players (the referee who breaks up a clinch, the cornermen with their sponges and towels, the cut man, the doctor who scrutinizes the wounds, the announcer with his fantastic tuxedo, the judges attentively looking on, the bell man), and all of that on an elevated and perfectly illumined space, filled with silks and colors, blood spattering, the flash of the cameras, the shouts and whistles, the drama of the knockdown (will he get up or won't he?), the crowd on its feet, the cheering, the winner's upraised arm. It's no surprise that the people of the Caribbean should be good boxers and also, of course, good musicians, good singers, good dancers, and good writers.

From Literature to Carnival

One might think that literature is a solitary art as private and quiet as prayer. Not true. Literature is one of the most exhibitionistic expressions in the world. This is because it is a stream of texts and there are few things as exhibitionist as a text. It should be remembered that what a performer writes—the word *author* has justifiably fallen into disuse—is not a text, but something previous and qualitatively different: a pre-text. For a pre-text to transform itself into a text, certain stages, certain requisites, which I won't list for reasons of space and argument, must be gone through. I'll content myself by saying that the text is born when it is read by the Other: the reader. From this moment on text and reader connect with each other like a machine of reciprocal seductions. With each reading the reader seduces the text, transforms it, makes it his own; with each reading the text seduces the reader, transforms him, makes him its own. If this double seduction reaches the intensity of "a certain kind of way," both the text and the reader will transcend their statistical limits and will drift toward the decentered center of the paradoxical. This possible impossibility has been studied philosophically, epistemologically, through the discourse of poststructuralism. But poststructuralist discourse corresponds to postindustrial discourse, both discourses of so-called postmodernity. Caribbean discourse is in many respects prestructuralist and preindustrial, and to make matters worse, a contrapuntal discourse that when seen à la Caribbean would look like a *rumba,* and when seen à la Europe like a perpetually moving baroque fugue, in which the voices meet once never to meet again. I mean by this that the space of "a certain kind of way" is explained by poststructuralist thought as episteme—for example, Derrida's notion of *différance*—while Caribbean discourse, as well as being capable of occupying it in theoretical terms, floods it with a poetic and vital stream navigated by Eros and Dionysus, by Oshun and Elegua, by the Great Mother of the Arawaks and the Virgen de la Caridad del Cobre, all of them defusing violence, the blind violence with which the Caribbean social dynamics collide, the violence organized by slavery, despotic colonialism, and the Plantation.

And so the Caribbean text is excessive, dense, uncanny, asymmetrical, entropic, hermetic, all this because, in the fashion of a zoo or bestiary, it opens its doors to two great orders of reading: one of a secondary type, epistemological, profane, diurnal, and linked to the West—the world outside—where the text uncoils itself and quivers like a fantastic beast to be the object of knowledge and desire; another the principal order, teleological, ritual, nocturnal, and referring to the Caribbean itself, where the text unfolds its bisexual sphinxlike monstrosity toward the void of its impossible origin, and dreams that it incorporates this, or is incorporated by it.

A pertinent question would be: how can we begin to talk of Caribbean literature when its very existence is questionable? The question, of course, would allude more than anything to the polylingualism that seems to divide irreparably the letters of the Caribbean. But I would respond to this question with another: is it any more prudent to consider *One Hundred Years of Solitude* as a representative example of the Spanish novel, or the work of Césaire as an achievement of French poetry, or Machado de Assis as a Portuguese writer, or Wilson Harris as an English writer who left his homeland (Guyana) to live as an exile in England? Certainly not. Clearly, one could quickly argue that what I've just said doesn't prove the existence of a Caribbean literature, and that what in fact exist are local literatures, written from within the Caribbean's different linguistic blocs. I agree with this proposition, but only in terms of a first reading. Beneath the turbulence of *árbol, arbre,* tree, etc., there is an island that repeats itself until transforming into a meta-archipelago and reaching the most widely separated transhistorical frontiers of the globe. There's no center or circumference, but there are common dynamics that express themselves in a more or less regular way within the chaos and then, gradually, begin assimilating into African, European, Indoamerican, and Asian contexts up to the vanishing point. What's a good example of this trip to the source? The field of literature is always conflictive (narrow nationalism, resentments, rivalries); my example will not be a literary but a political performer: Martin Luther King. This man was able to be a Caribbean person without ceasing to be a North American, and vice versa. His African ancestry, the texture of his humanism, the ancient wisdom embodied in his pronouncements and strategies, his improvisatory vocation, his ability to seduce and be seduced, and, above all, his vehement condition as a dreamer (*I have a dream . . .*) and as an authentic performer make up the Caribbean side of a man unquestionably idiosyncratic in North America. Martin Luther King occupies and fills the space in which the Caribbean connects to the North American, a space of which jazz is also a sign.

To persevere in the attempt to refer the culture of the Caribbean to geography—other than to call it a meta-archipelago—is a debilitating and scarcely productive project. There are performers who were born in the Caribbean and who are not Caribbean by their performance; there are others who were born near or far away and nevertheless *are.* This doesn't excuse the fact, which I pointed out earlier, that there are common tropisms, and that these are seen with greater frequency within the marine flows that extend from the mouth of the Amazon to the Mississippi delta, that bathe the north coasts of South and Central America, the old Arawak-Carib island bridge, and parts of the United States that are not completely integrated into its technological marrow; furthermore, we would perhaps have to count New York, a city where the density of Caribbean population is noticeable, but, as I said, these geographical speculations leave a lot to be desired. Antilleans, for example, tend to roam the entire world in search of the centers of their Caribbeanness, constituting one of our century's most notable migratory flows. The Antilleans' insularity does not impel them toward isolation, but on the contrary, toward travel, toward exploration, toward the search for fluvial and marine routes. One needn't forget that it was men from the Antilles who constructed the Panama Canal.

Well then, it is necessary to mention at least some of the common regularities which, in a state of flight, the Caribbean's multilinguistic literature presents. In this respect I think that the most perceptible movement that the Caribbean text carries out is, paradoxically, the one that tends to project it outside its generic ambit: a metonymic displacement toward scenic, ritual, and mythological forms, that is, toward machines that specialize in producing bifurcations and paradoxes. This attempt to evade the nets of strictly literary intertextuality always results, naturally, in a resounding failure. In the last analysis, a text is and will be a text ad infinitum, no matter how much it tries to hide itself as something else. Nonetheless, this failed project leaves its mark on the text's surface, and leaves it not so much as the trace of a frustrated act but rather as a will to persevere in flight. It can be said that Caribbean texts are fugitive by nature, constituting a marginal catalog that involves a desire for nonviolence. Thus we have it that the Caribbean *Bildungsroman* does not usually conclude with the hero's saying good-bye to the stage of apprenticeship in terms of a clean slate, nor does the dramatic structure of the Caribbean text ordinarily conclude with the phallic orgasm of climax, but rather with a kind of coda which, for example, would be interpreted in the Cuban popular theater by a rumba danced by the entire cast. If we look at the Caribbean's most representative novels we see that their narrative discourse is constantly disrupted, and at times almost annulled, by heteroclitic, fractal, baroque, or arboreal forms, which propose themselves as vehicles to drive the reader and the text to the marginal and ritually initiating territory of the absence of violence.

All of this refers, nevertheless, to a first reading of the Caribbean text. A rereading would require of us a stop to look at the rhythms proper to Caribbean literature. Here we will soon notice the presence of several rhythmic sources: Indoamerica, Africa, Asia, and Europe. Well, as we know, the polyrhythmic play that makes up the copper, black, yellow, and white rhythms (a conventional way of differentiating them) that issue from these sources has been described and analyzed in the most diverse ways and through the most varied disciplines. Clearly, nothing like that will be done here. In this book there will be discussion only of some regularities that break off from the interplay of those rhythms. For example, white rhythms, basically, articulate themselves in a binary fashion; here is the rhythm of steps marching or running, of territorializing; it is the narrative of conquest and colonization, of the assembly line, of technological knowledge, of computers and positivist ideologies; in general these rhythms are indifferent to their social impact; they are narcissistic rhythms, obsessed with their own legitimation, carrying guilt, alienation, and signs of death which they hide by proposing themselves as the best rhythms existing now or ever. The copper, black, and yellow rhythms, if quite different from one another, have something in common: they belong to the Peoples of the Sea. These rhythms, when compared to the ones mentioned earlier, appear as turbulent and erratic, or, if you like, as eruptions of gases and lava that issue from an elemental stratum, still in formation; in this respect they are rhythms without a past, or better, rhythms whose past is in the present, and they legitimize themselves by themselves. One might think that there is an irremediable contradiction between the two kinds of rhythms, and in fact there is, but only within the confines of a first reading. The dialectic of this contradiction would take us to the moment of synthesis: *mestizo* rhythm, *mulato* rhythm. But a rereading would make it apparent that *mestizaje* is not a synthesis, but rather the opposite. It can't be such a thing because nothing that is ostensibly syncretic constitutes a stable point. The high regard for *mestizaje,* the *mestizaje* solution, did not originate in Africa or Indoamerica or with any People of the Sea. It involves a positivistic and logocentric argument, an argument that sees in the biological, economic, and cultural whitening of Caribbean society a series of successive steps toward "progress." And as such it refers to conquest, to slavery, neocolonialism, and dependence. Within the realities of a rereading, *mestizaje* is nothing more than a concentration of differences, a tangle of dynamics obtained by means of a greater density of the Caribbean object, as we saw in the case of the Virgen del Cobre, who, by the way, is known as "la Virgen mulata." Then, at a given moment in our rereading, the binary oppositions Europe/Indoamerica, Europe/Africa, and Europe/Asia do not resolve themselves into the synthesis of *mestizaje,* but rather they resolve into insoluble differential equations, which repeat their unknowns through the ages of the meta-archipelago. The literature of the Caribbean can be read as a *mestizo* text, but also as a stream of texts in flight, in intense differentiation among themselves and within whose complex coexistence there are vague regularities, usually paradoxical. The Caribbean poem and novel are not only projects for ironizing a set of values taken as universal; they are, also, projects that communicate their own turbulence, their own clash, and their own void, the swirling black hole of social violence produced by the *encomienda* and the plantation, that is, their otherness, their peripheral asymmetry with regard to the West.

Thus Caribbean literature cannot free itself totally of the multiethnic society upon which it floats, and it tells us of its fragmentation and instability: that of the Negro who studied in London or in Paris, that of the white who believes in voodoo, that of the Negro who wants to find his identity in Africa, that of the mulatto who wants to be white, that of the white man who loves a black woman and vice versa, that of the rich black man and poor white man, that of the mulatto woman who passes for white and has a black child, that of the mulatto who says that the races do not exist. Add to these differences those that resulted—and still result in certain regions—from the encounter of the Indoamerican with the European and of the latter with the Asian. Finally, add to all of this the unstable system of relations which, amid uncompromising alliances and conflicts, brings together and separates the Native American and the African, the Native American and the Asian, the Asian and the African, but why go on with this? What model of the human sciences can predict what will happen in the Caribbean next year, next month, next week? We are dealing obviously with an unpredictable society that originated in the most violent currents and eddies of modern history where sexual and class differences are overlaid with differences of an ethnographic nature. Nevertheless, to reduce the Caribbean to the single factor of its instability would also be an error; the Caribbean is that and much more, including much more than what will be dealt with in this book.

In any case, the impossibility of being able to assume a stable identity, even the color that one wears in his skin, can only be made right through the possibility of existing "in a certain kind of way" in the midst of the sound and fury of chaos. To this end, the most viable route to take, it's clear, is that of the meta-archipelago itself, above all the paths that lead to the semipagan hagiography of the Middle Ages and to African beliefs. It is in this space that the majority of the Caribbean cults are articulated, cults that by their nature unleash multiple popular expressions: myth, music, dance, song, theater. This is why the Caribbean text, to transcend its own cloister, must avail itself of these models in search of routes that might lead, at least symbolically, to an extratextual point of social nonviolence and psychic reconstitution of the Self. The routes, iridescent and transitory as a rainbow, cross at all points the network of binary dynamics extended by the West. The result is a text that speaks of a critical coexistence of rhythms, a polyrhythmic ensemble whose central binary rhythm is decentered when the performer (writer/reader) and the text try to escape "in a certain kind of way."

It will be said that this coexistence is false, that finally it ends up as a system formed by the opposition Peoples of the Sea/Europe and its historical derivations. A rereading of this point, nevertheless, would have more imaginative consequences. Relations between Peoples of the Sea and the West, like all power relations, are not simply antagonistic. For example, at bottom, all the Peoples of the Sea want to occupy the place that they occupy geographically, but they would also like to occupy the place of the West, and vice versa. Put differently, any Person of the Sea, without ceasing to be such, would like at bottom to have an industrial machine, one of flow and interruption, to be perhaps in the world of theory, science, and technology. In a parallel fashion, the world made by the Industrial Revolution, without ceasing to be such, would like at times to be in the place of the Peoples of the Sea, where it once was; it would like to live immersed in Nature and in the poetic, that is, it would like once more to own a machine that flows and interrupts at the same time. The signs of the existence of this double paradox of desire are wherever you look—the New Age movement and the environmental movement in the United States and Europe, the industrializing plans and taste for the artificial in the Third World—and I'll return to this contradictory theme in the last chapter. With matters in this state, the opposition of theoretical machine versus poetic machine, epistemological machine versus teleological machine, power machine versus resistance machine, and others of the like will be quite other than fixed poles that always face each other as enemies. In reality, the supposed fixity of these poles would be undermined by an entire gamut of relations that are not necessarily antagonistic, to open up a complex and unstable kind of existing that points to the void, to the lack of something, to repetitive and rhythmic insufficiency which, finally, is the most visible determinism to be drawn in the Caribbean.

And finally I want to make it clear that to undertake a rereading of the Caribbean gives one no license to fall into idealizations. In the first place, as Freud would see, the popular tradition is also in the last analysis a machine that is not free from repression. Certainly it is no technologico-positivist machine that is indifferent to the conserving of certain social linkages, but in its ahistoricity it perpetuates myths and fables that attempt to legitimate the law of patriarchy and hide the violence inherent in every sociological origin. Further—following Rene Girard's reasoning—we can agree that the ritual sacrifice practiced in the symbolic societies implied a desire to sublimate public violence, but this desire was emitted from the sphere of power and pursued objectives of social control.

In the second place, the critical coexistence that I have spoken of tends to unfold in the most unpredictable and diverse forms. An island can, at a given moment, bring closer together or move farther apart cultural components of diverse origins with the worst of possible results—which, luckily, is not the rule—while on a contiguous island the seething and constant interplay of transcontinental spume generates a fortunate product. This chance circumstance makes it possible that, for example, the degree of Africanization in each local culture will vary from island to island, and that the Plantation's acculturating impact will make itself known asymmetrically.

As to the rest, the Caribbean text shows the specific features of the supersyncretic culture from which it emerges. It is, without a doubt, a consummate performer, with recourse to the most daring improvisations to keep from being trapped within its own textuality. In its most spontaneous form it can be seen in terms of the *carnaval*, the great Caribbean celebration that spreads out through the most varied systems of signs: music, song, dance, myth, language, food, dress, body expression. There is something strongly feminine in this extraordinary *fiesta*: its flux, its diffuse sensuality, its generative force, its capacity to nourish and conserve (juices, spring, pollen, rain, seed, shoot, ritual sacrifice—these are words that come to stay). Think of the dancing flourishes, the rhythms of the conga, the samba, the masks, the hoods, the men dressed and painted as women, the bottles of rum, the sweets, the confetti and colored streamers, the hubbub, the carousal, the flutes, the drums, the cornet and the trombone, the teasing, the jealousy, the whistles and the faces, the razor that draws blood, death, life, reality in forward and reverse, torrents of people who flood the streets, the night lit up like an endless dream, the figure of a centipede that comes together and then breaks up, that winds and stretches beneath the ritual's rhythm, that flees the rhythm without escaping it, putting off its defeat, stealing off and hiding itself, imbedding itself finally in the rhythm, always in the rhythm, the beat of the chaos of the islands.

Works Cited

García Márquez, Gabriel. *One Hundred Years of Solitude*. Gregory Rabassa, trans. New York: Harper & Row, 1970.

Guerra y Sánchez, Ramiro. *Sugar and Society in the Caribbean: an Economic History of Cuban Agriculture*. New York: Yale University Press, 1964.

Rodney, Walter. *How Europe Underdeveloped Africa*. London: Bogle-L'Ouverhure Publications, 1988.

Williams, Eric E. *Capitalism and Slavery*. Chapel Hill, N.C.: University of North Carolina Press, 1944.

ON BRAZIL-MEXICO-THE U.S. LATINO:

TUPINICÓPOLIS: THE CITY OF RETRO-FUTURISTIC INDIANS
Celeste Olalquiaga

> *Tupy, or not Tupy, that is the question.*
>
> Oswald de Andrade, 1928

If atrocity exhibitions and junk gardens are counterpoints to hi-tech, what about employing both electronics and its waste to construct a dancing retrofuturistic Indian city?[1] Or confronting a still life of a dead turkey with its referent, both on identical kitchen tables, surrounded by vegetables and culinary implements? This kind of postindustrial-culture-with-a-twist is typical of Third World urban centers, a sardonic reminder that postindustrialism is not exclusively a metropolitan phenomenon, but rather a condition particular to all those cultures, including postcolonial ones, where a fast, if irregular, industrialization has taken place.[2]

Latin America's own version of international culture tends toward a hyperrealism of uniquely parodic attributes. This "magical hyperrealism" often inverts the image of a colonized people humbly subservient to metropolitan discoveries into one of a cynical audience rolling over with laughter at what it perceives as the sterile nuances of cultures with very little sense of their own self-aggrandizement. Banalizing issues and objects by either making them literal or dramatizing their function is part of a long tradition of dealing with the unexpected changes and imposed or makeshift policies postcolonial countries are usually forced to face. Thus, contrary to Fredric Jameson's definition of contemporary pastiche (a blank collage), I will argue here that Latin America's current

---

[1]Reprinted from *Megalopolis; Contemporary Cultural Sensibilities* (Minneapolis: University of Minnesota Press, 1992).

[2]On how postindustrialism affects Latin American culture see Néstor García Canclini, *Culturas híbridas: estrategias para entrar y salir de la modernidad.*

use of pastiche redeems some of the traditional qualities of parody, although with a layer of cynicism that was absent until now from its discourse.[3]

While the appropriation and transformation of elements that are felt as threatening is an old process, it is in these past years that it has reached the highest degree of complexity. This is mainly due to an unprecedented degree of reciprocal appropriation and mutual transformation, whereby cultural change can no longer be said to be a matter of simple vertical imposition or ransacking, but is rather an intricate horizontal movement of exchange. Despite the inherent inequalities of sources and processes, this system of social recycling constitutes culture into a somewhat duty-free space in which, as in Hong Kong, Manaus (Brazil), and Isla de Margarita (Venezuela), all hierarchies are disrupted and humanistic justifications put aside in order to guarantee the free and prompt flow of cash for goods sold at wholesale value.[4]

For Latin American culture both at home and in the United States, this means at least three distinct types of cultural recycling that, as was seen in Chapter Three to be true of kitsch, cohabit in synchronized difference. The matter of direct, unmediated adaptation aside, the processes of cultural transformation that involve Latin America as an object, a subject, or both, are: the Latinization of urban culture in the United States, the formation of hybrid cultures such as the Chicano and Nuyorican, and what I will call the pop recycling of U.S. icons of both Latin American and U.S. culture itself at the moment of postindustrialization.[5]

---

[3]See Fredric Jameson, "Postmodernism; or The Cultural Logic of Late Capitalism." An interesting comparative account of how this process of banalizing or parodying U.S. cultural production is done in Brazilian film may be found in Joao Luiz Vieira and Robert Stam, "Parody and Marginality: The Case of Brazilian Cinema." Thanks to George Yúdice for this reference as well as for his suggestions and support during the writing of this chapter.

[4]This image of postmodernity corresponds to the notion of wholesale changes in capital formation and their adaptation and reformulation by social representations as discussed in Paul Smith, "Visiting the Banana Republic." However lucid this article may be, Smith, like Jameson in "Postmodernism," doesn't seem to take into account postcolonial strategies of resistance. For a good overview of the main issues of the postmodernist polemic, see Andreas Huyssen, "Mapping the Postmodern."

[5]The question of unmediated adaptation has been discussed by theorists of imperialism and neocolonization. Néstor García Canclini, in *Culturas híbridas*, goes to great lengths to discuss the degree and implications of such adaptation, showing that it is seldom as mechanical as it has been made out to be. He pro-

The Latinization of the United States

A survey of the first two types of acculturation will illustrate the peculiar characteristics of the third, especially the parodic attributes suggested above as the counterpart to contemporary melancholia. Latinization is a process whereby the United States' culture and daily practices become increasingly permeated by elements of Latin American culture imported by Spanish-speaking immigrants from Central and South America, as well as the Caribbean. Inspired by an ever-growing population that is currently estimated at 30 million people, Latinization is obviously stronger in those areas where this immigration is more concentrated, for instance in New York City, Florida, Texas, and California.[6]

The several kinds of elements absorbed by U.S. mainstream culture differ in their degree of permeation. The most simple and elementary kind occurs with all foreign cultures that have come to the U.S. and is part of the "melting pot" ideology: the commercial circulation of food and clothing, appreciated mostly for their exotic quality. Constantly reinforced as part of a distancing strategy that attempts to keep clear boundaries, the importance of this exoticism becomes most apparent in the distinction between the "American" and the "ethnic." These two widely misused terms ignore the physical frontiers of the United States and the social mélange on which its culture is based in order to promote a sense of original belonging and reinforce the isolation of incoming communities. Consequently, the consumption of exotica has very little influence on the culture within which it takes place.

Although it may seem that such isolation runs counter to the "melting pot" ideology, I would like to propose that in fact these two complement one another, for implicit in the notion of melting is the disappearance of peculiar traits, the erasure of those attributes that distinguish different cultures, making them potentially disruptive to an established system. In short, both as exotica and as alloy foreign cultures in the United States would seem to be doomed: in one case to perpetual marginality, in the other to a critical integration. Amidst the myriad struggles such limited options have triggered, it is interesting to note that even the term "melting pot" is beginning to age, giving way to more dynamic reformulations of the intricate cohabitation of cultures. An example of this is the

---

poses that the irregularities of both the nationalism and modernizing processes in Latin America are made apparent by postmodernism's flattening of distinctions.

[6]On the reaction to Latinization see Thomas B. Morgan, "The Latinization of America."

recent official description of New York City as a "mosaic," a place where elements come together not to be dissolved, but to construct together a panorama.

This first type of acculturation process gains in complexity when mainstream culture begins to be infiltrated by fragmented and scattered elements of language, music, film and iconography. Beyond Latino restaurants, outlets, and communities, Spanish has begun to invade advertising and colloquial speech. Started mainly as a marketing strategy to address the growing Spanish-speaking population, this trend has been picked up by cityspeak, where the regular use of words like *adiós*, *café* (coffee), *nada*, among others, indicates a certain popular recognition of the confluence of Latino and mainstream cultures in the United States. In a city like New York, this phenomenon is not new: many words have been borrowed from other languages, particularly Yiddish, and adapted as colloquialisms. The case of Spanish, however, is a national phenomenon, whose increasing diffusion is perceived as so culturally destabilizing that a purist reaction against it has been launched; movements like English Only have succeeded in imposing English as the legal official language in many states.

The effort to appropriate and reformulate Latino culture into an "American" version extends also to food, music, film and iconography. I have already discussed the current fashion of Catholic religious iconography in Chapter Three. As for food, the 1980s witnessed the proliferation of mixed restaurants that basically take one of two directions. The first could be called the hi-tech rendition of "ethnic" foods: different staples are transformed into fast food, as in the case of Tex-Mex food, derived from Mexican cooking. The second is a less drastic transformation, and it consists in the blending of mainstream packaging strategies and administration with the typical food and decor of the country in question. The outcome is places like Bayamo and Benny's Burritos, which offer savory mixing and matching of the basic ingredients and staples of Chino-Latino (Chinese-Cuban) and Mexican cuisine respectively--in pink and green neon-lit restaurants. This atmospheric artificiality is meant to evoke the color and icon saturation with which most of Latin America and the Caribbean culture is associated. Benny's Burritos does it metonymically through colors, Bayamo by creating an elaborate mise-en-scène of tropical motifs, namely an excess of coconut trees.[7]

Latin American musical instruments, rhythms, and popular songs are also being steadily adopted. In part, this has to do with the current "worldbeat" and "go global" music, eager to incorporate postcolonial rhythms. Movements like 1988's We Are the World and SOS-Racisme (France) have both capitalized

---

[7]Paul Smith in "Visiting the Banana Republic" shows how the Banana Republic stores effect a similar process to neutralize and legitimize colonial discourse.

on this music and thrust it to the limelight. American singer-composer David Byrne has adopted Caribbean and Brazilian melodies, and his recycled versions are barely distinguishable from the originals, adding to the prevailing pastiche of genres and nationalities.

Mainstream films that attempt to broach the question of Latino cultural integration approach it from a conventional point of view. Two recent ones are coincidentally about musicians: *La Bamba* (Luis Valdez, 1987), about 1950s rock singer Ritchie Valens, and *Crossover Dreams* (Leon Ichaso, 1985), about 1970s and 1980s salsa singer Rubén Blades. In these two rags-to-riches stories, the issue of maintaining Latino identity in relation to becoming a mainstream musician is diffused by the highly emotional narrative through which it is rendered. In the Valens film it becomes a question of being accepted by his girlfriend's father, and Valens' final and successful discovery of the intensity and marketability of his legacy's music happens totally by accident. In the other film, Blades' failed crossover is schematic and full of dogma: blinded by money and success, he abandons his own community only to discover that he can't make it in the outside world, which wanted him precisely for his ethnicity.

Rather than presenting the complexities of acculturation within the social context in which they are negotiated—market competition, cultural prejudice, the distinct degrees of success and failure other musicians have achieved—both films decontextualize their main characters in order to make them individual success (or failure) stories. In this sense, the films accept a preexisting cultural narrative that measures the success of Latino integration into mainstream culture through outstanding achievement. By ignoring the more quotidian practices of integration of such a large community, these films reinforce the notion that marginalized groups have to excel in order to be accepted in the dominating culture.

These films stand in contrast to the more sophisticated treatment of second-generation immigrants in *Le Thé Au Hare* (Mehdi Charef, 1986) and *My Beautiful Laundrette* (Stephan Frears, 1985), in which the difficult integration of Arab and Pakistani youths in Paris and London respectively is shown as part of a broader context that includes their families, their peers, and their relationship to the labor market. Furthermore, in these two films the ambivalent and shifting feelings of the main characters toward their cultural identity is portrayed as a reformulation of the underlying conflict between modernity and tradition, a duality that has been shattered by the contemporary globalization of ethnic attributes.

Nostalgia as a Cultural Hindrance

It is within the paradigms of this duality that the second type of Latin American acculturation takes place: the emergence of hybrid cultures—Chicano, Nuyorican—that struggle to find a place within the United States while keeping intact a sense of belonging to quite a different tradition. Whereas Latinization implies the fragmentary incorporation of Latino elements into a fairly technologized discourse, as in the case of food, the formation of hybrid cultures tends to pull toward a more traditional setting, connected to the nostalgia for the homeland that characterizes first-generation immigrants. This nostalgia permeates the second generation in the form of highly ethnocentric values--or resistance to them, an adamant denial of the legacy--and a family-centered behaviour that, coupled with inadequate housing, education, and job opportunities, promote the isolation they should fight against.

Perhaps one of the most extreme representations of Latino nostalgia may be found in the *casitas*, the small houses built on vacant lots by Puerto Ricans in the Bronx and Manhattan. Used as weekend clubs, *casitas* enact an altogether different space, that of memory. Resembling homeland architecture and colors, they install a piece of Puerto Rico right in the middle of New York City, enabling builders and neighbors to imaginarily transport themselves in time and space.[8]

On the other hand, the mixing of traditional and modern elements is not only fundamental to the survival of many artists but often the main issue of their work. Nuyoricans Pepón Osorio and Merián Soto, one a visual designer and the other a choreographer, work together to produce performances in which a visually exuberant scenario sets the scene for the questioning and reformulation of classic Latino values—machismo, women's roles—through mixed media (video, slides, etc.).[9] The little-known Latin Empire signed with Atlantic Records in 1989 for the first Spanglish Hip Hop single: "Puerto Rican and Proud"; one of its artists goes by the pseudonym Puerto Rock.[10] The complexities and implications of the constitution of Latino culture being beyond the scope of this chapter,

---

[8]On the *casitas* see Joseph Sciorra, "I Feel Like I'm in My Country." Also see Dinitia Smith, "Secret Lives of New York."

[9]On Pepón Osorio and Merián Soto, see Joan Acocella, "Loisaida Story" and my "El difícil arte de montar escenarios."

[10]See Guy Trebay, "Hip Hop in Spanglish." For more on Latinization see Juan Flores and George Yúdice, "Living Borders/Buscando América: Languages of Latino Self-Formation."

it is important to note that it has been precisely this nostalgia that has kept the majority of Latino communities from developing the parodic distance characteristic of the third type of acculturation.

Latin American Postindustrial Pop

While Chicano and Nuyorican cultures are bent on protecting an identity continually threatened by both bias and market voracity, there is a tendency in Latin America and in some Latino groups in the United States to turn inside out the Latin American stereotypes produced by the United States and the postindustrial iconography thought to be primarily from the First World. This inversion succeeds in casting its own light over postindustrialism, throwing back the stereotypes reproduced in that iconography and capitalizing on the U.S. image of the postcolonial. Based on the strategies of anthropophagy and carnivalization, this recycling generates a pastiche that parodies the iconographic production of mainstream culture. However, beyond a mere transitory laugh, this parody enables the formulation of a peculiar Latin American and Latino questioning of the issues of tradition, modernity, and postmodernity, and often a method that benefits economically from overturning them.[11]

Parody and role inversion are not only examples of how to resist colonial practices to the advantage of marginalized cultures, but also processes whose political and social implications indicate a more dynamic mode of acculturation than that of Latinization. This is probably due to the fact that Latinization takes place mainly through commodification, corporations having rapidly understood the market potential of both Latinos and Latin iconography. As opposed to this, the overturning strategies to be discussed here may be considered popular or spontaneous practices in which consumption is either secondary or fully displayed as consumption. The contrast between Latinization and Latin American postindustrial pop shows the versatility of a practice like appropriation.

An interesting illustration of the way postcolonial parody works can be found in an episode of what must be the most well-known South American popular festivity—Brazilian carnival. An old tradition involving both the local community, which prepares year round for the three-day extravaganza, and the

---

[11]See João Luiz Vieira and Robert Stam, "Parody and Marginality," which follows the notion of carnivalization put forth by Mikhail Bakhtin. See also Afranio M. Catani and Jose I. de Melo Souza, *A chanchada no cinema brasileiro*; Celso F. Favaretto, *Tropicalia: alegoria, alegria*; Benedito Nunes, *Oswald Canibal*; Haroldo de Campos, "Da razão antropofágica: a Europa sob o signo da devoração."

international marketing of touristic goods, the carnival features as its main spectacle the parade of samba schools. Each school parades an *enredo*, or theme, with a magnificent display of outfits and dances called *fantasias* (fantasies). Made up of thousands of dancers and singers, and several *carros alegóricos* (allegorical carriages) where the theme is recreated, each school dances its *enredo* for forty-five minutes along the Sambódromo, a long stadium that acts as an artificial avenue.

Built in 1985 in an official attempt to control the carnival and its profits, the Sambódromo is already an interesting metaphor of the dynamics between tradition and modernity on which the carnival dances and that is often the topic of its *enredos*. Before the Sambódromo was built, the carnival used to parade down one of Rio de Janeiro's main downtown avenues, accessible to all. The construction of the mile-long avenue that comes to life once a year automatically stratified the event, since tickets to enter the Sambódromo are beyond the means of many Brazilians; furthermore, the place is segmented by price, ensuring that the private expensive rooms, occupied by wealthy politicians or tourists, get the best view at the expense of literally obstructing the sight of the lower-priced benches. Yet perhaps the biggest paradox of this popular event can be found right outside the Sambódromo's walls, in the very poor neighborhood whose inhabitants have to watch on television the spectacle that develops only a few feet away from them.

The contradictions and exclusions of the process of modernity are often addressed by the carnival's *enredos*. One of the most brilliant of such thematic allegories left the issue of national identity—through which this conflict is usually articulated—aside, focusing instead on the mechanics and consequences of global urban reality. A retrofuturistic Indian metropolis, *Tupinicópolis*, was the second finalist in the 1987 competition for best *samba*. Its theme described the Tupi Indians, happy inhabitants of an unbridled cosmopolis where, amid neon and trash, they ride supersonic Japanese motorcycles and play rock music, wearing the Tupi Look: brightly-colored sneakers, phosphorescent feathers, and blenders as head-gear. Its *carros alegóricos* showed a high-tech urban scenario of mirrors, chrome, and plastic, made in golden, silver, and electric colors and set up in expressionistic diagonals and spirals. In it were highways, skyscrapers, and neon signs: Shopping Center Boitatá, Tupinicopolitan Bank, Tupy Palace Hotel, and even a disco.

The humorous Tupinicopolitan aesthetic recycled Hollywood's postcolonial pop image, producing a sort of Carmen Miranda in 1987 Tokyo. It carnivalized both the perception of Latin America as "primitive" and the glamour and distance of high-tech by putting them together: executive Tupi Indians skating around glittery cityscapes and consuming city life to the utmost. In so doing, this *enredo* brought forward two constitutive issues for Latin American and

Latino culture. These issues help understand how the habit of simultaneously processing different cultures in Latin America anticipated postmodern pastiche and recycling to the point where it could be affirmed that Latin American culture, like most postcolonial or marginalized cultures, was in some ways postmodern before the First World, a pre-postmodernity, so to speak.[12]

The first of these issues is the ability to simultaneously handle multiple codes. The intersection of an alien perception of Latin America—whose supposed primitivity is ridiculed by turning its inhabitants into Indians—with the sophistication of a technological cityscape, however dramatized for the effects of parody, is an accurate representation of the cultural mix in which Latin America is developing. Accustomed to dealing with the arbitrary imposition of foreign products and practices, this culture has learned the tactics of selection and transformation to suit the foreign to its own idiosyncracy, thus developing popular integration mechanisms that are deliberately eclectic and flexible. Rather than reflecting a structural weakness, this infinite capacity for adaptation allows Latin American culture to select what is useful and discard what it deems unimportant.[13]

Having become a cultural trait, this acquired distance is practical in more ways than one: it enables a humoristic perspective that often reveals the relativity of problems that are felt elsewhere as unique and overriding. The tropicalization that "Tupinicópolis" makes of high-tech culture, for instance, heightens the perception of its impersonality and consumptiveness without a trace of demagogy. The transitoriness and short life span of advanced technology capped this allegorical reflection on city life: the last *carro alegórico* was the Tupilurb, a pile of debris (abandoned cars, refrigerators, televisions) painted in gold. "Watch all that happiness, it's a smiling city," Tupinicopolitans sang of the volatile urban experience, "even trash is a luxury as long as it's real." If First World postindustrial countries assume the decadence of the modern belief in progress with either melancholy or a disillusionment that stylizes ruins—as punk does—"underdevelopment" carnavalizes this decadence. In a paradoxical anthropophagy, the postcolonial turns postindustrial culture into pop, making its emptiness kitsch.

The second issue that "Tupinicópolis" brings to the surface regarding the postmodern *avant la lettre* character of Latin American and Latino cultures has to do with its depiction of the self-referentiality of urban discourse. The growing visual and iconic qualities of contemporary perception have turned to the city as

---

[12]This idea has been suggested by, among others, Guillermo Gómez-Peña in "New Artistic Continent."

[13]On Latin American selective adaptation and transformation in literature see Angel Rama, "Los procesos de transculturación en la narrativa latinoamericana."

the foremost scenario, an endless source of ever-changing images. Intensified by the mirror reflections of corporate architecture, cities become a place to be seen rather than to be lived in. This spectacular self-consciousness (the consciousness of being a spectacle) is familiar to cultures that have been regarded "from above" by colonization. What can be more conscious than the allegorical parade of an imaginary city on an artificial avenue?

The familiarity of being observed possibly accounts for the qualitative distance of two exhibits dealing with the contemporary production of images. *A trama do gosto: Um outro olhar no cotidiano* (The Constitution of Taste: Another Look at Everyday Life) took place in 1987 in São Paulo and was part of that city's anniversary celebrations. Imageworld is a retrospective that opened at the Whitney Museum of American Art in New York City in fall 1989. In dealing with the same topic, these two exhibits followed two completely different paths. What is relevant here is the unconventionality and humor of the Brazilian exhibit in comparison to the traditional way the Whitney installed its show. Whereas the Whitney scarcely ventured (except in its precious few video installations) to upset the predictability of the museum walk, which was mainly linear and without opportunities for viewers to participate, the Brazilian exhibit portrayed the contemporary relationship to images in the format in which it is usually lived: the experience of being in a city.

Using an avenue, the Avenida Babalurbe, as an organizing figure, the particular shows of *A trama do gosto* were arranged so as to simulate the urban façades of stores, buildings, and parks that urbanites can appreciate while walking or riding in a car. From the daily exchange of postcards to the more educated pleasure of visiting art galleries, the show tracked down how looking is culturally constituted. One of the more striking presentations was *Arranha-Céu* (Skyscraper), where, protected by darkness and standing on a rooftop, the public could spy with binoculars through "windows," looking into video monitors that depicted domestic scenes. The cinematic fascination of anonymous spying was confirmed by this presentation's popularity: a long line had climbed to the rooftop, and once they were there, viewers were glued to the binoculars. Not a guard was in sight in this exhibit, which was complete with sidewalk cafés and performances. Quite a contrast to the heavily guarded, hands-off show the Whitney presented as its own version of an image world, whose seriousness, authority, and conventional spatial disposition were hardly dislocated by the scattered video installations.

Be it the transitoriness of technology or the visual constitution of contemporary sensibility, both Tupinicópolis and *A trama do gosto* clearly represent a humorous approach to contemporary experience. In this way, threatening situations and intricate issues become familiar to a mass audience that would otherwise remain marginalized from such sophisticated reflections on urban life.

Consequently, these shows indicate not only the ability of Latin American culture to deal with the complexities of postindustrialism, but also how such humorous reversals can promote an awareness of these issues at a popular level and, in the final instance, show them within a broader context than their First World counterparts ever do.

Reinventing Roles in Postcolonial Culture

Extreme examples of the recycling of First World icons may be found in a sort of cultural transvestism whereby these icons, rather than being overturned, are driven to the limit. This kind of subversion acts not by a deconstructive dismantling, but rather by saturation. The imposition of added layers of meaning (through the use of multiple codes and a self-conscious theatricality) transforms the icon into a baroque object whose weight distorts the effectivity of any one signification. Two examples of such cultural transvestism may be found in the emergence of Superbarrio from the ruins of Mexico City's 1985 earthquake and in the casual adoption of punk gear by Chilean youth. The generalized establishment of Latin American cultural transvestism can be appreciated in the intrinsic differences of these examples, since Superbarrio is a popular political phenomenon engaged in the social struggle to assist Mexico City's poor, whereas Chilean weekend punks are middle-class youths concerned mainly with fashion. Both, nevertheless, succeed in reformulating the original roles and exposing the mechanisms that articulated them in the first place.

Superbarrio (Superslum) is a masked stranger who indirectly grew out of the governmental inefficiency in handling the 1985 earthquake that destroyed vast areas of Mexico City, and who has come to represent a growing popular mobilization that is dramatically rearticulating social policies in Latin America.[14] Superbarrio first appeared in 1987 to assist the newly-formed Assembly of Barrios, an alliance of groups that pressed the government for rapid reconstruction of the city's devastated neighborhoods, in continuing its demands for housing reforms for the poor. Although anonymous behind his mask and outfit (red tights, gold cape, and shirt inscribed with the initials SB), Superbarrio has become a well-known national figure who is received in high government offices, and has extended his agenda to denouncing and fighting police corruption, pollution, and transportation problems—an ambitious undertaking that, according to popular mythology, is really covered by four Superbarrios.

---

[14]For the recent popular movements in Latin America see "The Homeless Organize," a special issue on this topic. Thanks to Jean Franco for this reference and for her suggestions on the writing of this chapter.

Rather than turning reality into a dream, which is what happens through mainstream media in the United States, Superbarrio, complete with a telephone hotline, a Barriomobile and a Barrio Cave, inverted the formula: taking the superhero figure quite literally, he put it to work at the service of the needy. Whereas in the United States, superheroes like Superman and Batman do little more than promote consumer goods and reinforce the good guys versus bad guys national ideology, in Mexico City popular appropriation of the superhero has replaced leisure consumption with the need for basic goods and a schematic narrative by a street struggle for the basic rights of the poor: "Our enemies are not imaginary, but real," says Superbarrio. Consistent with the popular power that enables his existence, Superbarrio keeps his mask on on the grounds that it allows collective identity (Rohter).

The case of Chilean punks is a role-reversal of quite a different type. If Superbarrio politicizes the superhero figure, Chilean punks have managed to carry to the extreme the fashion industry's co-optation of punk. Initially, punk was a trend that sought to corporize the disillusionment of modernity and of the early 1970s hippie revolution in an aesthetics of bleakness and decay (in many ways like the one described in chapter 4, "Nature Morte"). The hard-core years of punk (roughly 1976 through the early 1980s) produced a dress code, music, and a graphic language that used violence as a means of resistance to an apathetically established counterculture. This violence took the form of loud, dissonant music with accompanying melancholic or politically provocative lyrics; ragged black clothes that conveyed a state of physical deterioration; a lifestyle marked by an absence of past or future and therefore basically transient—without a permanent home or job, feeding off junk or stolen food; and an anarchist lack of belief in any kind of institution (Hebdige).

In many ways, punk was the most conspicuous resistance to the cultural mainstream to come from within its native ranks. Mainly a white phenomenon, it grew out of the depressed London inner cities and was taken up soon after in New York City by middle-class youth, which makes Chilean weekend punks into an icon at second remove. Blank and defiant to the world and tied internally by a strong sense of peer alliance, punk soon began to emerge from the margins of cosmopolitan cities worldwide. Such a dramatic statement of style was rapidly co-opted by the fashion and musical industries, which turned the aesthetics of decay into yet another mode of consumption. However obvious this may be in New York or London, it is in the Chilean making of punk into a pop icon of hipness that the contrast between its origins and its later versions can be best appreciated.

The "punk fashion" in Santiago, as portrayed in Gonzalo Justiniano's video *Guerreros pacíficos* (1985), must be distinguished from the punk underground that developed there, however small or contradictory it is. By contrast,

Chilean weekend punks live a relatively established life and don punk outfits as party costumes. Delighted at the local commotion they cause, they wear elaborate makeup, dance rowdily, and gang up, but neither their aesthetics nor their attitude is connected to the bleakness and violence. Instead, they are punk because *es la onda* (it's cool), and their detachment from the punk subculture as well as their highly iconic experience of it is perhaps best portrayed in their naive use of pins that say "Punk." By openly adopting punk as a fashion that in no way alters the rest of their life, Chilean weekend punks break the illusion that adopting a certain type of clothing can automatically grant a certain kind of experience, a founding illusion of U.S. advertisement, which equates aesthetics with style and style with fashion, implying that in buying into the fashion you can acquire the aesthetics. Unwittingly, Chilean weekend punks assist in exposing the mechanics of the fashion industry.

The iconic radicalism of Superbarrio and Chilean weekend punks is politically and artistically explored by San Diego's Border Art Workshop/Taller de Arte Fronterizo, a multidisciplinary group of Chicano, Mexican, and American artists who work to subvert the images of the border region that have been created by the media. Fascinated by crosscultural phenomena, the Taller de Arte Fronterizo is bent on understanding and reproducing hybrid cultures and uses the frontier as a metaphor for a place where different discourses intersect. To this effect, it recycles stereotypical iconography, in particular iconography that addresses the mixture of U.S. and Mexican clichés, as a politically powerful discourse, highlighting the potential strength of hybrid cultures over purist nationalistic exclusivities. The workshop explicitly addresses the brutal governmental tactics of U.S. border control in its installations and performances, many of which take place on site: on the border.

Among other interesting cases of cultural transvestism is the tongue-in-cheek acceptance of the primary icon for commercial uses. This is the case of innumerable tourist industries that simulate traditions and situations to fit tourists' expectations as a means of survival. As opposed to an organized tourism that creates a reality of its own, these industries are on the fringe of that market and benefit from it but are the product of the survival skills and the ingenuity of a people accustomed to having to meet others' demands and finally cashing in on those demands. Thus, the Hollywood transformation of Carmen Miranda into an icon of luscious tropicality finds its counterpoint in, say, a trio of astute Mexicans who, under the guise of being "Authentic Aztec Dancers," make a living from the gullibility of tourists in Niagara Falls.[15] These "authentics" manage to capitalize on the belief that Latin America is a "primitive" culture by

---

[15]As told by Guillermo Gómez Peña, one of the founding members of the Taller de Arte Fronterizo.

practicing a sophisticated cultural transvestism that allows them to become what they are expected to be without the schizophrenia it usually engenders in the First World. Their ability to benefit from the icons of themselves by putting them on stage for a profit goes a lot farther in undoing racist clichés than most theoretical deconstructions. By appropriating such icons and manipulating them at will, popular culture demonstrates its unequaled mastery in recycling, the game only a high-culture postmodernity was supposed to play.[16]

It is in this third type of acculturation, the one that banks on its hybrid character to participate in and overturn the paradigms produced by the First World, that the most exciting cultural proposals of the moment can be found. Leaving behind postindustrial melancholia and identity nostalgia, and to the side market globalization of ethnicity, the humorous overturning of mass media images, like the artistic exposure of scientific disciplines I have discussed elsewhere,[17] works exclusively within the iconic realm to proclaim it a flexible language that may be bent, twisted, and turned to satisfy far more needs than the ones that produced those icons in the first place. Trained by a long history of intertwining codes and spectacular roles, postcolonial cultures show in this reversal how the world can also be a scenario for their own directorial and spectatorial delight.

Works Cited

Acocella, Joan. "Loisaida Story." *7 Days*, November 9, 1988.

Campos, Haroldo de. "Da razão antropofágica: a Europa sob o signo da devoração," in *Obras completas de Oswald de Andrade*, vol. 2. Rio de Janeiro: Civilização Brasileria, 1971.

Catani, Alfranio M., and Jose I. de Melo Souza. *A chanchada no cinema brasileiro*. São Paulo: Brasliense, 1983.

Favaretto, Celso F. *Tropicalia: alegoria, alegria*. São Paulo: Kairos, 1979.

Flores, Juan, and George Yúdice. "Living Borders/Buscando América: Languages of Latino Self-Formation." *Social Text* 24 (1990): 57-84.

García Canclini, Néstor. *Culturas híbridas: estrategias para entrar y salir de la modernidad*. México: Grijalbo, 1990.

Gómez-Peña, Guillermo. "A New Artistic Continent." *High Performance* 9.3 (1986): 24-31

---

[16]A similar ridiculization of and profit from tourists' expectations is depicted in *Cannibal Tours* (Dennis O'Rourke, 1988).

[17]See my "Nature Morte."

Hebdige, Dick. *Subculture: The Meaning of Style*. London: Methuen, 1979.

"The Homeless Organize." *NACLA* 4 (November-December 1989).

Huyssen, Andreas. "Mapping the Postmodern." *New German Critique* 33 (1984): 5-52.

Jameson, Fredric. "Postmodernism; or The Cultural Logic of Late Capitalism." *New Left Review* 146 (July-August 1984): 53-92.

Morgan, Thomas B. "The Latinization of America." *Esquire* 99 (May 1983): 47-56.

Nunes, Benedito. *Oswald Canibal*. São Paulo: Perspectiva, 1979.

Olalquiaga, Celeste. "El difícil arte de montar escenarios." *Más*, Winter 1989: 71.

—. "Nature Morte." *Megalopolis. Contemporary Cultural Sensibilities*. Minneapolis, Oxford: University of Minnesota Press, 1992.

Rama, Angel. "Los procesos de transculturación en la narrativa latinoamericana." *La novela en América Latina: panoramas 1920-1980*. Colombia: Procultura, 1982: 203-34.

Rohter, Larry. "The Poor Man's Superman, Scourge of Landlords." *New York Times*, August 15, 1988, 4.

Sciorra, Joseph. "I Feel Like I'm in My Country." *TDR* 34 (Winter 1990): 156-98.

Smith, Dinitia. "Secret Lives of New York." *New York*, December 11, 1989: 41-42.

Smith, Paul. "Visiting the Banana Republic." *Universal Abandon? The Politics of Postmodernism*. Ross, Andrew, ed. Minneapolis: University of Minnesota Press, 1988. 128-48.

Trebay, Guy. "Hip Hop in Spanglish." *Village Voice*, April 11, 1989: 19-20.

Vieira, João Luiz and Robert Stam. "Parody and Marginality: The Case of Brazilian Cinema." *Framework* 29 (1985): 20-49.

ON CUBA:

INTERTEXTUALITY AS *DIFFÉRANCE* IN JULIETA CAMPOS' *EL MIEDO DE PERDER A EURÍDICE*: A SYMPTOMATIC CASE OF LATIN AMERICAN POSTMODERNISM
Cynthia M. Tompkins

Julieta Campos was born in Havana, Cuba, on May 8, 1932.[1] She received her doctorate from the School of Philosophy and Letters at the University of Havana. Later on, she won a scholarship from the Alianza Francesa, which enabled her to study at the Sorbonne (1953-54), where she received a diploma in contemporary French Literature (Cortés 114-15). In Paris, she married Mexican political scientist Enrique González Pedrero. She has a son, Emiliano, and has resided in Mexico since 1955 (Lagos-Pope 128).

Campos began contributing literary criticism for cultural supplements in 1956. Upon her mother's death, Campos wrote her first novel, *Muerte por agua* (Death by Water), which appeared in 1965, in conjunction with *La imagen en el espejo* (The Image in the Mirror) a collection of critical essays on Virginia Woolf, Malcolm Lowry, Michel Butor, Nathalie Sarraute, Alain Robbe-Grillet, François Mauriac, Ernest Hemingway, Simone de Beauvoir, Alejo Carpentier, Agustín Yáñez and Juan Rulfo (Flores 157).

In terms of literary criticism, Campos published *El Oficio de Leer* (On Reading) in 1971, *Función de la novela* (Purpose of the Novel) in 1973, and *La herencia obstinada* (The Obstinant Inheritance) in 1982. Campos' fiction includes *Celina o los gatos* (Selina and the Cats), which appeared in 1968, *Tiene los cabellos rojizos y se llama Sabina* (She Has Reddish Hair and her Name is Sabina) in 1974, and *El miedo de perder a Eurídice* (The Fear of Losing Eurydice) in 1979 (Cortés 115).

In addition to the parallel production of novels and essays, Campos has translated over thirty-eight books in social sciences, history, and psychoanalysis (Flores 157) for both the Fondo de Cultura Económica and the publishing house Siglo XXI (Barrea-Marlys 115). In 1974 Campos received the Xavier Villaurrutia

---

[1]Different stages of this project have been funded by the Scholarship, Research and Creative Activities Grant Program at Arizona State University West (Summer Stipends for 1992-93, 1993-94, and 1994-95).

prize for her novel *Tiene los cabellos rojizos y se llama Sabina*. Her play, *Jardín de Invierno*, was staged in 1986. Campos contributed to *Plural*. From 1981 to 1984 she edited the *Revista de la Universidad de México*. At present, Campos is a member of the editorial board of *Vuelta*. From 1976 to 1982 Campos taught literature at the Universidad Nacional Autónoma de México. During that period (1978-82) she was president of the P.E.N. club of Mexico (Flores 157).

Campos' sojourn at the Sorbonne (1953-54) would allow us to infer that she was exposed, directly or indirectly, to the *nouveau roman*. Her essay, "La novela de la ausencia (Butor, Sarraute, Robbe-Grillet)," which appeared in *La imagen en el espejo* (1965), buttresses this argument. Furthermore, critics argue that Campos' *Muerte por agua*, which is "representative of the 'nouveau roman' among Hispanic Americans" (Cortés 115), "synthesizes Woolf and Sarraute" (Bruce-Novoa 43). According to Evelyn Picón-Garfield, the "points of contact [between *Muerte* and] the French 'new novel'" include:

> the similar protagonist-narrator who subjectively selects and obsessively zeroes in on certain objects: the absence of the dynamics inherent in a traditional plot; and, above all, a subliminal dialogue similar to that found in Nathalie Sarraute's novels, like a "muted battle in which a true sense of life and death vie to emerge amidst commonplaces." (Picón-Garfield 77)

In describing the practices of the *nouveau roman*, "authors place an emphasis on subjectivity and on the creation of new temporal dimensions, disregarding linear time, external descriptions, plot, and intrigue,"[2] Campos may have

---

[2]Certain connections could also be established with the Surrealist novel, given:

> [the] primacy of the imagination over the demands of a material universe; dismissal of the psychological novel as inept in a world in which psychology has no more place than reason; hermeticism; flagrant unconcern for certain basic features of the realistic novel . . . and sharply ironical dismissal of realism as pure illusion; [characters which represent] aspirations [of their creator become] embodiment of desire[s] often . . . placed in a universe released from the restraint of reason, morality, and social convention. (Matthews 8-12)

According to Matthews, the Surrealist novel is also defined by a hero who "stands at once for refusal to accept certain restraints and for the affirmation of certain liberties, considered in surrealism to be essential to the fuller development of man [and conversely characters] conceived in desire [who] appeal outside the

been referring to her own work (Lagos-Pope 130). This link with the French New Novel led to an "ur" *écriture féminine* which Campos would further develop in *Tiene los cabellos rojizos y se llama Sabina* (1974).

Another connection with the *nouveau roman* arises from the stylistic similarities shared by *El miedo de perder a Eurídice* and Marguerite Duras' *The Ravishing of Lol Stein*,[3] "over and over speakers retell or re-invent multiple reconstructions of inaccessible, absent stories" (Cohen 178). Furthermore, these texts rely on a pattern of repetition with variation, "repetition with revision" (Willis 139), "repetition but also transformation, recurrence but also displacement" (Hill 64) of a paratactic nature—based on juxtaposition rather than on subordination. In other words, both Duras and Campos "coordinate parataxis with repetition" (Cohen 194; Glassman 11) "reducing the forward momentum of [the] narrative in favor of a temporal expansion" (Glassman 11), which, in turn, "abolishes the distance and the polarity of reading and writing, precisely by displaying their interaction in the ongoing *production* of the narrative" (Willis 135).

The Latin American "boom" conjures up formal experimentation (Borges' *Ficciones*, Julio Cortázar's *Rayuela*, *Relatos*, *El Libro de Manuel*, Mario Vargas Llosa's *La casa verde)*, and its corollary, the active participation of the reader.[4] A list of typical narrative devices, self-referentiality, intertextuality, parody, *pastiche*, Chinese boxes and interwoven narratives, suggests an affinity between the "boom" and Postmodernism.

Similarly, the connection with the cultural models proposed by the Latin American "boom" may be traced to Campos' critical essays and editorial duties in established literary journals. Furthermore, Picón-Garfield's observation about the experimental nature of the fiction produced during the Latin American "boom," specifically the "novelistic structures which create an atmosphere of simultaneity"—which allows us to establish similarities between Cortázar, Vargas

---

realm of naturalistic authenticity" (Matthews 9).

[3]See Hill for a summary on Xavière Gauthier's and Hélène Cixous' attempts to claim Duras as an "exponent of *écriture féminine*" (Hill 27).

[4]According to Ralph Yarrow, texts by Borges and Robbe-Grillet are similar in that they "demand for the active participation of the reader in the creation of the work" (Yarrow 73). Moreover, focusing on the question of the enigma, Yarrow then compares Borges' "Garden of the Forking Paths" to Robbe-Grillet (detectives—*Les Gommes*, *La Maison de Rendez-Vous*, labyrinths in *Dans le Labyrinthe*, *Topologie d'une Cité Fontôme*), Butor (*Passage du Milan*) and Beckett (*Molloy*). Moreover, Yarrow then closes the circuit by adding Postmodernism (Pyncheon's *The Crying of Lot 49*) to the *nouveau roman* (Yarrow 75).

Llosa, Cabrera Infante and the Campos of *Sabina* (Picón-Garfield 78)—is all the more pertinent concerning *Eurídice*.

Bibliographical searches on Campos highlight the dearth of critical attention received by her work. In addition to references on autobiographical pieces or interviews—two in total, the MLA data base search led to one entry on *Muerte*, one on *Celina*, two articles arguing for thematic correspondences in Campos' *oeuvre*, and eight (minus one translation) on *Sabina*. According to Juan Bruce-Novoa, Campos'

> two books of experimental prose—*Tiene los cabellos rojizos y se llama Sabina* and *El miedo de perder a Eurídice*—which for lack of a more exact description are known as novels, placed her in the vanguard of Latin American innovative writing. Both are difficult texts and present unusual challenges to critics, which partially explains the scarcity of critical attention they have elicited. (Bruce-Novoa 43)

However, Bruce-Novoa declines to intervene, "[i]n this essay I focus on *Sabina*, reserving *Eurídice* for future treatment" (Bruce-Novoa 43).

The link with the automatic writing of Surrealism is self-referential in *Sabina*: "[h]e descubierto que la única manera de escribir algo que no se muera enseguida es dándose una libertad, digamos de asociación, que se parece mucho a la escritura automática" (Campos 142-43; I have discovered that the only way to write something that doesn't perish immediately is granting ourselves freedom, such as that of free association, which resembles automatic writing—my translation). However, Campos argues that though

> the method was similar to that of free association in psychoanalysis. . . . *Sabina* is not surrealist automatic writing because there was a deliberate system, an outline for *Sabina*. The associations are free only up to a certain point; free but oriented, guided. (Picón-Garfield 85-87)

Among the numerous psychoanalytic approaches to *Sabina*, Ksenjia Bilbija resorts to Julia Kristeva's notions of "genotext" and "phenotext" to highlight the semiotic fabric of the novel, which would allow for another type of connection with *écriture féminine* (Bilbija 233-234).

Julieta Campos' *El miedo de perder a Eurídice* (*The Fear of Losing Eurydice* 1979; 1993) showcases Postmodernism by staging intertextuality as *différance.*[5] Moreover, the stylistic ties to Surrealism, the *nouveau roman* and the Latin American "boom" lead us to claim that the text constitutes a paradigmatic example of a two-way cross-fertilization between Structuralism, Post-Structuralism, High-Modernism and Post-Modernism across the Atlantic.[6] Thus, in addition to restating Campos' importance as a forerunner of *écriture féminine,* we reclaim the canonical value of Campos' *Eurídice* as among the most vital examples of Latin American Postmodernism.[7]

"Intertextuality as *Différance* in Julieta Campos' *El miedo de perder a Eurídice*: a Symptomatic Case of Latin American Postmodernism" is part of a larger project aimed at developing a theoretical framework on the intersection(s) between Postmodernism, feminism and Latin American literary criticism, and at identifying postmodern features in texts by contemporary Latin American women writers.

The question of Latin American Postmodernism requires taking a critical stance to avoid reproducing hegemonic discourse(s), and/or essentializing positions. However, rather than dwelling on etymological questions (Hassan *Dismemberment of Orpheus* 260-61, Toro 48), on definitions or genealogies (Bertens 9-

---

[5]Though the Derridean concept precludes logocentric definitions, we shall include the following approximations: Differánce is described as the play between difference and deferral in so far as "every concept is inscribed in a chain or in a system within which it refers to the other, to other concepts, by means of a systematic play of differences. Such a play, *differánce*, is thus no longer simply a concept, but rather the possibility of conceptuality, of a conceptual process and a system in general. . ." (Derrida 63); "What is written as differánce, then, will be playing movement that 'produces'—by means of something that is not simply and activity—these differences, these effects of difference. . . . Differánce is the nonfull, nonsimple, structured and differentiating origin of differences."(Derrida 64); "we will designate as differánce the movement according to which language, or any code, any system of referral in general, is constituted 'historically' as a weave of differences" (Derrida 65).

[6]I owe this insight to Norma Alarcón's comments on my introductory material on Latin American Postmodernism.

[7]Hélène Cixous states, "it is impossible to *define* a feminine practice of writing, and this is an impossibility that will remain, for this practice can never be theorized . . . which doesn't mean that it doesn't exist. But it will always surpass the discourse that regulates the phallocentric system; it does and will take place in areas other than those subordinated to philosophico-theoretical domination. It will be conceived of only by subjects who are breakers of automatisms, by peripheral figures that no authority can ever subjugate" (Cixous "Laugh of the Medusa" 253).

51, Díaz 19-33, Foster ix-xvi, Hassan *Dismemberment* 259-71, *The Postmodern Turn* 84-96, Hutcheon 3-21, Huyssen 179-221, Jameson 53-92, McCafferty xiv-xviii, Lyotard 1-16, Richard "Latinoamérica y la Post-Modernidad" 15-19, Toro 47-51), or even on the controversial status of Postmodernism (Habermas, "Modernity—An Incomplete Project" 3-15, "Modernity versus Postmodernity" 91-104) per se,[8] we shall survey different positions on Postmodernism in Latin America. Noting, however, that the impact of feminism(s) (Flax 623-26, Giroux 39-88, Richard *Masculino/Femenino* 77-92, Suleiman 111-130, Waugh 119-64) and ethnic movements (Giroux 111-46—both in Owens 57-82, and Hutcheon 59-73) on Postmodernism has been as widely acknowledged as has the concern about the politics of Postmodernism.[9]

Bernardo Subercaseaux's models of Latin American Cultural Politics: the model of Cultural Reproduction and the Model of Appropriation allow us to zero-in on the question of Latin American Postmodernism. The former, which takes for granted the Latin American reproduction of European culture and ideas, is the underlying assumption of theoretical frameworks articulated in terms of neocolonialism and dependency, as well as debates on premises such as center vs. margins and metropolis vs. underdevelopment. Rather than presupposing a dichotomy between the existence of an indigenous or rural pre-Columbian component and the élite, the Model of Appropriation legitimized by current socio-

---

[8]I endorse Linda Hutcheon's approach on the Postmodernist double movement (inscription and subversion), which interrelates concepts formally deployed by critics such as Hassan ("Dismemberment" 267-268), to distinguish Postmodernism from Modernism: "The postmodern . . . effects two simultaneous moves. It reinstalls historical contexts as significant and even determining, but in so doing, it problematizes the entire notion of historical knowledge." (Hutcheon 89) Hutcheon adds, "postmodern parody [i]s a form of ironic rupture with the past [but] there is always a paradox at the heart of that 'post': irony does indeed mark the difference from the past, but the intertextual echoing simultaneously works to affirm—textually and hermeneutically—the connection with the past" (Hutcheon 125).

[9]A number of critics such as Hutcheon, Giroux and Waugh, fear that by delegitimizing questions of identity and agency, which are at the core of feminist, ethnic and post-colonial agendas, the notion of the "death of the subject" may result in a neo-conservative backlash.

cultural conditions, emphasizes the cross-fertilization that takes place during the process of adaptation (Subercaseaux 221-35).[10]

Attitudes toward Postmodernism appear to be polarized around these models, since the negative reactions among supporters of the Model of Reproduction offset the mixed or positive ones among those who favor the Model of Cultural Appropriation. However, the broad range of variations and cross-overs within each model ultimately subvert the dichotomy.[11]

Among supporters of the Model of Reproduction, María Cristina Reigadas is wary about the impact of "Euro-American" Postmodernism on agency:

> given that Latin American existence and dignity depend upon the formulation and operationalization of a collective project that, preserving and recreating difference, would prevent fragmentation and anarchy, allowing for cultural, economic and political survival in a world in

---

[10]Subercaseaux's Model of Reproduction also includes the belief that Latin American élites reproduce European philosophical or artistic trends prior to the full existence of the forces that resulted in those trends in the first place, which leads to arguments positing Baroque without Reformation, Liberalism without bourgeoisie, Positivism without Industrialization, Existentialism without World War II, Postmodernism without Postmodernity. On the other hand, the Model of Appropriation leads to conceiving of Latin America as an intellectual and cultural construct (Subercaseaux 221-35).

[11]Within the Model of Appropriation Subercaseaux distinguishes three matrixes: 1) According to prevalent ideology in the Caribbean and Central America, development of culture and thought is contingent upon structural change. In addition to denouncing foreign manipulation, this discourse posits the redemptive nature of agricultural popular culture, which, together with the struggle for emancipation will lead to cultural development; 2) Intellectuals from countries with a great indigenous population—such as Perú, Bolivia, Ecuador and Paraguay—who stress the genocide brought about by the conquest tend to resort to dichotomous cultural paradigms: native vs. Western, popular vs. high, traditional vs. modern, etc. In so far as they conceive of illiteracy as a gesture of resistance in a struggle defined by cultural terms, the most extreme of these intellectuals favor a matrix antithetical to contemporary Western culture. Subercaseaux notes the similarities between these two matrixes and the Model of Reproduction; 3) Intellectuals from the Southern Cone, Mexico and Brazil posit a matrix that synthesizes Latin American traditional culture and contemporary (Western) culture (Subercaseaux 234-35).

which the gap between the haves and the have nots, the powerful and the powerless, broadens proportionally. (Reigadas 142)[12]

The notion of a "post-modern effect" enjoys a certain consensus among the intelligentsia. According to Ricardo Gutiérrez Mouat:

in the Latin American context, the debate . . . about the continuity between modernity and postmodernism(s) is pointless, given that the area did not enjoy a fully established modernity . . . In fact, the region's characteristicallyuneven and marginal modernity produces a postmodern *effect* as national economies are inserted in a fragmented and differential manner in the world market. . . . [T]he process of economic insertion generates a cultural heterogeneity which can be "read" as a postmodern text.[13] (Gutiérrez Mouat 121)

Sergio Zermeño, who coincides in affirming that "Latin America is postmodern without having ever been modern" (Zermeño 65), claims that the region's economic stagnation leads to Postmodern frameworks:[14]

Latin American social, political and cultural life seems fragmented, its principles of progress and development broken, progressively distanced from the notion of (a social or state) hegemony which would be articulated by a political party. Thus, social strife and cultural and political life are shot through by countless, oftentimes contradictory dimensions, axis or systems, . . . which, within the space of the community appear to momentarily recreate restricted identities and defensive democracies; on other occasions, or even within the same impulse, they appear to respond to repeated State addresses aimed at chauvinistic (nationalistic) . . . mobilization of the masses; [simultaneously] endorsing and even adopting hegemonic class aspirations, or, inconsistently mixing them

---

[12]Translation of all citations is mine.

[13]Yúdice may be counted among the supporters of the notion of a Latin American Postmodernism resulting from cultural heterogeneity and a partial and restricted participation in the world market (Yúdice 119).

[14]In referring to economic factors in Latin America Zermeño quotes Alain Touraine: "a region in which the high levels of economic growth of the last twenty-five years have only polarized society by generating a radical exclusion of the masses regarding the benefits of development, due the modern transnationalized sector's minimum absorption of the traditional sector" (Zermeño 64).

with the values of an anti-authoritarian and apparently pluralistic society, better integrated to development, based on American consumerism patterns, or on materialistic individualism, and on the overarching impact of technology measured by personal computers and parabolic antennas. (Zermeño 65)[15]

In addition to neo-conservative discourses, such as Mario Heler's attack on "narcissistic hedonism" (Heler 108), the Model of Reproduction includes the articulation of hegemonic views based both on Euro-American paradigms, such as Beatriz Sarlo's *Una modernidad periférica: Buenos Aires 1920-1930* (Ferman 53-56) and/or on the notion of a "primeval" Latin American "origin" (Ferman 47-48 and Richard, *La Estratificación de los márgenes* 42). Variations on the "aboriginal ideology" include re-inscriptions of "Andean" solidarity and intersubjectivity derived from the satisfaction of collective labor and a sense of oneness with the world (Quijano 18),[16] and literary styles such as "magic realism" (Quijano 22).

Adhering to the Model of Cultural Appropriation, George Yúdice and Doris Sommer argue for an idiosyncratic Latin American Postmodernism:

contemporary writing in Latin America begins by being, if not postmodernist, then at least paramodernist, for it has never accommodated feature for feature, the hegemonic Western modernist episteme from its inception in the early seventeenth century to its high modernist swan song in the first three decades of the twentieth century. (Sommer and Yúdice 189)

Yúdice concurs with José Joaquín Brunner, who attributes the Latin American cultural malaise to an exasperation with the permanent crisis generated by modernity rather than to its exhaustion (Yúdice "¿Puede hablarse de postmdodernidad en América Latina?" 120). Nelly Richard synthesizes these points:

---

[15]Similarly, Marc Zimmerman emphasizes the hybrid nature of Latin America noting, "the paradoxical revitalization by repressive regimes of strong pre-capitalist [pre-independence, or pre-colonial] 'residual' sectors which never had been subjected" (Zimmerman 282).

[16]My translation. Ferman points out the danger of taking mythical reconstructions of pre-Columbian civilizations as touchstones by noting the similarities between a national identity built on the defeat of the natives and the Christian version of the Fall (Ferman 48).

Latin America's hybrid past and the heterogeneity of its traditions together with the multiplicity of transnational economic and communicational vectors that segment local behaviors and identities, result in the
fragmentation and dissemination that readily identifies the sensibility we
have come to accept as postmodern. (Richard, *Estratificación* 44)

As Yúdice and Sommer's view suggests, attitudes toward Postmodern
artistic expressions in Latin America vary. While Néstor García Canclini contends, "[p]ostmodernism is not a style but the tumultuous co-existence of all, the
cross-roads of art, history and folklore" (García Canclini 87), Alberto Moreiras
emphasizes reception, noting that Latin American Postmodern art is a practice
of resistance similar to the every day practices isolated by Michel de Certeau and
John Fiske in late capitalism. In other words, the text of popular culture embrac-
es (hegemonic) forces [as it] allows for their subversion (Moreiras 107). On the
other hand, Roberto González Echevarría highlights deconstructive gestures:

Latin American literature is revolutionary and modern because it cor-
rodes the core of Western tradition from its fringes, constantly reflecting
back a distorted and denuded image. . . . Rather than a radical, onto-
genetic distinction, a perverse and exaggerated similarity often constitutes the difference in Latin American literature. If the main theme in
Latin American literature is its newness and independence, its significance can only be gauged by its exaggerated topicality within the context of Modernity: born of Modernity, Latin American literature appears
to be condemned to the delusions of newness in order to expose them.
(González Echevarría 39, quoted in Ferman 66)

Along these lines Richard maintains that the consumption of modern and postmodern images has led the margins to a fine-tuned "culture of re-signification"
which questions imposed meanings and tailors "loans" to fit the local functional-
ity of a new critical design (Richard, *Estratificación* 55).[17] Finally, some critics
reclaim a Latin American origin for Postmodernism, hailing Jorge Luis Borges
as its founder (Jauss quoted by Ruffinelli 33; Fokkema by Ferman 69 and de
Toro 53-58).

The question of Latin American Postmodernism involves issues of
cultural identity, nationalism, colonialism and post-coloniality. According to
Richard:

---

[17]The New Left's (Jameson, Larsen, Yúdice, Zimmerman) interest in the
deployment of agency in "testimonial" narratives.

from the vantage point of postmodern 'collage,' Latin American identity may consist of the rhetorical exacerbation of the de-centering and re-appropriating procedures whereby the margins inscribe their 'signature' on the dominant culture's serialized sets of enunciations. (Richard, *Estratificación* 47)

Personally, being born and raised during Argentina's "hyperinflation," devaluations, state of siege, military juntas, "Dirty War," "Proceso," "Malvinas War," foreign debt, I would argue for a "postmodern" lived experience (the post-modern condition?) defined by the breakdown of master discourses, by irrational-ity [the defeat of Reason], by an ironic attitude toward institutions, and by the definite failure of neo-liberal capitalism.[18] However, the awareness of the two way nature (N-S; E-W) of the intellectual exchange(s) across the Atlantic results from having been raised on Borges and the Latin American "boom."[19]

Though Julieta Campos is part of the Mexican "establishment," her work has not received much critical attention. My intention is to showcase *Eurídice* as symptomatic of Latin American Postmodernism in its investment in and negotia-tion with a series of cultural movements on both sides of the Atlantic. *Eurídice* deploys narrative strategies associated with the *nouveau roman*, with the so-called Latin American "boom," and with the surrealist technique of automatic writing. This combination resulted in a Postmodern text which continues to be ignored. Since *Eurídice* also incorporates the practice of *écriture féminine* into Spanish American literature, by shedding some light on the significance of the novel I intend to reclaim Julieta Campos' position among the forbearers of Latin Ameri-can Postmodernism.[20]

---

[18]Subercaseaux coincides in attributing this "horizonte 'post'" [post-horizon] to political events in Chile. In addition to the crisis of utopias and historical certainties, Subercaseaux mentions the draining effect of "mourning" the tragedy (1973), especially by the generation that did not personally experience it; the loss of interest in politics as a possibility of personal development; the sudden experi-ence of technological modernization and the omnipresence of mass culture (Subercaseaux 306).

[19]See Emir Rodríguez Monegal's "Borges and Derrida: Apothecaries"; Gerry O' Sullivan's "The Library is on Fire: Intertextuality in Borges and Foucault" and Herman Rapaport's "Borges, De Man, and the Deconstruction of Reading" for examples of intellectual cross-overs.

[20]Hélène Cixous acclaimed Lispector's approach in *Vivre L'Orange* and "L'approche de Clarice Lispector." The translation of Lispector's *Agua Viva* (1973) also includes a foreword by Hélène Cixous. Along these lines, Gina

Retracing Campos' stylistic practices to the *nouveau roman*, the Latin American "boom," and the automatic writing of the surrealists will result in a pendular movement between structuralist and post-structuralist paradigms. Nonetheless, we should bear in mind that, far from remaining dissected, these practices are always already in constant movement triggered by difference and deferral.

Our interpretation of *différance* presupposes the Bakhtinian social inscription of discourse in the novel:

> any concrete discourse (utterance) [is] shot through with shared thoughts, points of view, alien value judgments and accents . . . and all this . . . may leave a trace in all its semantic layers. [H]aving taken meaning and shape at a particular historical moment in a socially specific environment, [t]he living utterance . . . cannot fail to become an active participant in social dialogue. (Bakhtin, *Discourse* 276)[21]

In addition to the social inscription of the utterance, Campos' extensive use of quotation adds another level to the question of intertextuality:

> Inevitably a fragment and displacement, every quotation distorts and redefines the 'primary' utterance by relocating it within another linguistic and cultural context. Therefore, despite any intentional quest on the part of the quoting author to engage in an intersubjective activity, the quotation itself generates a tension between belief both in original and

---

Michelle Collins argues that "we can interpret Cixous' link of women's writing to the body in terms of Lispector's feminine discourse as an attempt to evoke writing as directed from and by the 'it'/id, the non-rational, undifferentiated drives which Western civilization has worked so hard to control" (Collins 123).

[21] As Julia Kristeva notes:

> By introducing the *status of the word* as a minimal structural unit, Bakhtin situates the text within history and society, which are then seen as texts by the writer, and into which he inserts himself by rewriting them. Diachrony is transformed into synchrony, and in light of this transformation, *linear* history appears as abstraction. The only way a writer can participate in history is by transgressing this abstraction through a process of reading: writing; that is, through the practice of a signifying structure in relation or opposition to another structure. History and morality are written and read within the infrastructure of texts. The poetic word, polyvalent and multi-determined, adheres to a logic exceeding that of codified discourse. (Kristeva 65)

originating integrity and in the possibility of (re)integration and an awareness of infinite deferral and dissemination of meaning. Quotation as fragmentation does indeed generate centrifugality in reading, but it also generates centripetality, focusing the reader's attention on textual functioning rather than on hermeneutics. (Worton 11)

Along these lines, Campos' extensive use of *collage/montage* and the resulting deconstruction of mimesis highlight the similarities between *Eurídice* (1979) and Jacques Derrida's *Glas* (1974).[22] Perhaps the cornerstone of both intertextuality and dissemination is the very notion of "iterability":

the possibility of extraction and citational grafting which belongs to the very structure of every mark, spoken or written, and which constitutes every mark as writing even before and outside every horizon of semio-linguistic communication; as writing, that is, as a possibility of function-ing cut off, at a certain point, from its 'original' meaning and from its belonging to a saturable and constraining context. Every sign, linguistic or nonlinguistic, spoken or written (in the usual sense of this opposi-tion), as a small or large unity, can be *cited*, put between quotation marks; thereby it can break with every given context, and engender infinitely new contexts in an absolutely nonsaturable fashion. (Derrida 97)[23]

---

[22]Effect of collage, according to Derrida:

[H]eterogeneity . . . imposes itself on the reading as stimulation to pro-duce a signification which could be neither univocal nor stable. Each cited element breaks the continuity or the linearity of the discourse and leads necessarily to a double reading: that of the fragment perceived in relation to its text of origin; that of the same fragment as incorporated into a new whole, a different totality. The trick of collage consists also of never entirely suppressing the alterity of these elements reunited in a temporary composition. Thus the art of collage proves to be one of the most effective strategies in the putting into question of all the illu-sions of representation. (Collages 34-35, Ulmer 88)

[23]Originally cited as "Signature Event Context" *Glyph* 1 (1977): 185, in Ulmer (89).

However, in addition to the different levels of intertextuality[24] and dissemination inherent in language itself ("iterability" and the social inscription of the utterance), and risking the danger of a structuralist reading, my contention is that Campos stages the play between difference and deferral through intertextuality,[25] through the "undecidable reading effect, oscillating between presence and absence" (Ulmer 88) of *collage*, through the subversion of typographically built-in expectations, through the constant thematic displacement between these "fields," and the dissemination or reverberation resulting from the fluid incorporation/mirroring of themes and characterization.

The very structure of *Eurídice* is elusive in that Campos both installs and subverts textual expectations. At first glance the typographical inscription engenders a tripartite structure: narrow strands, marginal quotes, and the so-called "standard" text. The narrow strands are the locus of the love stories. The isolated quotes anchored on the outer margins of these strands iconically represent their content, since they refer to "real" or fictitious islands. In addition to resonating [thematically] in the "main" text, the quotes echo each other creating multiple variations and reverberations. This pattern could be likened to a Moëbius braid in which the diachronic reversal is constantly criss-crossed synchronically. The "standard" typographical page format is the locus of the implied narrator(s). However, a fourth type follows along these lines, since the initial parodic rendition of the Biblical story of creation stands both apart and in between the three fields. Like the marginal quotes, it is an island, typographically anchored in the middle of the text. Thematically, the passage weaves in the three narrative strands: the couple, the island, and the act of writing: "Con [la serpiente] penetró en el paraíso una seducción nocturna y la Isla, espacio de utopía, devino espacio de poesía" 'With [the serpent] a nocturnal seductiveness penetrated paradise, and the Island, this utopian space, became the space of poetry' (Campos 7; 1).[26] The same typographical format reappears toward the end of the text in the carnival-

---

[24]According to María Teresa Marrero's "Repensar el amor a fines del siglo XX: *El miedo de perder a Eurídice* de Julieta Campos" (unpublished manuscript), the marginal quotes inscribe the Western literary tradition beginning with the first Roman novels.

[25]Discourses drawn into intertextuality: literary references(including writers), geographical data (islands), film (including technique), opera (scores included), songs and paintings.

[26]Hereinafter all references to Campos' texts will be cited parenthetically.

ized speech of the Harlequin (153-166; 110-119).[27] Once again, the text stands both apart and between the three fields. Carnival gives way to a "Túnel del amor" 'Tunnel of Love', which highlights the relationship, "Todos se han ido. La isla se ha quedado vacía. Somos, tú y yo, la isla" 'Everyone has gone. The island is empty. You and I, we are the island' (163; 117). Soon enough the island, the couple, and Monsieur N. turn into an old photo and the recurrent drawing on "una servilleta blanca" 'a white napkin' (166; 119).

Yet, the reader's provisional cartographies are de-familiarized by means of thematic displacements. The references to islands which star the margins are incorporated into the standard text when Monsieur N. begins his "ISLARIO" 'ISLANDIARY' (62; 41). Free-associating leads Monsieur N. to define "*Isla*: imagen del deseo" '*Island*: image of desire' (142; 102) which, in turn is linked to writing, "Todos los textos, todo lo que ha sido escrito hasta el instante en que escribo estas palabras dibuja la imagen de esa cartografía del deseo. Todos los textos son islas" 'Every text, everything ever written up to the moment I write these words, outlines the image of that cartography of desire. Every text is an island' (142; 102). The coupling between desire/writing and islands is then developed as Adamic possession through naming along the field we have come to associate with the series of love stories (143-52; 102-109).

The play engendered by the thematic "contamination" and the displacement between the typographical fields is anchored by self-reflexive references to the seduction of a self-assuringly high but finite number of permutations:

> ¿Y si el Diario no fuera más que la inminencia de algo que siempre estaría a punto de ocurrir sin llegar a, de algo que no acabará nunca de revelarse? ¿O si disimulara simplemente un libro con tres capítulos dispersos en una secuencia caótica de notas de lectura: I La Isla II La pareja III El naufragio o I La pareja II El naufragio III La Isla o I El naufragio II La isla y III La pareja? (130)

> what if the diary were nothing more than something imminent, always on the verge of coming into being without ever managing to, something that will in the end never be revealed? Or what if it simply concealed a book with three chapters dispersed in a chaotic sequence of notes from his readings: I: the Island, II: the couple, III: the shipwreck; or else I:

---

[27]The speech of the Harlequin is reminiscent of Bakhtin's depiction of the Medieval "*life of the carnival square*, free and unrestricted, full of ambivalent laughter, blasphemy, the profanation of everything sacred, full of debasing and obscenities, familiar contact with everyone and everything" (Bakhtin, *Problems* 129-30).

the couple, II: the shipwreck, III: the Island; or else I: the shipwreck, II: the Island, III: the couple? (93)

Fully aware of the danger of understating the constant movement and displacement generated by difference and deferral, we freeze it momentarily to sort out stylistic devices along the principles of 'similarity' or 'contiguity'(Adams 1113),[28] though they are always already interrelated. The linearity of the reading process and the endless series of associations stress the significance of the metonymic alignment; however, we could also consider each element of the series as an autonomous unit. The initial case is paradigmatic:

> Abelard and Héloïse, Venus and Tannhäuser, Hamlet and Ophelia, Agathe and Ulrich, Solomon and the Shulamite maiden, the Consul and Yvonne, Daphnis and Chlöe, Percy and Mary Shelley, the narrator and Albertine, Jocasta and Oedipus, Hans Castorp and Claudia Chauchat, Pygmalion and Galatea, Othello and Desdemona, Penelope and Ulysses, Baudelaire and Jeanne Duval, Laura and Petrarch, Humbert Humbert and Lolita, Elizabeth Barrett and Robert Browning, Alonso Quijano and Dulcinea, Leda and the Swan, Adam and Eve, Wagner and Cosima, Pelléas and Mélisandre, Cleopatra and Mark Antony, Calisto and Melibea, Faust and Gretchen, Orpheus and Eurydice, Romeo and Juliet, Heathcliff and Cathy, Tristan and Isolde, Rilke and Lou Andreas-Salome, Jason and Medea, Miranda and Ferdinand, Kafka and Milena, Electra and Agamemnon, Don Juan and Thisbe, von Aschenbach and Tadzio, Poe and Annabel Lee, Borges and Matilde Urbach. (3-4)

Difference and deferral are deployed in the enumeration of couples, defined in a seemingly endless (and random) series of units (signs), connoting different positionalities and socio-historical inscriptions linked by some manifestation of "love." Thus, the heterogenous origin of the characters (mythology, the Bible, different literary periods and cultural traditions, poets, novelists, musicians), the range of experience represented, and the richness of the intertextual allusions are put under erasure by a free-floating signifier ("love"); thus, both in spite of and because of their differences, each couple becomes an avatar of:

---

[28]Jakobson explored the stylistic impact of the 'metaphoric' and 'metonymic poles:'"the primacy of the metaphoric process in the literary schools of Romanticism and symbolism has been repeatedly acknowledged, but it is still insufficiently realized that it is the predominance of metonomy which underlies and actually pre-determines the so-called realistic trend" (Adams 1114).

la pareja arquetípica, la que reuniría en su...rostro los rasgos de todos los amantes de la historia, de los que hubieran podido amarse, de los que han imaginado los poetas, y de los que no han sido imaginados todavía. (11)

the ideal couple, the perfect couple, the archetypal couple, who would combine in their . . . faces the features of all the lovers of history, all those who might have been able to fall in love with each other, all those ever imagined by the poets, and all those unimagined yet. (3)

While the metonymic pole includes: repetition, *montage, pastiche*, and surrealist associations leading to *écriture féminine*, the metaphoric pole aligns: self-referentiality, paradox, parody and Chinese boxes.

Metonymic pole

1. *Repetition*

1.1. *Recurrent terms:* "Virgen de las rocas" 'Virgin of the Rocks' as a parameter of similarity drawn between Monsieur N.'s drawing and the woman he watches at the bar (34; 21); (45; 29); "island . . . drawn on a napkin" 'isla dibujada en una servilleta' (45; 29); (54; 35); (74; 51); (168; 120).

1.2. *Repetition with variations*: in addition to *metathesis*[29] "*¿pasiflora laurifolia? ¿pasifolia lauriflora? ¿lauriflora pasifolia?"* (48;31) this category encompasses different types of enumeration, such as the series of brief narratives defining islands (143-149; 102-106), which gives way to a listing of proper names followed by the term "island" (149; 107), before reverting into flora and fauna (149-51; 107-108) and closing with brief narratives (151-52; 108-109). At another level we may include the numerous interwoven narratives such as Count Uccello's in Venice (91-101; 67-71) and a woman's suicide (127-28; 90-91).

2. *Montage:* "piscina...volcanes nevados" 'swimming pool . . . snowcapped volcanoes' (33; 19-20); "Ciudad y bosque superpuestos" 'superimposed city and forest' (83; 57; my trans.).

3. *Pastiche:* (pseudo newspaper article) "los jóvenes de la isla Kangaroo aspiran al suicidio como liberación de un paraíso sin meta" 'the young people of Kanga-

---

[29]Transposition of letters out of normal order in a word (Lanham 196).

roo Island aspire to suicide as freeing them from a paradise without any objectives' (137; 98).

4. Surreal Associations: Toward écriture féminine

4.1. Enumeration—Thematic links

> el viento estremeció las copas de los mangos, cimbró los hules y silbó con cierta fiereza entre los penachos de las palmeras. Los cipreses y los acantos brotaron al unísono y la isla se volvió un islote del Mar Egeo. (14)

> the wind shook the crowns of the mango trees, made their oilskins rattle, and whistled through the crests of the palm trees with some ferocity. The cypresses and acanthuses sprang up in unison and the island turned into an islet in the Aegean Sea. (5)

4.2. Surreal Association—Pseudo generic link

"El escribió entonces un poema, que se le olvidó pronto porque las palabras, persiguiendo a las hojas, se dispersaron..." 'He wrote a poem which he then forgot because the words, pursuing the leaves, simply scattered. . . .' (16; 7)

4.3. Surrealist Images—Shattered Expectations

"Del tulipán africano se desprenden infinidad de hostias transparentes que platean por un instante la columna de sol donde reverbera el fulgor súbito de la primavera" 'From the African tulip tree great numbers of transparent wafers drop, [momentarily] silvering the column of sunlight where the sudden stridency of spring reverberat[es]' (32; 19; my trans.) or "y los párpados son pétalos mojados en plomo, infinitamente pesados" 'and her eyelids are petals dipped in lead' (41-42; 26).

4.4. Personification

"los laureles eran robles fatigados por tanto heno que les crece entre los brazos como túnicas flotantes de incongruentes fantasmas" 'the laurels used to be oak trees weary from so much moss growing from their arms like the flowing tunics of incongruous ghosts' (44; 28); or "la sensación de traer arrastrando entre los pies el cadáver de un día escuálido, pero recalcitrante, renuente a recibir sepultura" 'the sensation of dragging along between her feet the body of a squalid but recalcitrant day, ill-disposed to receive burial' (45; 28-29); or "Los cristales, fatigados de sobreactuar...han dejado de finjir la transparencia y enturbian las siluetas...que se divisan desde adentro como caballos demasiado grandes, con largas cabelleras que los protegen del viento" 'The windows, exhausted from overacting . . . have ceased pretending transparency and are muddying up the silhouettes . . . which can be divined from within like [huge] horses, with long coats of hair [which] protect them from the wind' (38; 24); or:

> El tigre dice: 'Nunca te había sentido tan mía... ¿No sientes la electri-cidad? Podría poner a arder un bosque... Te voy a devorar dulcemente. No habrá efusión de sangre. Todos podrán verlo: la película se llamará 'Asesinato en el parque.' (43-44)

> The tiger says, 'I have never felt you so much mine. . . . Don't you feel the electricity? I could set the forest afire. . . . I am going to devour you gently. There won't be a lot of blood. Everyone will be able to see it: the film will be called Murder in the Park.' (27-28)

4.5. *Pastiche*

> Un tigre de fosforescencia dulce y violenta, que se perdió de repente, de un salto, sobre el río de orillas arenosas, sobre la plaza de Venecia, sobre el bosque un poco dorado y la obligó a perseguirlo, como si no hubiera acabado de despertar, por las galerías de un recinto sin techo. (40-41)

> A sweet, violent, phosphorescent tiger that lost itself suddenly in one leap over the river with its sandy banks, over the piazza of Venice, over the slightly gilded forest, and it forced her to follow along, as if she had not just awakened, through the galleries of a roofless labyrinth. (25)

As may be inferred from the above, "suture" results from some type of feature bonding enumerations. Similarly, weather (night, lightning, rain (13; 4-5) serves as an "editing" device:

> Fue entonces cuando la isla empezó a brotar dulcemente del mar como una venus con los pies mojados por las ondas. Engendrada en una noche *tormentosa*, nació predestinada...los *relámpagos* empezaron a iluminar la entrada de la bahía alrededor de las once y, en esos *destellos* súbitos, el paisaje reveló una intimidad que el día había disimulado. Después *llovió*. Las luces del puerto *temblaron* ligeramente y, en la bocana, el

barco blanco profusamente encendido se fue volviendo un buque fantasma... (13, my emphasis)

That was the moment when the island began to break softly from the
sea like a Venus with her feet dampened by the waves. Begotten on a
stormy night, it was born predestined . . . *lightning* began to illuminate
the entrance of the bay, and in the light of those *sudden flashes* the
landscape revealed an intimacy that the day had concealed. Then it
rained. The lights of the port were *quivering* lightly, and at the entrance
the white ship, profusely illuminated, gradually turned into a ghostly
boat. . . . (4-5)

Metaphoric pole

1. *Self-referentiality*

1.1. *Thematic links—Repetition with variations*

"YO voy a contar una historia... Voy a contar, pues, la historia de un sueño..."
'I am going to tell a story. . . . So I am going to tell the story of a dream' (11;
3);

"*Yo* he dicho que me propongo contar una historia. Que esa historia será una
historia de amor y, en consecuencia, la historia de un sueño" '*I* have said that I
propose to tell a story. That this story will be a love story and consequently the
story of a dream' (27; 15);

> Yo que he dicho...que voy a contar una historia; yo...que, si desapare-
> ciera, me llevaría...a la pareja y a Monsieur N.,...yo que me imagino
> omnipotente y omnisciente y que disfruto suponiendo que, sin mi inter-
> vención, el hombre que toma notas...y la pareja que empieza a interes-
> sarle...irían retrocediendo...como las figuras proyectadas por una cinta
> cinematográfica de vuelta... Me temo que soy un accidente... Porque mi
> voluntad apenas representa aquí el pobre papel de un relevo que recibe
> y entrega: traduzco y, al traducir, me escribo y, fuera de la página que
> escribo,... Bebo cocteles helados...y, a la vez, trazo el contorno de una
> isla sobre una servilleta blanca...como todo el mundo, estoy a cada rato
> en un tris de no ser nadie. (45-46)

> I, the one who has said . . . that I am going to tell a story . . . if it were
> to disappear, I would [take] the couple and Monsieur N; . . . I who
> imagine myself omnipotent and omniscient and who enjoy assuming
> that without my intervention, the man taking notes . . . and the couple
> who are beginning to interest him . . . would gradually recede . . . like
> the figures [of a] film when the reel is run backward. I fear I am merely
> an accident. . . . Because only with difficulty does my will act out the
> barren role of a relay who merely receives and transmits: I translate,
> and upon translating I write, and outside of the page I am writing,
> . . . I drink frozen cocktails . . . while. . . . I trace the outlines of an
> island on a white napkin. . . . [L]ike everyone else, I am constantly
> within an ace of not being anyone at all. (29)

"Y yo escribo como si soñara. O sueño como si escribiera... La historia de amor
es un sueño que me escribe... La pareja, al engendrarse, me sueña y es mi sueño"
'And I write as I were dreaming. Or dream as if I were writing. . . . The
[love]story is a dream that is writing me. . . . On coming into existence the couple dreams me and is my dream' (74; 51);

"Y yo vuelvo al punto en que digo: "voy a contar una historia" con la fascinación
y el miedo de regresar a una escena primitiva...que condena al voyeurismo" 'And
I return to the point at which I say, "I am going to tell a story," with the fascination and dread of returning to a primal scene . . . a scene that condemns one to
voyeurism' (135; 96);

"La historia que yo quería contar y que he contado habría podido ser contada,
también, de otra manera" 'The story that I had wished to relate and that I have
told might also have been told in some other way' (153; 110)];

2. *Paradox—Multiple Options*

Paradox appeals to the law of non-contradiction; however, rather than cancelling
each other out, the multiple possibilities are put under erasure. While the pleasure
of the text increases as it is postponed, the totalizing quest for meaning is ob-
structed by the suspension of chronology and causality, as well as by the slippage
between terms (lovers = shipwrecked crew), the circularity brought about by the
thematic displacement along the different "fields" and the recurrent permutations.

1.1. *Events take place simultaneously in different locations*

"La escena ocurre a la vez en la banca del parque, en algún piso elevado de una moderna torre de cristales y en la penumbra de un pabellón recatado... Los escenarios son intercambiables" 'This scene takes place simultaneously on the bench in the park, in some upper floor of a modern glass tower, and in the half-light of a secluded summerhouse. . . . The sets are interchangeable' (17; 7)];[30]

1.2. *Contradictory statements*

> La imagen de una mujer que recorre una ciudad laberíntica se obstina en desplazar todas las otras imágenes. Hace frío y llovizna. Son las dos y media de la tarde. Pero es de noche y ha oscurecido. Comienza entonces a dibujar a la mujer como si la recordara. (34)

> The image of a woman passing through a labyrinthine city stubbornly displaces all other images. It is cold and rainy. Two-thirty in the afternoon. But it is nighttime and now dark. He begins, then to draw the woman as if he were recalling her. (21)

1.3. *Options which appear to cancel each other out*

Monsieur N. returns to the habitual bar only to discover, "1) un anuncio que advierte: CERRADO POR REFORMAS-PROXIMA REAPERTURA; 2) el local sellado y clausurado... 3) un terreno baldío, sin huellas de demolición, derrumbe o incendio..." '1) a sign announcing: CLOSED FOR REPAIRS. REOPENING SOON; 2) the place closed and sealed shut. . . . 3) an empty lot, without the slightest trace of demolition, collapse, or fire' (167; 120). Furthermore, these options lead to contradictory results:

---

[30]Another example of events taking place simultaneously in different locations:

> La lluvia desplaza la presencia indiferente de otros transeúntes. Sobre el pavimento ruedan, junto a los autos, los resplandores azulados de los faroles: es una lluvia de hojas plateadas que desciende sobre los dos desde un escenario. Un escenario donde hay cerezos en flor y mujeres vestidas de lino blanco. (66-67)

> The rain removes the indifferent presence of the other passersby. Above the pavement, next to the cars, the bluish splendors of the streetlamps are falling; it is a rain of silvered leaves descending on the two of them from a stage set. A set where there are cherry trees in bloom and women dressed in white linen. (45)

Si 1) ó 2) corre, en un arranque de decisión, a comprar un boleto para visitar la Isla de Coral, islote artificial, con feria y parque de diversiones, que han instalado en medio del lago Si 3) después de una breve turbación entra, como todos los días, saluda al camarero, ordena vino... (167)

If 1) or 2), he runs in a sudden burst of decision to buy a ticket for a visit to Coral Island, an artificial isle with a carnival and amusement park set up in the middle of the lake; if 3, after a brief moment of confusion, he enters as on every day, greets the waiter, orders wine. . . (120)

3. Parody

3.1. Stylistic

Imitation of Jorge Luis Borges' style in "fábulas sufís sobre la condición humana" 'Sufi Fables on the Human Condition' (137-140; 98-100).

3.2. Thematic

Staging of the plotline of Bioy Casares' *La Invención de Morel* (131-32; 93-94) or the narrative which arises from an apple in a Magritte picture (63-65; 42-43).

4. Chinese Boxes

The apparent retelling of Truffaut's film—*The Story of Adèle H* (107-115; 76-82) becomes the plotline of another movie.[31]

In sum, granting *différance* at the semiological level of language, and the social inscription of discourse in the novel, Campos' *El miedo de perder a Eurídice* stages intertextuality as *différance* through the constant play between difference and deferral engendered by the paratactical articulation of the devices provisionally aligned with the metonymic and metaphoric poles, namely: repetition, montage, pastiche, and surreal associations leading to *écriture féminine* and self-referentiality, paradox, parody and Chinese boxes. As we mentioned earlier on, these devices always already depend on the constant interrelation of these poles. In addition, intertextuality engages in the constant play between difference

---

[31]At present, intertextuality would echo Suzana Amaral's film on Clarice Lispector's *The Hour of the Star*.

and deferral by virtue of the marginal "quotes" about islands that thematically echo the central strands of narrative. However, this paratactical articulation is emphasized by the endless series of repetition with variations, by the thematic displacement along the typographical fields, by the possibility of multiple options, by self-referentiality, by thematic contamination and the mirroring of characters. Bearing in mind that intertextuality results not only from the variety of specific references to items from discourses as varied as music (popular and opera), film, painting and literature but also from the juxtaposition of narrative kernels aligned in the endless series of enumerations, there seems to be no doubt that Campos successfully stages intertextuality as *différance* in *The Fear of Losing Eurydice.*

Campos' paratactical articulation precludes principles of logical causality, temporality and non-contradiction, forcing the reader to consider writing and desire as s/he becomes an ongoing producer of meaning (Willis 135). The encyclopedic range of references deployed in the staging of intertextuality, the stunning images resulting from surreal associations, and the cerebral playfulness of the text lead us to reclaim Campos' *El miedo de perder a Eurídice* as a canonical text of Latin American Postmodernism.

Works Cited

Bakhtin, Mikhail. "Discourse in the Novel." *The Dialogic Imagination.* Michael Holquist, ed. Caryl Emerson, and Michael Holquist, trans. Austin: U of Texas P, 1981. 258-422.

—. *Problems of Dostoevsky's Poetics.* Caryl Emerson, trans. Minneapolis: U of Minnesota P, 1984.

Barrea-Marlys, Mirta. "Julieta Campos." *Dictionary of Mexican Literature.* Eladio Cortés, ed. Westport, CT: Greenwood Press, 1992. 114-15.

Bertens, Hans. "The Postmodern *Weltanschauung* and its Relation with Modernism: An Introductory Survey." *Approaching Postmodernism.* Douwe Fokkema, and Hans Bertens, eds. Amsterdam: John Benjamins Publishing Company, 1986. 9-51.

Bilbija, Ksenija. "Tiene los cabellos rojizos y se llama Sabina." *La palabra y el hombre: revista de la Universidad Veracruzana* 84 (Oct.-Dec. 1992): 228-39.

Bruce-Novoa, Juan. "Julieta Campos' *Sabina*: In the Labyrinth of Intertextuality." *Third Woman* 2.2. (1984): 43-63.

Campos, Julieta. *Celina o los gatos.* México: Siglo XXI, 1968.

—. *The Fear of Losing Eurydice.* Leland H. Chambers, trans. Normal, IL: Dalkey Archive Press, 1993.

—. *Función de la novela.* México: Editorial Joaquín Mortiz, 1973.

—. *La herencia obstinada: análisis de cuentos nahuas.* México: Fondo de Cultura Económica, 1982.

—. *La imagen en el espejo.* México: Universidad Nacional Autónoma de México, 1965.

—. *El miedo de perder a Eurídice.* México: Editorial Joaquín Mortiz, 1979.

—. *Muerte por agua.* México: Fondo de Cultura Económica, 1965.

—. *El oficio de leer.* México: Fondo de Cultura Económica, 1971.

Cixous, Hélène. "L'approche de Clarice Lispector." *Poétique* 40 (Nov. 1979): 408-19.

—. "The Laugh of the Medusa." *New French Feminisms.* Keith Cohen and Paula Cohen, trans. Elaine Marks, and Isabelle de Courtivron, eds. New York: Schocken Books, 1981. 244-64.

—. *Vivre l'orange.* Paris: Ed. des Femmes, 1979.

Cohen, Susan D. *Women and Discourse in the Fiction of Marguerite Duras.* London: Macmillan, 1993.

Collins, Gina Michelle. "Translating a Feminine Discourse: Clarice Lispector's *Agua Viva.*" *Translation Perspective.* Binghamton: SUNY, 1984. 119-24.

Derrida, Jacques. *A Derrida Reader.* Peggy Kamuf, ed. New York: Columbia UP, 1991.

Díaz, Esther. "Qué es la Postmodernidad?" *Posmodernidad?* Prólogo de Enrique Marí. Buenos Aires: Editorial Biblos, 1988. 17-43.

Duras, Marguerite. *The Ravishing of Lol Stein.* Trans. Richard Seaver. New York: Pantheon Books, 1966.

Ferman, Claudia. *Política y posmodernidad: hacia una lectura de la anti-modernidad en Latinoamérica.* Miami: Iberian Studies Institute, 1993.

Flax, Jane. "Postmodernism and Gender Relations in Feminist Theory." *Signs* 12.4 (1987): 621-43.

Flores, Angel. *Spanish American Authors: The Twentieth Century.* New York: Wilson Publishing, 1992.

García Canclini, Néstor. "El debate posmoderno en Iberoamérica." *Cuadernos hispanoamericanos* 463 (Jan. 1989): 79-92.

Giroux, Henry. *Border Crossings: Cultural Workers and the Politics of Education.* New York: Routledge, 1992.

Glassman, Deborah N. *Marguerite Duras: Fascinating Vision and Narrative Cure.* Rutherford, NJ: Associated University Presses, 1991.

Gutiérrez Mouat, Ricardo. "Autoridad moderna y posmoderna en la narrativa hispanoamericana." *Nuevo texto crítico* 3.6 (1990): 121-34.

Habermas, Jürgen. "Modernity—An Incomplete Project." *The Anti-Aesthetic: Essays on Postmodern Culture.* Hal Foster, ed. Port Townsend, WA: Bay Press, 1983. 3-15.

—. "Modernity versus Postmodernity." *A Postmodern Reader.* Joseph Natoli and Linda Hutcheon, eds. Albany: State U of New York P, 1993. 91-104.

Hassan, Ihab. "Postface 1982: Toward a Concept of Postmodernism." *The Dismemberment of Orpheus: Toward a Postmodern Literature.* 2nd. ed. Madison: U Wisconsin P, 1982. 259-71.

—. *The Postmodern Turn: Essays in Postmodern Theory and Culture.* Athens: Ohio State UP, 1987.

Heler, Mario. "La postmodernidad o una interpretación falaz." *¿Posmodernidad?* Prólogo de Enrique Marí. Buenos Aires: Editorial Biblos, 1988. 83-111.

Hill, Leslie. *Marguerite Duras: Apocalyptic Desires.* London: Routledge, 1993.

Huyssen, Andreas. "Mapping the Postmodern." *After the Great Divide: Modernism, Mass Culture, Postmodernism.* Bloomington: Indiana UP, 1986. 179-221.

Jakobson, Roman. "The Metaphoric and Metonymic Poles." *Critical Theory Since Plato.* Hazard Adams, ed. New York: Harcourt Brace Jovanovich, 1971. 1113-16.

Jameson, Fredric. "Postmodernism, or The Cultural Logic of Late Capitalism." *New Left Review* 146 (July-Aug. 1984): 56-92.

Kristeva, Julia. "Word, Dialogue, and Novel." *Desire in Language: A Semiotic Approach to Literature and Art.* Leon S. Roudiez, ed. Thomas Gora, Alice Jardine, and Leon S. Roudiez, trans. New York: Columbia UP, 1980. 64-91.

Lagos-Pope, María Inés. "Julieta Campos." *Spanish American Women Writers: A Bio-Bibliographical Source Book.* Diane E. Marting, Ed. Gabriela Mahn, trans. New York: Greenwood Press, 1990. 128-39.

Larsen, Neil. "Postmodernism and Imperialism: Theory and Politics in Latin America." *Postmodern Culture* 1.1 (September 1990): 1-45. Trans. by Ignacio Corona-Gutiérrez as "Postmodernismo e imperialismo: teoría y política en América Latina." *Nuevo texto crítico* 6 (1990): 77-94.

Lispector, Clarice. *The Hour of the Star.* Giovanni Pontiero, trans. New York: Carcanet Press, 1986.

—. *The Stream of Life.* Elizabeth Lowe and Earl Fitz, trans. Minneapolis: U of Minnesota P, 1989.

Lyotard, Jean-François. *The Post-Modern Explained.* Minneapolis, U of Minnesota P, 1992.

Matthews, J.H. *Surrealism and the Novel.* Ann Arbor: U of Michigan P, 1966.

McCafferty, Larry. "Introduction." *Postmodern Fiction: A Bio-Bibliographical Guide.* New York: Greenwood P, 1986. xi-xviii.

Moreiras, Alberto. "Transculturación y pérdida del sentido. El diseño de la posmodernidad en América Latina." *Nuevo texto crítico* 3.6 (1990): 105-119.

O'Sullivan, Gerry. "The Library is on Fire: Intertextuality in Borges and Foucault." *Borges and His Successors: The Borgesian Impact on Literature and the Arts.* Edna Aizenberg, ed. Columbia: U of Missouri P, 1990. 109-21.

Owens, Craig. "The Discourse of Others: Feminists and Postmodernism." *The Anti-Aesthetic: Essays on Postmodern Culture.* Hal Foster, ed. Port Townsend, WA: Bay Press, 1983. 57-82.

Picón-Garfield, Evelyn. *Women's Voices from Latin America: Interviews with Six Contemporary Authors.* Detroit: Wayne State UP, 1985.

Quijano, Aníbal. "Modernidad, Identidad y Utopía en América Latina." *Imágenes desconocidas: la modernidad en la encrucijada postmoderna.* " Fernando Calderón, ed. Buenos Aires: Consejo Latinoamericano de Ciencias Sociales, 1988. 17-24.

Rapaport, Herman. "Borges, De Man, and the Deconstruction of Reading." *Borges and His Successors: The Borgesian Impact on Literature and the Arts.* Edna Aizenberg, ed. Columbia: U of Missouri P, 1990. 139-54.

Reigadas, María Cristina. "Neomodernidad y posmodernidad: preguntando desde América Latina." *¿Posmodernidad?* Prólogo de Enrique Marí. Buenos Aires: Editorial Biblos, 1988. 83-145.

Richard, Nelly. *La estratificación de los márgenes.* Santiago de Chile: Francisco Zegers Editor, 1989.

—. "Latinoamérica y la Post-modernidad." *Revista de crítica cultural* 3 (Abril, 1991): 15-19.

—. *Masculino/femenino: prácticas de la diferencia y cultura democrática.* Santiago, Chile: Francisco Zegers Editor, 1993.

Rodríguez Monegal, Emir. "Borges and Derrida: Apothecaries." *Borges and His Successors: The Borgesian Impact on Literature and the Arts.* Edna Aizenberg, ed. Columbia: U of Missouri P, 1990. 128-38.

Ruffinelli, Jorge. "Los 80: ¿ingreso a la posmodernidad?" *Nuevo texto crítico* 3.6 (1990): 31-42.

Shipley, Joseph T. *Dictionary of World Literary Terms.* Boston: The Writer Inc. Publishers, 1943; rpt. 1970.

Sommer, Doris, and George Yúdice. "Latin American Literature from the 'Boom' On." *Postmodern Fiction: A Bio-Bibliographical Guide.* Larry McCafferty, ed. New York: Greenwood Press, 1986. 189-214.

Sturrock, John. *The French New Novel: Claude Simon, Michel Butor, Alain Robbe-Grillet.* London: Oxford UP, 1969.

Subercaseaux, Bernardo. *Historia, literatura y sociedad: ensayos de hermenéutica cultural.* Santiago, Chile: Documentas, 1991.

Suleiman, Susan Rubin. "Feminism and Postmodernism: A Question of Politics." *Zeitgeist in Babel: The Postmodernist Controversy.* Ingeborg Hoesterey, ed. Bloomington: Indiana UP, 1991. 111-27.

Toro, Alfonso, de. "Posmodernidad y Latinoamérica." *Plural: revista cultural de Excélsior* 233 (Feb. 1991): 47-61.

Ulmer, Gregory L. "The Object of Post-Criticism." *The Anti-Aesthetic: Essays on Postmodern Culture.* Hal Foster, ed. Port Townsend, WA: Bay Press, 1983. 83-110.

Waugh, Patricia. *Practising Postmodernism Reading Modernism.* London: Edward Arnold, 1992.

Willis, Sharon. *Marguerite Duras: Writing on the Body.* Urbana: U of Illinois P, 1987.

Worton, Michael, and Judith Still, eds. *Intertextuality: Theories and Practices.* Manchester: Manchester UP, 1990.

Wright, Doris T. "Fantastic Labyrinths in Fictions by Borges, Cortázar, and Robbe-Grillet. *The Comparatist* 13 (May 1989): 29-36.

Yarrow, Ralph. "Irony Grows in My Garden: Generative Process in Borges' "The Garden of Forking Paths." *The Fantastic in World Literature and the Arts.* Donald E. Morse, ed. New York: Greenwood Press, 1984. 73-86.

Yúdice, George. "¿Puede hablarse de posmodernidad en América Latina?" *Revista de crítica literaria latinoamericana* 15.29 (1989): 105-28.

—. "Testimonio and Postmodernism." *Latin American Perspectives* 18.3 (Summer, 1991): 15-33.

Zermeño, Sergio. "La posmodernidad: una visión desde América Latina." *Revista mexicana de sociología* 5.3 (July-Sept. 1988): 61-70.

Zimmerman, Marc. "Orientaciones de la cultura popular latinoamericana." *Nuevo texto crítico* 9.10 (1992): 277-95.

ON NICARAGUA:

GIOCONDA BELLI: THE MAGIC AND/OF EROTICISM
Arturo Arias

In the same way that the narrative of the 1970s preceded the political crisis of the end of that decade, the narrative that began to emerge in the mid-1980s precedes the new period that began fully in 1990 with the electoral defeat of the Sandinista Front.

Furthermore, in the same way that the narrative of the seventies did not pretend to start from scratch, the narrative movement that began approximately in the mid-eighties did not attempt to represent a rupture, but rather to build on the narrative body which preceded it. In some way, the writers of the eighties are a generation that no longer have to prove their revolutionary credentials through literary experimentation, but assume as their own the experiences of the end of the seventies and eighties. Now, they are attempting to reencounter the magic of illusion and fantasy; to close the chapter on the shattering of their lives as a result of their own political militancy as well as because of the revolutionary struggles in the region.

For U.S. audiences, the eighties have been synonymous with political crisis in Central America. Lost in the uproar, however, is the fact that because of the rapid pace of economic, social and political change, Central Americans have also begun to change the way they think of themselves and their place in the world.

These changes are apparent in the literature that has emerged in the region during the decade of the eighties. If we agree that novels are systems of symbolic representations that generate "truth effects" through their discursive practices, it is evident that they register these subjective changes in the perception of being. Thus their study should allow us to explore transitions both in identity and in ideology.[1]

---

[1]Discourses are areas of organized and ordered knowledge that suggest specific ways of apprehending truth and power, and that are formed by linguistic statements. Language doesn't reveal knowledge per se, but rather captures and contains it, generating its own "truth effect" which is expressed symbolically through literature.

In the same vein, the writers of the eighties took for granted the linguistic fascination that enveloped the narrators of the previous decade, and were searching for new routes in avenues yet to be explored. These spaces coincided with certain features that have been outlined by postmodernism, such as ascribing a positive value to intimacy and the private space, the emergence of feminism as a discursive practice, and the fascination with irrational and anti-scientific phenomena such as magic. Other features included a questioning of the hard-line revolutionary subject as a mechanism through which to reencounter the spaces of sensual perception (understood as "sensation" or "feeling," and not exclusively in its erotic definition), and a fascination with various manifestations of popular culture, such as schmaltz and sentimentality. What is emerging is a kind of fatigue with the grandiose pretensions of the previous literary decade, and an attempt to recover conventional forms. Naturally, the latter implies a new kind of formal game, a deliberate return to forms that have been explicitly inherited from tradition to allow them to unfold in a different context.

In another work we have shown how the decade of the seventies represented a *boom* of Central American narrative which can be compared to the so-called narrative *boom* in the rest of the continent during the preceding decade (A. Arias). Although this occurrence was influenced by events elsewhere in the continent, it acquired its own attributes. However, these have hardly been studied by literary critics. We believe this is because Central American literature is still seen as peripheral to the rest of Latin American literature (in which it is customary to examine Mexico and South America; occasionally Cuba or Puerto Rico). This, in spite of the Nobel Prize awarded to Miguel Angel Asturias in 1967, and the presence of other first rate Central American figures such as Augusto Monterroso, Ernesto Cardenal or Luis Cardoza y Aragón.

In Central America the narrative of the seventies did not pretend to start from scratch. Rather, it tried to build on the achievements of the generation that preceded it. For the writers of the seventies, progress consisted in having discovered that literary texts created a linguistic reality, which implied linking the production/reproduction of ideologems. Writing became a practice that "worked" the ideology, without confusing literariness with the socio-historical discourse.

This is the space in which the rupture with the traditional discourse of the period prior to the seventies takes place. Though maintaining the importance of the narrative as a representation of the world, the new trends understand the latter on a primarily linguistic level, that is to say, on the level of literary discourse itself. Thus, the literary evolution that the Central American narrative of the seventies proposes is not a change in "discursive themes," but rather an evolution on the discursive level.

On the symbolic level, this literature preceded the political crises, revolutions and civil wars that the Central American countries experienced from the mid-seventies through the eighties.

If the novels of the early seventies mimicked the collapse of bourgeois coherence, the novels from the mid-eighties onward attempt to transcend it by means of creating an apparently lucid surface that masks these contradictions. These also appear in the emotional domain, in the non-rational, non-conscious or ideological sphere. It is in these areas that the continuity with bourgeois morality has been preserved, even in the revolutionary ranks. While formal or linguistic work is quite evident in the novels of the seventies, the literary craft is hidden below the surface in the narrative of the second half of the eighties. In the first there is a totalizing effort to systematize a historical picture in order to show the inevitability of the struggle for socialism. But in the latter there is an attempt to examine meticulously partial and contained aspects of daily life, generally tied to sensitivity and tenderness.

To explore these issues further, we will take a closer look at two novels written by Nicaragua's Gioconda Belli in the 1980s. They are *La mujer habitada* and *Sofía de los presagios*. We consider her novels emblematic of both emerging postmodern traits in Central America, as well as a turning point in feminist literature for the region.

La mujer habitada (*The Inhabited Woman*)[2] begins with an Indian woman named Itzá going into an orange grove. It is moving back to indigenous cultural roots, and it is also an invocation of 19th-century literature that romanticizes indigenous characters, such as *Tabaré* by Juan Zorrilla de San Martín, or the novels of the Mexican Ignacio Altamirano. Nevertheless, this going back to the roots is not a going back to recreate the image of national identity, or else to re-mystify the figure of the Indian, as it happened with 19th-century literature. Rather, it is a reconstruction of this earlier project to reaffirm the image and identity of women, of the combatant, and of the revolution that seeks to destroy the image of the national state which emerged a century and a half earlier. Thus, the textual project places itself squarely in the context of tradition in order to break it down from the inside, instead of blowing it up from the outside, as the *boom* writers and the Central American narrators of the seventies attempted to do.

This process is personified in Lavinia, the main character in this novel. Lavinia breaks stereotypes right from the start. Her first appearance in the book is a sentimental moment, taken from a heartthrob romance or else from parodies by Manuel Puig. Still sleepy, she smells the scent of orange blossoms as she goes into the bathroom. However, at this very moment a game is established in which

---

[2]All the quotes from this book are our translation.

the orange grove circulates between two axiological spaces, Itzá's and Lavinia's. In Itzá's case, it identifies the survival of the ethnic group and its cultural universe. In Lavinia's case, it provides the space of sensuality that appears combined with strength, wholeness and courage.

Let's see how this process develops. At first, Lavinia appears following the description of Itzá in the tree. The first thing we hear about her from the narrative voice is that she is "perezosa," lazy (11). Next we are informed that Lavinia goes into the bathroom where she scrubs her body, combs her long hair, muses about her face, and about being in sync with rock music, hippie style. Finally, we find out that she has abandoned her paternal home, and that she is a "woman who is alone, young and independent" ("mujer sola, joven e independiente"; 11). All this information in a Central American novel is innovative in itself. However, we will touch on this later. At this point, we want to emphasize the tension between Itzá's discourse and Lavinia's that manifests the apparent contradiction between Itzá's world and Lavinia's world. The latter having "features resembling those of the invaders' women" ("rasgos parecidos a las mujeres de los invasores"; 10), functions as the structural element of the text on a semantic level. We can see immediately how this generative knot reveals, at the level of narrative discourse, the hybridization of two discourses that are only antagonistic in appearance. These are the poetic, mythological discourse of the indigenous woman, and the discourse of the modern woman of the end of the 20th century. The precise point of intersection is that they are both women combatants. Both are ex-centric women.

Itzá says:

> Me pregunto qué quedaría de nosotros, de mi madre,
> a quien nunca más volví a ver después que me fui con Yarince.
> *Nunca entendió que no podía simplemente quedarme en la*
> *casa. Jamás le perdonó a Citlalcoatl que me enseñara a usar*
> *el arco y la flecha.*

> I wonder what was left of us, of my mother, whom I
> never saw again after I left with Yarince. *She never understood*
> *that I couldn't simply stay home. She never forgave Citlalcoatl*
> *for showing me how to use the bow and arrow.* (19, emphasis
> added)

As for Lavinia, she makes a big show of being rebellious even before she joins a political organization. When she is introduced to Felipe in the firm that hires her as the first woman architect, Lavinia recalls:

Los dos hombres parecían disfrutar su actitud de paternidad laboral. Lavinia se sintió en desventaja. Hizo una reverencia interna a la complicidad masculina y deseó que las presentacionesterminaran. No le gustaba sentirse en escaparate. Le recordaba su regreso de Europa, cuando sus padres la llevaban a fiestas, engalanada, y la soltaban para que la husmearan animalitos de sacos y corbatas. Animalitos domésticos buscando quién les diera hijos robustos y frondosos, les hiciera la comida, les arreglara los cuartos. Bajo arañas de cristal y luces despampanantes la exhibían como porcelana *Limoges* o *Sevres* en aquel mercado persa de casamientos con olor a subasta. Y ella lo odiaba. No quería más eso. Por escaparlo estaba allí.

The two men appeared to enjoy their attitude of labor paternalism. Lavinia felt at a disadvantage. She took an internal bow to masculine complicity, and wished that the introductions would be over. She didn't like feeling like she was on display. It reminded her of her return from Europe, when her parents used to take her to parties all dressed up, and would let her loose to be sniffed by little animals in coats and ties. Little domestic animals on the prowl for someone who could give them robust and fertile children, cook their meals and pick up their rooms. They exhibited her under crystal chandeliers and dazzling lights, as Limoges or Sevres china in a Persian wedding market that smelled like an auction. And she hated it. She didn't want that anymore. She was there to escape it. (16)

The contrast between the two voices is marked by differences in narrative focus. Lavinia's discourse is in the third person. Itzá's is in the first person. At the same time, the ideological framework is set by Itzá's discourse, while Lavinia's world unfolds gradually through the plot. For example, Itzá says:

Lentamente voy comprendiendo este tiempo. Me preparo. He observado a la mujer. Las mujeres parecen ya no ser subordinadas, sino personas principales. Hasta tienen servidumbre por sí mismas. Y trabajan fuera del hogar. Ella, por ejemplo, sale a trabajar por las mañanas. (27)

I am slowly understanding this time. I'm getting ready. I've observed the woman. Women seem not to be subordinated anymore, but rather they are the main characters. They even have their own servants.

And they work outside the home. She, for example, leaves in the morning to go to work.

Nevertheless, at the same time in the narrative, Lavinia has not yet understood her role, is not conscious of the decisions she will have to make later. She is still "landing" from her previous situation. In other words, Itzá's discourse appears as the ideological rector, as the visible symbol of critical and contextual thinking, indicating the path that Lavinia will have to travel on in narrative time.

The tension between both discourses reveals clearly that both the past and the present are discursive practices. Both constitute systems of meaning. Through them we confer meaning to the past and establish its continuity with the present, not just by ordering it discursively, but by linking both times on the symbolic level. In the narrative flow, this occurs when Lavinia drinks the juice from the oranges, and the spirit of Itzá enters her veins.

> Ella nos abrió de un tajo... Luego los dedos asiendo la cáscara y el fluir del jugo... Los gajos abriéndose. Las delicadas pieles liberando sus cuidadosas lágrimas retenidas en aquel mundo redondo. Y posarnos en la mesa. Desde la vasija transparente la observo. Espero que me lleve a los labios. Espero que se consumen los ritos, se unan los círculos. (44-45)

> She cut it right open. . . . Then her fingers grasped our peeling and the juice seeped out. . . . The sections opened. The delicate skins liberated their tears, carefully retained in that round world. She placed us on the table. I observe her from the transparent bowl. I want her to take me to her lips. I wait for the rites to be consummated, for the circles to be joined.

This symbolic fusion also transforms Itzá. She's not only a combatant, she's also a woman, with her own demands. Both combatants, both women struggling to defend their identity as women in the face of their own companions in arms, be it Yarince or Felipe.

This process of self-reflection cannot be separated from the notion of difference. But it is only an apparent difference. The historical context is reinstated in order to reestablish the present for the sake of the past, the past continuing toward the present and the future, as a river flows toward the sea. This is revealed in the final poem that closes the text:

> He cumplido un ciclo: mi destino de semilla germinada, el designio de mis antepasados.

Lavinia es ahora tierra y humus. Su espíritu danza en el viento
de las tardes. Su cuerpo abona campos fecundos.
Desde su sangre vi el triunfo de los ximiqui justicieros.
Recuperaron a sus hermanos. Vencieron sobre el odio con
serenidad y teas de ocote ardientes.
La luz está encendida. Nadie podrá apagarla. Nadie apagará el
sonido de los tambores batientes.
Veo grandes multitudes avanzando en los caminos abiertos por
Yarince y los guerreros, los de hoy, los de entonces...
...Ni ella y yo (sic) hemos muerto sin designio ni herencia.
Volvimos a la tierra desde donde de nuevo viviremos...
...Nadie que ama muere jamás. (338)

I've completed one cycle: my destiny as a fertilized seed, the
design of my ancestors.
Lavinia is now earth and humus. Her spirit dances in the after-
noon wind. Her body fertilizes fruitful grounds.
From her blood I saw the triumph of the avenging ximiqui.
They are recovering their brothers. They triumphed over hate
with serenity and burning torches of pine.
The light is burning. No one can extinguish it. No one will
extinguish the sound of the beating drums.
I see great multitudes advancing on the paths cleared by Yarin-
ce and the warriors, today's, those of other days. . . .
. . .Neither she nor I have died without design or inheritance.
We returned to the earth where we will once again live. . . .
. . .No one who loves ever dies.

There exists in this mixture of voices (Itzá/Lavinia) a deliberate contamination of the historical environment with a didactic element, which questions the
transparency of the representation. Simultaneously, it questions the code through
which the Nicaraguan Indian past has been interpreted traditionally. *La mujer
habitada* reminds us that, although indigenous people did exist in an empirical
past, we name them and establish them as a historical fact depending on our
choice and narrative stance. Furthermore, we know her past not only by the
discourse that expresses it, but also by the scent of her presence in the present.
The past repeats itself in the present. Itzá is Lavinia, Yarince is Felipe. The
entire text is a kind of dialogical relationship, Bakhtinian style, between Lavinia's discourse and Itzá's.

On a symbolic level we witness a reconciliation between both characters.
As the poem quoted above indicates, they become one: we have a dialectic

synthesis that resolves the contradiction. Nevertheless, there is no synthesis or reconciliation on the level of discourse. The two discourses are in a dialogical relationship, and they will never come together. It is precisely in this lack of fusion that we find the conflict between fiction and history, narrative art, and the perception of reality.

The other element that the textual movement expresses clearly is eroticism, which in this case plays a positive and liberating role, a subversive pleasure of another kind.

From the beginning of the text, Lavinia is aware of her physical attractiveness, of her body, and the effect it has on men. In the first chapter, Lavinia appears naked, in the bath, surrounded by the scent of orange blossoms. Then she goes to her job as an architect in a miniskirt, conscious of the effect her clothes have on Julián and Felipe. Almost all of the following scenes contain a reference to her physical appearance.

For example, the texts tells us that Lavinia "sudaba. El sudor corría por sus piernas ajustándole los pantalones a la piel, la camiseta roja a la espalda. El maquillaje manchaba el *kleenex* con que se secaba la cara." 'She perspired. The perspiration trickled down her thighs so that her pants clung to her skin, her red t-shirt to her back. Her makeup stained the kleenex she used to dry her face' (24). "Estaba consciente de la blusa aún mojada, pegándosele a la piel; los pezones alzados en el frío del aire acondicionado." 'She was conscious of her damp blouse clinging tightly to her skin; her nipples erect in the cold of the air conditioner' (25). "Se sacudió la blusa, soplándose dentro, ventilándose los pechos. Estaba acalorada." 'She shook her blouse out, blowing air on herself inside, fanning her breasts. She was hot' (25). "Le gustaba frotar el jabón hasta hacerse bordados de espuma en el cuerpo desnudo, ver los vellos del pubis tornarse blancos, reconocerse aquel cuerpo asignado misteriosamente para toda la vida..." 'She liked to scrub with soap until she embroidered her naked body with lather, to see her pubic hair turn white, recognize herself in that body mysteriously assigned to her for her entire life...' (28). "Le bailó pretendiendo no verlo, consciente de que lo hacía para provocarlo, disfrutando el exhibicionismo, la sensualidad del baile, la euforia de pensar que por fin se encontrarían fuera de la oficina. Llevaba una de sus más cortas minifaldas, tacones altos, camisa desgajada de un hombro—pura imagen del pecado, había pensado de sí misma antes de salir— y había fumado un poco de monte." 'She danced for him, while pretending not to see him, aware that she was doing it to provoke him, enjoying the exhibitionism, the sensuality of the dance, the euphoria of thinking that they would finally meet outside of the office. She was wearing one of her shortest miniskirts, high heels, a short sleeve blouse that laid bare one shoulder—the very image of sin, as she had thought of herself just before she left—and she had smoked a bit of grass' (31).

The eroticism plays the role of transgressor language here. Eroticism, marginalized from the discursive practices of the Central American novel, confronts the ideological rigidities that informed the previous dialogue, generating a fusion between erotic and political vitality. The erotic discourse in *La mujer habitada* emphasizes its energy as a liberating element that breaks with the framework of traditions that fossilizes Central American society. The tradition appears represented by Lavinia's family, naturally, but also by Sara and Adrián, "un retrato hablado del matrimonio perfecto"; 'a verbal portrait of the perfect marriage' (39). Lavinia, who represents the opposite pole, admits that "siempre le había costado imaginar a Sara haciendo el amor..." 'She had always had trouble imagining Sara making love...' (39).

As Bakhtin indicated, eroticism appears as a central element in the carnival, and its roots date back to the Dionysian festivities of the Greeks' and Romans' Saturnalias (Bakhtin 5). Part of its function is to play a symbolic role as a vision of an alternative world, characterized by a playful undermining of conventional norms. The body once again takes a central role as an instrument of play that dissolves the dogma, the authoritarianism, and the narrow severity that social hierarchies always imply. Laughter and eroticism, instrumentalized as if they were Zen rituals, become signs of a free and critical consciousness that mocks dogmatism and fanaticism. Eroticism makes it possible to recover the forbidden, the repressed, the grotesque, the irrational. The body ceases to be a self-contained system, and becomes a space of tolerance and liberating multiplicity.

The affirmation of carnivalesque eroticism that appears in Bakhtin comes together with the rebellion against rationality that Foucault expresses. The latter celebrates the spirit of creative disorder, of destructuring, of the end of the attempt to explain the world with the blinders imposed by the myth of progress and scientific pretense. Thus, at the same time, it turns towards a reaffirmation of the subjectivity of knowledge, which is contained in imagination and irrationality.

The origins of both trends—the Bakhtinian and the Foucaultian—can be found in the postmodern space, facilitating the recognition of a cultural production that emphasizes the self-creation of a new subject by other than rational means. In this sense, Gioconda Belli's work is an expression of the fact that this trend has entered Central America hand in hand with the transformations in the space of consciousness that began to operate during the second half of the eighties in that part of the world.

The environment in which Belli's second novel, *Sofía de los presagios* (*Sofía of the Forebodings*)[3] is going to operate is made clear from the very first moment:

> Es de noche y el mundo está quieto. Hay que entrar de punti-
> llas al Diriá, pueblo de brujos, pueblo que crece sobre el cerro que en
> lo alto se quiebra y baja hacia la inmensa laguna de Apoyo. (11)

> It's nighttime, and the world is still. You have to tiptoe into the
> Diriá, the world of the witches, a town that grows on the mountain that
> breaks at the peak and goes down toward the immense Apoyo lagoon.

The first chapter ends with the phrase: "Xintal, la bruja vieja que habita en el Mombacho siente un aire de presagios en el ambiente y pone rajas de canela en la puerta de su casa." 'Xintal, the old witch who inhabits the Momba-cho, senses an air of forebodings in the environment, and places some cinnamon sticks on the door of her home' (13). We know from the very beginning that we are in another world, the world of sorcery. We find ourselves in a place of un-ambiguous irrationality, and it is from here that the novelesque discourse is going to flow. At the same time, the tone clearly signals a return to the art of story-telling, of the narrative. It is a tone that approximates oral tales, close to the kind of tone used by domestic servants when they tell about their villages steeped in superstitions, where the border between fantasy and reality is nonexistent. The narrative voice could well have been that of Lucrecia, Lavinia's servant in *La mujer habitada*. The narration moves the story onward in a linear fashion, similar to the way which Roberto González Echevarría describes when he speaks of the "narrative apotheosis" that exists in Severo Sarduy's *Colibrí* (59).

Sofía de los presagios is both a rebellion against the premodern patriar-chal oppression that still dominates social relations in most of the Third World, and a quest for its destruction. In a much more explicit way than *La mujer habi-tada*, the struggle is centered around feminism.

The transition experienced around the subject in the Central American novel shifts from the dominating bourgeois man (*criollista* novel), to the mestizo revolutionary woman (*La mujer habitada*), to the marginal woman defending her existence as a woman (*Sofía de los presagios*). Also included in the latter literary trend are the texts of other traditionally marginated sectors such as indigenous peoples. Their narrative begins to appear with force both in fictional texts, such as Luis de Lión's *El mundo principia en Xibalbá* (1985) or Víctor Montejo's *El K'anil. El pájaro que limpia el mundo* (1989); in poetry such as Humberto

---

[3] All the quotes from this book are our translation.

Ak'abal's, or testimonies such as Rigoberta Menchu's. In other words, what we see here is an emerging process in which identities traditionally marginalized and discriminated against are now affirmed. In this process, they are breaking out of the mythological world they were condemned to, and are attempting to affirm themselves as conscious subjects capable of controlling their own destiny.

Texts such as *Sofía de los presagios* deliberately question subjectivity, including the way in which their own identity has been represented in literature and in society. Obviously, this questioning is of a political nature, even though it doesn't appear in the texts as an explicitly political struggle. Sofía, for example, is neither a combatant like Lavinia, nor a feminist. She simply wants to control her own destiny; to own her life. This "simply," however, becomes a tremendous obstacle, due to the reigning prejudices and social restrictions of rural Nicaraguan society. In fact, Sofía's search becomes a political confrontation, even though the character in question never "reads" her situation as such.

To this end, a relationship is established between Xintal and Sofía that operates in a way that is analogous to the relationship between Itzá and Lavinia in *La mujer habitada*. Here, the poetic/mythological discourse belongs to Xintal, and it establishes the continuity of identity that opens and closes the text. As in the final poem in *La mujer habitada*, Xintal's last discourse establishes the continuity of time and identity:

> Xintal introduce una mano en el agua, pero ya el reflejo no se bifurca como antes; el destino de la muchacha se ve limpio y claro...
> A través del agua, Xintal tiene la visión del tiempo rompiendo el círculo y liberando a la mujer de los designios torcidos de la madre; vislumbra la disolución del rencor y el hechizo del abandono y sabe la ceremonia del rocío surtió efecto... Sofía había llegado al fin desu búsqueda, podría mirar su imagen en el espejo, reconciliarse con la oscuridad de su origen, romper las profecías y empezar a vivir su propia vida. (373-74)

> Xintal puts her hand in the water, but her reflection doesn't split as it used to; the girl's destiny looks clean and clear. . . . Through the water, Xintal has a vision of time breaking the circle and liberating the woman from her mother's twisted designs; she can glimmer the dissipation of the rancor, and the spell cast on her by her abandonment, and she knows that the ceremony of the dew was effective. . . . Sofía had come to the end of her search, she could see her image in the mirror, reconcile herself to the darkness of her origins, break with the prophecies and begin to live her own life.

Sofía, as Lavinia, expresses the discourse of the women of our time. In this second text we don't see the contrast between both voices marked by differences in narrative focalization, to use Gerard Genette's terminology for defining narrative voice. Both discourses appear in the third person. Nevertheless, the ideological framework is marked from the beginning by Xintal's discourse, while Sofía's world advances gradually as the plot unfolds. The forebodings that Xintal senses in the environment of Mombacho at the beginning of the text will be experienced by Sofía a lot later, and assimilated consciously even much later.

The division between the feminine discourses allows for the representation of women as a split subject. On the one hand, they participate in the privileges of the dominant sector, of the liberal humanistic discourse of freedom, self-determination, and rationality. At the same time, however, they partake of the specifically female discourse of submission, insufficiency, and irrational intuition.[4]

Here again, the contradiction between eroticism and "bourgeois conventions" is represented. Sofía drives the men in the region crazy because of her sensuality, which explodes at the party that Don Ramón organizes to marry her off:

> Baila Sofía y los hombres no pierden la ocasión de mirarla bailar. Sitúan a sus parejas de manera que puedan enfocar a la Sofía con los ojos entre vuelta y vuelta. El vestido amarillo de organza se convierte en vestido rojo de bailaora de flamenco... Los que pueden la asedian para que les conceda el don de tocarle la cintura menuda y ver si ella se deja apretar más que las otras. Las muchachas están inquietas y sienten que pierden la competencia... (27)

> Sofía dances, and the men don't miss a chance to watch her dance. They place their partners in such a way that they can focus their eyes on Sofía between each turn. The yellow organdy dress becomes a red flamenco dancer's dress. . . . Those who can beseige her with requests so as to be granted the gift of touching her small waist, and to see if she will allow them to dance closer than the rest. The girls are anxious and feel that they are losing the competition. . . .

René's aspirations, however, are to marry Sofía. "Y cuando sea su mujer, nadie más le va a tocar ni un pelo de la cabeza. El mismo la va a acompañar a la iglesia los domingos y la va a mantener cargada como escopeta de

---

[4]These aspects coincide with Linda Hutcheon's analysis of the feminine discourse.

hacienda, preñada, hasta que se le acabe la cinturita y se le pongan dulces y maternales esos ojos oscuros que brillan demasiado, que son un peligro para ella que ni cuenta se da como queda viendo a los idiotas que se derriten cuando ella los mira." 'And when she becomes his woman, no one else will touch even a hair on her head. He will go with her to church on Sundays, and he's going to keep her loaded like a farm rifle, pregnant, until her small waist is gone, and those black eyes that shine too much become sweet and maternal. Those eyes which are too dangerous for her. She doesn't even realize how the idiots melt when she looks at them' (28).

Here we have more than a dichotomy between two contradictory views of the world. We have a struggle between rationalism and irrationalism, between rigid social conventions and erotic, carnivalesque subversion.

Since Sofía is unaware of her own subjectivity, she agrees to marry René to satisfy Don Ramón. She also believes that marriage "marcará el principio de su vida adulta," 'signals the beginning of her adult life' and that "lo importante es poder hacer lo que uno quiere," 'what matters is to be able to do what one wants' (31). Nevertheless, none of these two things will happen. René, in his obsession for controlling and objectifying Sofía, undergoes a regression that makes it impossible for him to be an adult and to allow her to be one as well. Sofía, for her part, is unaware of the context of power in which she operates as the subjected party.

The conflict between René and Sofía symbolizes the clash between their two worlds, and is expressed from the moment of the wedding onward. Sofía insists on riding horseback into the church, but she escapes at a gallop just at that moment. "...galopa, y galopa hasta que se siente más tranquila. Entonces endereza las riendas y todos la ven aparecer entre la polvareda, cuando ya creen que habrá que suspender la boda porque al fin ha podido más la sangre gitana." '. . .(she) gallops and gallops until she feels calmer. Then she straightens the reins, and they all watch her appear through the dust. They had come to believe that the wedding would have to be cancelled because the gypsy blood had prevailed' (36).

> En silencio, los invitados, que han vuelto al interior de la iglesia, la ven pasar. Sofía lleva la espalda recta y sobre el vestido blanquísimo, se ven las manchas del polvo. El sudor de las ancas del caballo ha ensuciado el ruedo y un lado de la ancha falda de satín, el pelo de la muchacha está desordenado. (36)

> In silence, the guests who had gone back inside the Church watch her go by. Sofía's back is erect and her absolutely white dress is

spotted with dust. The sweat of the horse's flank has sullied the hem and one side of the wide satin skirt, and her hair is dishevelled.

For Sofía, it was an inexplicable, though a natural, wish. For René, the incident was humiliating socially, "él que quería una novia blanca e impecable para esponjarse de orgullo." '. . .he who wanted a white and impeccable bride to be proud of. . .' (37). He tells her that all gypsies are whores. Since that moment, they are left in a real state of war. René locks Sofía up in the house. Sofía refuses to get pregnant, and takes birth control pills on the sly. "Ella no podrá tener lo que quiere, pero tampoco lo tendrá René." 'She won't be able to get what she wants, but René won't be able to either' (47).

Here we have a parody of the macho subject who is attempting to be the dominant figure in both the public and the private arenas. By extension, the parody that expresses the constitution of this subject appears to flourish. The macho ideology of patriarchal society is broken down, not from the standpoint of an antithetical feminist ideology, but from an anti-rationalistic affirmation of feminine subjectivity.

At the same time, the novel expresses a lack of concurrence between the notion of "women" as a discursive practice of patriarchal society, and the oppressive reality experienced by women subjected to such practices. The novel takes place after the 1979 Nicaraguan revolution—there are several references to the revolution as a phenomenon almost alien to the Diriá. For example, Fausto receives a scholarship soon after the triumph of the revolution (31), and Sofía thinks about poisoning René with strychnine, because she has read *Castigo divino*, a novel by Sergio Ramírez, who published it when he was vice-president of the country (63). The fact that it seems so alien appears to confirm the continuity of the patterns of the patriarchal society, even within the historical time frame of the revolution.

The revolution does not really touch the irrational spaces, the domestic spaces that constitute the life of rural society. It is assumed that the revolution affects the ideological sphere exclusively, since this is the sphere of knowledge that is subjected to Cartesian rationality. The world of the instincts, of magic, the world that symbolically represents a gypsy who disowns her parents and her roots, is a world that is so devoid of ideologies that it is going to be besieged and punished by the decision to rationalize existence, as Sofía is punished by René. The world of magic and eroticism will resist the hounding of reason, just as Sofía does, and will emerge triumphant in time and space.

In other words, *Sofía de los presagios* represents a challenge to the premise upon which the entire humanist discourse is anchored. Men no longer represent the senses. They are embodied by women, who create a counter-discourse that is anti-rational and anti-humanist, to express a new coherence built around their existence as coherent subjects. Tradition becomes the container of oppression. The language of the novel becomes a source for the constitution of a subject who will have to negate it in order to continue with the liberating task of all subjects who are oppressed by the humanist yoke.

In the article by González Echevarría quoted above, the critic works out a certain parallelism between the postmodern narrative element and the Latin American narrative of the post-boom era. Then he reaches a series of preliminary conclusions about the same. These include the apotheosis of narration, the absence of a metadiscourse, the elimination of ironic reflexibility, and a certain superficiality (69-71).

If we examine Gioconda Belli's texts under this light, we find a strong compatibility with the first three characteristics, and a marked difference with the last one. Let's take a closer look at all this.

Gonzalez Echevarría's concept of the "apotheosis of narration" refers to a reaffirmation of the plot as the basic vehicle for the movement of narrative action. According to him, *boom* novels such as *Hopscotch* by Julio Cortázar or *Three Sad Tigers* by Guillermo Cabrera Infante obstruct the plot, pulverizing it most of the time. In the Central American case, we can detect similar characteristics in the novels of the seventies, such as *Pobrecito poeta que era yo* (*What a Sad Poet I Was*) or *Caperucita en la zona roja* (*Little Red Riding Hood in the Red Light District*). Nevertheless, the narrative of the eighties once again liberates the plot, the story, and emphasizes its linear development. We see the latter in *La mujer habitada* as well as in *Sofía de los presagios*. In both cases, the plot flows linearly, uninterrupted, from beginning to end.

At the same time, the *boom* novels contained a critical political and cultural metadiscourse. Perhaps the most explicit case is *Hopscotch* with its own literary theory formulated by Morelli, in what are called the "dispensable chapters." In the Central American case, this appears as a more explicitly political concern. Once again, we can see this in a special way in *Pobrecito poeta que era yo* in which the metadiscourse is a guideline for training militants: José's option, counterpoised to the option of the other group members.

Nevertheless, the post-boom novels eliminate this metadiscoursive element. When they cease to aspire to totalization, all that the novel has to say appears within the narrative matrix, and not revolving around it. Stories are privileged as such, instead of a metadiscourse that appears to be almost separate from, or an obstacle to, their development. Once again, this is the case in *La mujer habitada* and *Sofía de los presagios*. The entire meditation on militancy, or the identity problem, appears in the context of the narrative action, or else in dialogues within the scenes in which movement and the relationship between sequences are clearly evident. Time is never stopped; movement is never paralyzed while an external meditation to the flow of the plot is taking place.

As for the elimination of ironic reflexivity, this refers to that trait of *boom* novels in which the plot contained the history of how the novel was written, in an attempt to destroy the boundaries between reality and fiction. Generally, the implicit author[5] as Genette defines it (213) ended by self-immolating at the altar of language. The most remarkable case is the ending of *One Hundred Years of Solitude*. When the last Aureliano deciphers the Melquiades manuscripts written in sanskrit, he understands that the story they contain is his own story, the story of the novel, of his death, of Macondo, and that everything will be demolished by the wind and erased from memory.

In the narrative of the post-boom, the narrative conscience is not above the story itself, and generally, the author does not appear as a literary figure. Once again, we find this case in Gioconda Belli's novels. The third person narrative voice predominates—zero focalization in Gerard Génette's scheme (189-94)—without the temporal complexity in order, duration, or frequency. There are also no games with the narrative voice that imply variability in the focalizing perspective, nor intradiegetic or metadiegetic tricks. There is an overabundance of these traits in some of the novels which immediately precede Belli's, such as *¿Te dio miedo la sangre?* by Sergio Ramírez or *Función con móbiles y tentetiesos* by Marcos Carías, but they are totally absent in Gioconda Belli's work.

Finally, we come to the accusation of superficiality. According to Gonzalez Echevarría, in the post-boom narrative neither the language, nor the characters, nor the figure of the author, promise depth or understanding. It's all color, narrative, action. There's no breaking with the conventions of grammar, or with rhetoric. The post-boom narrative can be described as "narrative entertainment." Such is the case with the last novels by Manuel Puig and Osvaldo Soriano, or with the "light literature" emerging from Mexico.[6]

It is precisely on this point that I differ with González Echevarría regarding Gioconda Belli's novels as well as the general tendencies of postmodern

---

[5]The "implicit author" is the agent which builds and organizes the structure of the text, the one who gives it shape. By implication, it is the implicit author who represents the principles through which value judgements are made. It is the implicit author who either veils or reveals the characters' thoughts, who chooses among various kinds of discourses, the chronological order and the ruptures in time.

[6]Contemporary Mexican critics are describing as "light literature" contemporary novels published in their own country which are short, accessible to a mass audience, usually become best-sellers, yet retain valuable literary and ideological traits which also makes them recognizable as a literary, and not just a commercial, venture. Among those titles included in this category would be Laura Esquivel's *Like Water for Chocolate*.

narrative in Central America. Although, in the case of Belli, her narrative is conventional in general terms, the objective is not just color, action, or entertainment. Rather, under this apparent stylistic convention, we find the marked ideological break mentioned above. Belli, in fact, questions the traditional notions of the subject and of women's marginality.

As Mary O'Connor indicates, feminine literature has been motivated by the imperative of women's search for identity and acting on this knowledge (200). In this process, it discovers that the masculine identity is also a fabrication, and ideological artifact, as is the case with Sofía and René in *Sofía de los presagios*. Freedom in the postmodern world must come from analyzing and subverting all the ideologically constructed identities, especially those that place any subject in an exploitative position. Women still have to deconstruct their patriarchal image as silent, submissive beings, objects for pleasure and possession. This in turn generates an identity crisis, as they attempt to construct their own identity, after being the object of the other's gaze. It is the same process that indigenous peoples, homosexuals, Afro-Latinos, and any other group marginalized by the social patterns set by Modernity, must embark on.

Thus Belli's novels embody this process of metamorphosis of identity, that new process of the subject's developing consciousness. The subject Lavinia, and the subject Sofía, break with the identity conferred on them by the "other," and rediscover a new identity which allows them to harmonize, through their own life experience, the different polarities of their own life.

Lavinia's and Sofía's process is the process of self-actualization and of reconciliation with themselves. Both of them first find the limits and the confinement of the other's gaze, which objectifies them and ravages their nature. Both struggle with themselves to position themselves ideologically in a situation that confronts this gaze. They are both transformed as they act on their own conscious will to change. Both grow as self-sufficient people, establishing a new ethical/ideological space of their own, separate from the confinement of a society that is still attempting to negate them. Finally, they project themselves on the world with their own energy and affirmation.

The search the two women are embarked on is an ethical search. This ethos, however, cannot be found on the level of conscious rationalization. Rather, it is found on the instinctive level, on the level of aesthetic perception. Their process, then, involves breaking the rationalist dichotomy that forces beings to define themselves as one thing or another, with no control over their own destiny. In this space, beings have no recognition of the singularity of their place in the world. They are in a merely reactive position vis-à-vis all of the ethical-cognitive determinants that make it possible for subjects to configure their own meaning, and to define their own identity.[7]

There is no superficiality here. To the contrary, this is a legitimate search for identity, which in passing happens to coincide with the ideological project of the novels that preceded it. The process of searching continues. However, the nature of the search is different, as is the subject who searches. In this process, the new subject will sometimes clash with the subject of the preceding novels. Today, this has become one of the obstacles on the path of the new subjects, who are in turn struggling to free themselves from other kinds of oppression. There is no "last word," nor will there ever be one, as long as there continues to be a dialogue between subjects struggling in search of their own self-affirmation.

Works Cited

Arias, Arturo. "Consciousness of the Word: Some Features of the New Central American Narrative." *Hispamerica* 21.61 (1992):41-58

Bakhtin, Mikhail. "Author and Hero in Aesthetic Activity." *Art and Answerability*. Austin: U of Texas P, 1990. 4-256.

—. *Rabelais and His World*. Bloomington: Indiana UP, 1984.

Belli, Gioconda. *La mujer habitada*. Managua: Editorial Vanguardia, 1988.

—. *Sofía de los Presagios*. Managua: Editorial Vanguardia, 1990.

Esquivel, Laura. *Like Water for Chocolate: A Novel in Monthly Installments, with Recipes, Romances, and Home Remedies*. Carol Christenson, and Thomas Christensen, trans. New York: Doubleday, 1992.

Foucault, Michel. *The Archeology of Knowledge*. New York: Pantheon Books, 1972.

Génette, Gerard. *Narrative Discourse: An Essay in Method*. Trans. Jane E. Lewin. Ithaca: Cornell UP, 1980.

González Echevarría, Roberto. "Severo Sarduy, the Boom and the Post-Boom." *Latin American Literary Review* 15.29 (Jan.-June 1987): 57-72.

Hutcheon, Linda. "Subject in/of/to History and his Story." *A Poetics of Postmodernism*. New York: Routledge, 1988. 158-77.

---

[7]Here the text coincides with some of the objectives of the early Bakhtin expressed in "Author and Hero in Aesthetic Activity," regarding the way to carry out the task of transplanting the internal voice to the language of the public utterance (133), thus allowing the self-constitution of the subject as a human being among others who recognize him as such.

O'Connor, Mary. "Subject, Voice and Women in Some Contemporary Black American Women's Writing." *Feminism, Bakhtin and the Dialogic.* Dale M. Bauer, and S. Jaret McKinstry, eds. Albany: State U of New York P, 1991. 199-218.

ON WHAT WE DO:

IMPURITY AND THE CULTURES OF DEMOCRACY IN LATIN AMERICA

Santiago Colás

I don't believe it's still necessary to argue—as it was for George Yúdice several years ago—that one **can** speak of postmodernity in Latin America ("¿Puede?"). It may, however, still be valuable to recall why we **should**. Of course, we may feel tempted to shun a term that has lent itself so easily to commercial and imperialist abuse. But perhaps **because** the term has come to occupy a central position—however nebulous or vague—in our popular social and cultural vocabulary (unlike, by the way, so many of the more specialized terms of our profession), we should invest more energy in shaping its meaning and function. This seems not only useful, but practically a matter of strategic necessity, especially if the debate over postmodernity in culture and politics is really about "new ways of thinking or imagining democracy" ("¿Puede?" 109). If so, and if "'liberal democracy' is being touted as the *ne plus ultra* of social systems for countries that are emerging from Soviet-style state socialism, Latin American military dictatorship, and Southern African regimes of racial domination" (Fraser 56), then we find ample justification for continuing to talk about postmodernity and for talking about its relationship to Latin American culture.

But we should not only ask what postmodernism theory can do for Latin America, but what Latin America can and has done for postmodernism theory. I propose that postmodern Latin American theory and culture has contributed a powerful political component—oriented toward the deepening and extension of democratic practices—to the international debate on postmodernity. To elaborate this proposition, I want to highlight one feature of Latin American contributions to the postmodernism debate—their rhetoric of impurity—and relate it, via a study of the function of representation in the *testimonio*, to ongoing and expanding attempts to transform existing democracy.

Elsewhere I have argued against the theoretical appropriation, on the part of such eminent North American theorists as Linda Hutcheon and Fredric Jameson, of Latin American literature and culture (Colás, *Postmodernity* and Colás "Third"). Even in the best cases, where Latin America's culture is considered in view of social and historical developments, these are reduced and homogenized to conform to a certain—often orthodox Marxist—view of the effects of advanced capitalism on peripheral societies like those of Latin America. But there is ample evidence that the development of capitalism produces neither a uniform landscape of complete modernization, nor a checkerboard of permanently developed or underdeveloped regions, but rather a panorama of variously conflicting, constantly shifting and overlapping cultural, political, and economic exchanges that defies such reductive categories as have been furnished by Marxist theories of imperialism to date (Appadurai 6; Lechner, "Some" 28). In short, it produces, as theorists in the discipline of geography have come to observe, a radical and dynamic heterogeneity (Smith 152).

Significantly, this image of dynamic heterogeneity—irreducible to older binary characterizations—as an effect of capitalism also pervades many Latin American discussions of postmodernity. Arturo Escobar characterizes the shift as follows: "It is as if the elegant discourses of the 1960s [he refers to dependency theory and revolution]. . . had been suspended, caught in mid air as they strove toward their zenith, and, like fragile bubbles, exploded, leaving a scrambled trace of their glorious path behind" (20). Indeed, there is a rhetoric common to many Latin American contributions to the postmodernism debate: a rhetoric of impurity. Pure categories, supposedly referring to equally pure real entities, are contaminated by internal differences, messy hybrids and multiple identities. Benjamín Arditi thus speaks of a "crisis" and "transformation of ways of seeing, apprehending, and making in the world" (170). Economically, politically, and culturally, stable concepts and fixed oppositions give way to more flexible, dynamic, and open-ended characterizations.

In each case, the crisis of the institutions and concepts of Western modernity is viewed as the possibility for a rethinking and renewal of its ideals in accordance with a changed reality. But this critique and renewal of modernity does not take place along the lines of "completing" a stunted, but still unilinear, project of modernity (Habermas). Rather, a more appropriate metaphor might be one of switching modern values of economic, political, and cultural democracy off the single track of Enlightenment modernity and onto the variety of new tracks—some long, some short, without necessarily having any fixed or unified end in sight—being produced by a heterogenous group of social actors today. Even within the Latin American postmodernism debate itself, these contributions transcend the standoff between assimilationist espousal and nativist rejection of European and North American theories.[1] These antagonistic positions, based on

---

[1]Even some of the most respected Latin Americanist critics fall into these positions. Roberto González Echevarría's otherwise remarkable reading of Severo Sarduy is probably the best known example of the insufficiently critical application of the stylistic checklists of postmodernism theory to Latin American writers (González Echevarría 243-51). On the other hand, Neil Larsen has consistently

clear demarcations of the "native" and the "foreign," appear inadequate for explaining global flows of capital, goods, culture, and people. Instead, Latin American thinkers critically engage the concepts of postmodernism theory, reorienting them toward addressing the specific economic, political, and cultural challenges of contemporary Latin American societies.

Economically, the opposing models of modernization and dependency theory give way to pragmatic, but critical strategies for negotiating and reconfiguring capitalism in Latin America. Modernization theory, developed in the U.S. during the Cold War, advocated a tighter relationship to industrial capitalism as a solution for Latin America's "backwardness." An infusion of capital and technology, along with entrepreneurial values, would wrench Latin America out of its traditional (read: Hispanic and Catholic) stagnation into modernity (Lipset and Solari). It is important to understand that this prescriptive theory depended on a dualistic vision of "modern" and "traditional" societies. This pure dualism is precisely what contemporary theories recognize to have been irremediably contaminated by the development of capitalism. Dependency theory meanwhile, despite its epistemological and political advantages over modernization theory, never finally shed this fundamental dualism. It did posit capitalism as the problem's cause rather than its solution. But it effectively did little more than give different names—"metropolis and satellite" or "core and periphery"—to Lipset's "modern" and "traditional" (Frank, *Capitalism* 8-12).[2] Otherwise, the broader polemic between modernization theory and dependency theory generated accordingly antagonistic and predictably one-tracked prescriptions for development. Modernization theory advocated "free market" capitalism and dependency theory championed "state-planned" socialism. Both these models characterized the problems of Latin American society in pure, black and white terms and offered only violently sweeping proposals for change.

---

rejected postmodernism theory as a foreign and imperialist discourse incapable of accounting for Latin American reality (Larsen, "Posmodernismo" and *Modernism*, esp. "Introduction" and Chapters Four and Five). For contributions specifically addressing these positions and the "problem" of "importing" postmodernism theory into Latin America, see Yúdice, "¿Puede" and Beverley, "Postmodernism." I thank John Beverley for generously sharing this manuscript.

[2]See also Frank's *Latin America: Underdevelopment or Revolution?* Not only does the title betray this dualistic thinking, so also do chapter titles such as "Sociology of Development and Underdevelopment of Sociology," "Functionalism and Dialectics," "Economic Politics or Political Economy," "Liberal Anthropology vs. Liberation Anthropology," and "Aid or Exploitation." "Core and periphery" are developed in Immanuel Wallerstein's "world systems" theory. See *The Capitalist World Economy*.

The distinctions between "metropolis" and "satellite" are not irrelevant today, but their explanatory power is severely taxed by the recent intensification of certain phenomena such as global flows of finance capital (the debt crisis), deindustrialization in certain previous industrial centers of the metropolis (the American Ohio Valley), the rise of the drug trade (Peru, Colombia, and Bolivia, but also U.S. inner cities) and so-called informal economies, the exportation of manufacturing to previously non-industrialized "satellite" regions (the U.S.-Mexican border), the movement of large numbers of people displaced by material necessity (former peasants squatting on the outskirts of Latin American cities like Lima, Buenos Aires, and Rio, undocumented workers in the U.S.), and the increased "deterritorialization" of the corporation as national entity ("Japanese" auto manufacturers, IBM, Coca-Cola). It is important to discuss the variety of specific impacts these changes have had on Latin America, but here, I only want to reiterate that many Latin American political and cultural theorists of postmodernity depart from this observation: that capitalist development produces neither uniform modernization, nor neatly demarcated regions of industrialization and underdevelopment, but rather an impure landscape of heterogeneity and difference (Laclau, *New* 41-59; Hopenhayn 16; Lechner, "Un desencanto," 32). They insist, furthermore, that any transformative politics must take this new conception of capitalist development as its basis.

At the same time, the real operation of those economies misleadingly designated—within the rhetoric of the cold war—as "free market" or "state planned" has been freshly examined to reveal that no such pure economies have existed in the post-war era (Laclau, *New* xiii-xv, Hopenhayn 16-7). The acceptance of this reality, and the abandonment of severe programs to realize these impossible economic myths, are fundamental to successfully renegotiating Latin American modernity (Hinkelammert 29, Hopenhayn 14-19). Finally, the very goal of "development"—shared by modernization and dependency theorists—has been reexamined. Escobar's study of its history reveals that "development" served U.S. and European governments, as well as Latin American elites and intellectuals, more than the impoverished "masses" of Latin Americans it was ostensibly promoted to aid (Escobar 22-28).[3] While most Latin American theorists of postmodernity still depart from a description of economic conditions, they increasingly value political and cultural practices—as opposed to the seizing of the economic means of production—as fundamental to social transformation.

Politically then, the pure projects of revolution and authoritarianism have all but dissolved into multiple and antagonistic versions of democracy and

---

[3]Andreas Huyssen has similarly pointed to the emancipatory potential of postmodernism's challenge to modernization's blind valorization of progress and the new at any cost (Huyssen 185-86).

new social movements. Within this shifting political field, Latin American theorists, drawing upon European and North American concepts of postmodernity, have made especially provocative contributions to postmodernism theory and to social transformation in Latin America. They begin by constructing an image of "modern politics" (Hinkelammert; Arditi; Hopenhayn; Lechner; Laclau and Mouffe; Laclau, *New* 5-41). First, modern politics rise up out of a need to stabilize the chaotic elements of societies shaken by the reformation, the discovery of "new worlds," and the rise of capitalism and industrialization. Bereft of traditional moorings, modern politics seeks to reground order on a human scale (Lechner, "Un desencanto" 5-7). Second, modern politics bases itself on the assumption that a single interpretive key—history is class struggle or the progress of reason—can decipher the code in which modern society "is written" and thus render it transparently legible (Lechner, "Un desencanto" 11-12; Arditi, "Una gramática" 171-75). Third, the actual modern political "subject" is restricted to a self-anointed vanguard (military, cultural, intellectual, or political) that masks its particular interpretations and interests as those of society as a whole (Hopenhayn 6-7, 21). And finally, modern programs for social transformation are utopian in sharing two characteristics. First, they are future based, meaning that they depend upon a rigid disavowal of the past and present in favor of a future society valorized just because it is new. And second, they are total, or final, meaning that the solution promised will solve **all** the problems of present society once and for **all** (Hinkelammert 21-24; Lechner, "Un desencanto" 7-8, 25-27; Holston 314-18).

With their equal suspicion of the pure, utopian "metanarratives" offered by liberalism, marxism, and fascism—to say nothing of the recent authoritarianism of Latin America (considered a neo-liberal/fascist fusion by Hinkelammert)—these writers may seem merely to be echoing Jean-François Lyotard's own definition of postmodernity as "incredulity toward metanarratives" (Lyotard xxiv). However, their appropriation of Lyotard's critique of modernity's metanarratives actually exemplifies the **critical** dimension of their engagement with European and North American theories of postmodernism (Hopenhayn 9-14). For Lyotard's critique implies political consequences that are all too familiar in contemporary Latin American societies suffering under the austerity measures dictated by its reintegration into "anarchocapitalism" (Hinkelammert 25, Hopenhayn 11).[4] Instead, with their ears to the tracks of popular social initiatives, these writers produce various, different but fundamentally related, alternative analyses and strategies for the reworking of modernity's egalitarian goals on the

---

[4]"Anarchocapitalism," the theory of which was formulated by David Friedman, the son of Chicago school economist Milton Friedman, advocates massive deregulation and privatization, akin to what is being offered as a "cure" in Eastern Europe and the former Soviet Union.

concrete terrain of contemporary Latin America. In short, these theorists trace the attempts by Latin Americans to **concretely redefine** utopia on the basis of and through the rhetoric of impurity.

The literature since the mid-1980s on the so-called "new social movements" within Latin America alone is already too vast to be reviewed properly here.[5] However, Benjamín Arditi offers a useful theoretical reflection—accompanied by concrete examples—on the challenges these movements pose to the modern social sciences. He also proposes a "new grammar" to make the initiatives more visible and their practices more highly valorized. Departing from an image of modernity and modernization similar to that sketched above, Arditi begins his proposal with a distinction between society and the social. "Society" refers to the imperfect realization (through institutions, laws, culture, etc.) of a particular—modern—dream of homogenizing (or purifying) the social in the name of a single "rationality" or interpretation of reality. Yet, all such realizations, however totalitarian and apparently successful, must be imperfect due to the impurity of the "social," a term Arditi reserves for that which exceeds the "nets" of "society." "Political" examples might include homeless or squatter initiatives, undocumented workers and even informal economies, greens, women's, gays', and minorities' rights movements. But also Arditi offers a sampling of more narrowly "cultural" examples: artistic vanguards, alternative families, feminist and punk subcultures, gangs and the drug culture, prostitution and premarital sex. All these exceed the visibility of the law and its grid of surveillance and registering apparatuses like the church, work, business, or construction permits, museums, and so forth. But it is not only a matter of rigorously distinguishing between two separate realms of human practices. Rather, society must be understood as the "crystallization" of social practices, some of which continue to exist uncrystallized as "the social" itself. Thus "the social" ultimately suggests practices in constant flux, some of which succeed temporarily in institutionalizing themselves in a dominant way via interconnections—"archipelagos," Arditi calls them—to form a society.[6]

In strategic terms, Arditi's account dictates a "politics of space." "Social" practices "surprise" society by contaminating those sites it has overlooked in its focus on the conventional, official terrains of struggle. In Arditi's words:

---

[5]For a brief account and bibliography see Escobar, "Imagining" 32-34. For a useful English-language collection see Slater and also, more recently, Escobar and Alvarez.

[6]Compare this to Laclau's discussion of "social imaginaries," articulation, and democracy in *New Reflections* 60-85.

> **some** transformations can be forged by way of a permanent nomadism on the plane of the 'social,' particularly in relation to the culture and common sense of society; **but to achieve the permanence of 'colonies' of the alternative**, at some point these rebellious drives should shape strategic knowledges that animate new wills to power to take over marked off spaces, to modify segments of society. (184, emphasis added)

Far from the utopian dream of a totally new, transcendent society purified of power relations, the "politics of space" recognizes the ineluctability of power and seeks to work through it to appropriate and redirect it. It forms new identities and temporarily crystallizes new institutions for an always only partial transformation of society.

In this, Arditi's strategy proposal resembles those proposed by others. Hopenhayn writes of "new logics of social dynamics" generated by the new social movements which displace politics from conventional avenues to locally based organizations and practices, and economics from the discourse of macro-development to that of economic human rights and needs satisfaction (Hopenhayn 22-23). Lechner advocates a politics that values existing social initiatives without completely renouncing visions of the future. He also proposes a reconception of social reform that does not devalue it in relation to a glorified total revolution (Lechner 32-34).

Arditi's account, as well as Hopenhayn's, also assigns a constitutive role to cultural practices in the transformation of the social (184; 23). José Joaquín Brunner argues that the exports of the US culture industry—which for a previous generation were seen as homogenous and imposed violently on Latin America—are instead received and creatively reinterpreted in accordance with local needs, much like the Catholic religion in the Christian Base Communities ("Notas" 33). Since modernization has produced heterogeneity and a multiplicity of "cultural logics" in Latin America, Brunner insists that this heterogeneous cultural medium must be the condition of possibility for any strategy for development, modernization, or progress in the realm of social justice ("Notas" 34). Similarly, Néstor García Canclini observes that modernization in Latin America has produced a "massification" of previously exclusive high culture and a commodification of popular culture ("El debate"). But this is not necessarily a bad thing since the "purity" of those realms in the past functioned more to oppress than to liberate: for example, by employing a "national" high culture to oppress native cultures, or by mythologizing "popular cultures" as a national heritage to mask the assault on the social groups and relations from which they emerge. Thus, for Canclini, postmodernity is a "peculiar kind of work being done on the ruins of modernity." The "hybrid cultures" of postmodernity in Latin America redefine the meaning of popular culture—rejecting ahistorical essentialisms and myths of authenticity—in terms of "sociocultural representativity" (*Culturas*). This means accepting a new inclusiveness. It means not prescribing or circumscribing, but rather "permitting" genuinely popular culture to draw on even the most impure of mediums in its attempts to combat political and economic marginalization (Landi).

These discourses and concrete instances of a newly appreciated economic, political, and cultural impurity in Latin America—together with the observations of radical geographers and some theorists of mass culture (like Huyssen) in Europe and North America—help lay the foundation for critiques of the universalizing, appropriating gestures of much postmodernism theory toward Latin America. Only from a perspective rooted in heterogeneity and impurity can one obtain a critical purchase on theories that reduce or purify it. They also suggest the contours a positive working concept of "Latin American postmodernity"—as a grammatical and material modification of postmodernity—might take. "Latin American postmodernity" demands that attention be given to the impurity that exists (and that continually reproduces and displaces itself) among the various artifacts produced under a variety of local social conditions and aesthetic traditions. But second, "Latin American postmodernity" demands that the "original," "native" or "unique" elements identified in those artifacts not be interpreted only in light of those local phenomena. They must simultaneously be interpreted in light of differentiating global economic, political, and cultural processes which, while not immediately present, exert an ineluctable pressure on them. In critical practice, this means tracing the various local and global, social and political, cultural and aesthetic strands that are incorporated and transformed through the formal and technical activity of a text.

The fact that global structures of domination survive on differentiation requires us to grasp the various, local postmodernities as related, but not therefore homogeneous or identical. As critics, we must retain, not pretend to resolve, a tension between what will remain an unsatisfactorily homogenizing term: postmodernism, and the heterogeneous local forms produced within and sometimes against its logic. Perhaps the formal articulation of this tension between local difference and global totality constitutes one form of postmodern politics. The Latin American and Latin Americanist response to homogenizing theories of postmodernity might be conceived of as the inscription, within broader concepts, of the details of various local forms of cultural politics. In this way, certain pure, global categories operative within global models of postmodernity can be provisionally rewritten with greater flexibility to assist us in understanding and articulating the impure forms of resistance culture functioning around the world today.

In this spirit, I undertook a longer study of Argentine fiction and politics from the time of the Cuban revolution through the democratization process of the mid-1980s. Against this general background, generated by Latin American post-modernism theorists, of a shift from a purist modernity to an impurist post-modernity, I projected three moments in recent Argentine history. Julio Cortá-zar's *Rayuela* (1963) served as the centerpiece for discussing Latin American modernity, Manuel Puig's *El beso de la mujer araña* (1976) was the focal point for examining a second, transitional, moment between Latin American modernity and Latin American postmodernity, and finally, Ricardo Piglia's *Respiración artificial* (1980) marked the coordinates of Latin American postmodernism as found in Argentina. There, I found that the shift from purity to impurity took the form of a redefinition of utopian projections on the terrain of historical representation.

But I came to recognize that it was ludicrous to claim that the transition from modernity to postmodernity in Argentina was reproduced identically throughout Latin America. In fact, it was impossible to suggest that the transition in the same nation—if tracked through popular music, or journalism for example—would look the same. Indeed, according to some observers, the "paradigm shifts" away from high culture described by Brunner, García Canclini and others define the postmodern and mark one of the limitations of my own work which continued to emphasize literature, albeit recognizing its imbrocation with other forms of cultural and political practice (Yúdice, et al.). If nothing else, fidelity to my own critique of U.S. postmodernism theory precludes such generalizing gestures. On the other hand, the impulse to catalogue all these shifts, as though one could exhaust them and thus "fill" the concept of Latin American post-modernity, must also be resisted. For this too goes against the spirit of the theories and practices just reviewed. Both these strategies—universalism and encyclo-pedism—remain caught with a logic of pure, "final solutions" more proper to modernity. Therefore, I tried to preserve the tension between the very specific image of the shift from modernity to postmodernity in Argentine narrative fiction and a more abstract, and shadowy, background of a general and uneven shift from modernity to postmodernity throughout the region. Among the gains of retaining this uncomfortable tension, I believe, is the possibility of linking, over the course of many different works and practices, the various heterogeneous Latin American postmodernities into an "archipelago" of initiatives for, as García Canclini puts it, "entering and leaving" Western modernity.

Let me now illustrate one such link a bit more concretely by articulating the rhetoric of impurity of Latin American postmodernism theory with another Latin American postmodernity. This line I will be drawing—along a geographical and formal axis to Central American narrative and politics—is, I must emphasize, only one of many intersecting lines that could be traced from innumerable points of departure to equally countless points of destination across the region and perhaps beyond.

It would appear at first glance that little could be farther from the sophisticated novels of Cortázar, Puig, and Piglia—geographically, politically, culturally, and technically speaking—than the *testimonios*, or testimonial narratives, of Central America.[7] Testimonial narratives are first-person narrations of a real individual's experiences during a significant event or period in his or her country's history. They are unusual because the protagonist/narrator is often illiterate. Thus, most often they orally narrate their life story—sometimes in response to questions—to an interlocutor, often a writer, journalist, anthopologist, or political activist. The interlocutor records, transcribes, and edits the oral narrative and, usually, takes charge of the procedures involved in publication.

Surely when we here in the United States think of Latin American resistance culture, it is these *testimonios* that spring immediately to mind. In an apparently straightforward first-person narrative these texts tell the grimly triumphant stories of individual and emergent collective subjects struggling on a daily basis to transform their conditions of existence. For the most part, their celebrated reception not only by Latin Americanist critics but by the public at large, derives from an appreciation for the difficulties surmounted in this incursion of the genuinely popular into the realm of high culture. Especially for early celebrants of the form, *testimonio* was different because it was a representation by, of, and for the people; in marked contrast to the well-intentioned but finally colonizing representations offered by better known cultural elites (Barnet). Moreover, the entrance into the previously exclusive domain of written expression in Latin America was hailed for its invigorating and transformative effects on the institution of literature. Meanwhile, for more contemporary critics, the *testimonio* is remarkable less for the changes it signals **within** literature, than for its explosion of the very institution. *Testimonio*, it is argued, is not a representation at all, but rather a practice: the practice of identity-formation (Yúdice, "El conflicto"). If nothing else, this view seems supported by the Nobel Prize committee's decision to award one testimonial author—Guatemala's Rigoberta Menchú—their prestigious award, not for literature, but for peace.

All this may suggest that the *testimonio* conforms more to first world notions of the cultural forms emerging from the third world as resistant, but emphatically **not** postmodern (Jameson 152; Yúdice, "*Testimonio*"; and Larsen, "Posmodernismo"). But there may also be grounds and good reasons for viewing the *testimonio* as a form of Latin American postmodern cultural resistance (Beverley and Zimmerman; Beverley, "'Through'"). The appearance of simplicity and

---

[7] For accounts that do deal with testimonial narrative in the Southern Cone see Colás "Latin America" and Moraña.

authenticity—of purity—are belied by both the complex system of mediations involved in the production of the *testimonio* and by sophisticated narrative techniques employed by the protagonist/narrator (Sommer). Indeed, the resistance value of the *testimonio* as cultural practice and artifact, far from resting on either its transparently realistic openness or its "a-representational" identity-forming praxis, seems rather to derive from the tension between these practically unrealizable theoretical poles. That is, even the most apparently pure, "realistic" representation involves an interpretive transformation of reality into the cultural medium. At the same time, the ostensibly purely "a-representational" identity-forming dimension of the *testimonio* depends upon its representational dimension. If the *testimonio* did not represent to the protagonist/narrator, to her people, and to various publics a plausible "truth" about their lives, its political efficacy would be extremely limited. Only by sustaining an impure tension between pure transparency and pure opacity can the *testimonio* function as resistance in the broad variety of circles it has.

Thus, it is not the *testimonio's* uncontaminated positing of some pure, truthful, native history that makes them so powerful, but rather their subversion of such a project. This may or may not run counter to the *testimonialista's* own beliefs or intentions regarding their project. In the case of Rigoberta Menchú, her migration into ever-widening circles outside her native culture—first she learns Spanish, then she learns to read, then she travels to France, and so forth—would suggest a recognition of the fact that it is only the mutability of the form given different contexts that ensures its continued viability as a form of cultural resistance. Indeed, confirmation of this notion comes, surprisingly and perhaps unfortunately, from the neoconservative cultural observer Dinesh D'Souza. For *Me llamo Rigoberta Menchú y así me nació la conciencia* (the title of Menchú's *testimonio*) figures prominently in his harangue on curriculum revision at Stanford University. What bothers him so much—and it is the intensity of his irritation that I take as an index of the efficacy of this *testimonio*—is not that she tells a different version of Guatemalan history. It is rather that she both presents the appearance of being a "genuine" Guatemalan Indian and frustrates our expectations with regard to the proper contents of such an identity. She tricks us by being a Euro-North American Marxist and feminist in Indian clothing (D'Souza 71-73). Not the stability of her identity nor the fixed truth of her discourse, but the protean character of these confounds D'Souza and lends her work such "dangerous" power.

The notion of representation behind this view of *testimonio* is, I believe, a uniquely postmodern one in that it sheds the utopian purity of both realist (representation as transparency) and modernist (representation as opacity) stances on the function of representation. Ernesto Laclau has articulated this impure view in the context of political representation as part of his understanding of the post-Marxist (and postmodernist) "radical democracy":

> representation cannot simply be the transmission belt of a will that has already been constituted, but must involve the construction of something new. There is thus a double process: on the one hand, to exist as such, a representation cannot operate completely behind the back of the person represented; and on the other, to be a representation at all requires the articulation of something new which is not just provided by the identity of what is being represented. . . . Absolute representation, the total transparency between the representative and the represented, means the extinction of the relationship of representation. If the representative and represented constitute the same and single will, the 're' of representation disappears since the same will is present in two different places. Representation can therefore only exist to the extent that the transparency entailed by the concept is never achieved; and that a permanent dislocation exists between the representative and the represented. (Laclau 38)

For representation to exist, and the efficacy of the *testimonio* requires that it does, Menchú cannot be identical to the oppressed of Guatemala and the *testimonio* can be neither identical to her spoken testimony nor to the experiences of identity-formation which it narrates. Thus it is not necessary that representation be abandoned in order for the *testimonio* to function as a resistant, community-forming practice. On the contrary, it is essential that representation (in Laclau's "impure" postmodern sense) be operant for the *testimonio* as practice to fulfill itself.

    This theoretical justification for articulating the *testimonio* to the Latin American postmodernity of Argentine narrative may thus be speculatively complemented by a more properly historical one. Consider the Sandinista revolution in Nicaragua. The link between *testimonio* and revolutionary struggle is not one that needs to be reestablished. *Testimonio* emerged out of the cultural developments following the Cuban revolution and it accompanied, as in Menchú's case, both successful and less successful revolutionary struggles in Central America. But the February 1990 electoral defeat of the Sandinistas in Nicaragua, together with both the wave of guerrilla groups turning in their arms for ballots throughout Latin America and the dismantling of communist regimes in Eastern Europe, have raised questions about the future of revolutionary struggles in Latin America and, thus, about the future of a cultural form that seemed to draw its urgent force from those struggles.

But on my reading, the *testimonio* involved either a departure from or a redefinition of (I tend toward the latter) revolutionary culture. Its ambiguity and power in such a variety of contexts far exceeds the limits imposed by official restrictions on culture production in revolutionary societies such as Cuba. But if the *testimonio* redefines revolutionary culture with, if we are to believe Laclau, a decidedly democratic—though not bourgeois—inflection, then perhaps one can reevaluate not only its future and its relationship to seemingly dormant revolutionary tendencies in Central America, but the very status of those tendencies themselves.

In the case of the Sandinistas an evaluation of the electoral defeat must be made in light of world events, particularly those unfolding since the defeat. Given the overwhelming tide of international sentiment, it is hard to see the Sandinistas' capitulation to even an unfair electoral process as anything other than a strategically foresightful move. Consider the consequence of rejecting electoral arrangements: the protraction and intensification of a civil war not likely to end, especially given the new U.S. president Bill Clinton's continuation of Reagan-Bush policies toward Cuba and the rest of the region. Instead, the Sandinistas submitted to an election whose results, despite their distortions by U.S. involvement, did reflect, as Beverley points out, the partial breakdown of the "identification between a radicalized intelligentsia . . . and the popular sectors" (Beverley, "Through" 21). But beyond this, the election signified a strategic retreat from an unwinnable position in favor of one that would secure first, the continued existence and effectiveness of the Sandinista front, and second and more importantly, its favorable public image as a flexible social force most interested in leaving a democratic legacy, even at the expense of its own power. Events in Nicaragua suggest that the possibility of a return of Sandinista power, this time through internationally sanctioned elections, is not so far-fetched (Woodford Bray and Dugan Abassi 4). In the event of such a development, the U.S. may not be in the same position internationally to offer the kind of gruesome response with which it greeted Salvador Allende's Unión Popluar government in Chile two decades ago.

> The insistence in advance on coalitional 'unity' as a goal assumes that solidarity, whatever its price, is a prerequisite for political action. But what sort of politics demands that kind of advance purchase on unity? Perhaps a coalition needs to acknowledge its contradictions and take action with those contradictions intact. Perhaps also part of what dialogic understanding entails is the acceptance of divergence, breakage, splinter, and fragmentation as part of the often torturous process of democratization. . . . Without the presupposition or goal of 'unity,' which is . . . always instituted at a conceptual level, provisional unities might

emerge in the context of concrete actions that have purposes other than the articulation of identity. (Butler 14-15)[8]

The project Judith Butler theorizes seems to be already in progress in those impure realms of cultural politics I have described. The notion of a concrete and radical social politics of fragmentation—irreducible, contrary to its detractors' claims, to an exclusively textual variety of poststructuralism—might finally be the more abstract, theoretical image superimposed over these various locales and practices of resistances. Ernesto Laclau has written that "the radicality of a politics will not result from the emergence of a subject that can embody the universal, but from the expansion and multiplication of the fragmentary, partial and limited subjects who enter the collective decision-making process" (Laclau, *New* xiv; Laclau and Mouffe). Such assertions have come under heavy attack from certain quarters of the left today. But perhaps in Latin America, at least in Argentina, such a politics may have resonance, but may also seem unimaginable to us in the First World today. Jean Franco has written of Argentina's *Madres de la Plaza de Mayo* for example, that "Movements such as those cannot be reproduced or essentialized. If we can learn anything from them, it is that they raise questions which may not have a single correct answer" (Franco, "Death" 15-16; Franco, "Going"). Following Franco's speculations, we might conclude that the oppositional politics of Latin American postmodernism renounce "the discourse of the universal and its implicit assumption of a privileged point of access to 'the truth', which can be reached only by a limited number of subjects" (Laclau and Mouffe 192).

It is thus the impurity of the Sandinista project with respect to previously dominant conceptions of revolution that establishes its affinities with both Latin American postmodernism theory and the *testimonio*, not to mention certain forms of Argentine narrative. In all these cases, the rigidity of a purist stance with respect to such issues as the economy, political power, intellectual activity, historical truth, cultural forms, and subjective and collective identity has begun to yield to a more pragmatic—but not therefore unprincipled—set of approaches to renegotiating Latin America's hitherto largely tragic attachment to Western modernity.

---

[8]See also Fraser, "Rethinking the Public Sphere" and essays in Butler and Scott, eds. esp. Alonso.

Works Cited

Appadurai, Arjun. "Disjuncture and Difference in the Global Cultural Economy." *Public Culture* 2.2 (Spring, 1990): 1-24.

Arditi, Benjamín Arditi. "Una gramática postmoderna para pensar lo social." *Cultura, política, y democratización.* Norbert Lechner, ed. Santiago de Chile: FLACSO/CLACSO/ICI, 1987. 169-87.

Barnet, Miguel. "La novela testimonio. Socio-literatura." *Testimonio y literatura.* René Jara, and Hernán Vidal, eds. Minneapolis: Institute for the Study of Ideologies and Literature, 1986. 280-302.

Beverley, John. "Postmodernism and Latin America." unpublished manuscript.

—. "'Through All Things Modern': Second Thoughts on *Testimonio.*" *boundary 2* 18.2 (Summer, 1991): 1-21.

—, and Marc Zimmerman. *Literature and Politics in the Central American Revolutions.* Austin: U Texas P, 1990.

Brunner, José Joaquín. "Notas sobre la modernidad y lo posmoderno en la cultura latinoamericana." *David y Goliath* 17.52 (Setiembre, 1987): 30-39.

—. "Políticas culturales y democracia: hacia una teoría de las oportunidades." *Políticas culturales en América Latina.* Néstor García Canclini et al., eds. México: Grijalbo, 1987. 175-203.

Butler, Judith. *Gender Trouble: Feminism and the Subversion of Identity.* New York: Routledge, 1990.

—, and Joan W. Scott. *Feminists Theorize the Political.* New York: Routledge, 1992.

Colás, Santiago. "Latin America and the Problem of Resistance Culture." *Polygraph* 4 (1990): 92-110.

—. *Postmodernity and Argentina: Fiction, History and Resistance.* Forthcoming Duke UP, 1994.

—. "The Third World in Jameson's *Postmodernism or the Cultural Logic of Late Capitalism.*" *Social Text* 31/2 (1990): 258-70.

D'Souza, Dinesh. *Illiberal Education.* New York: Free, 1991.

Escobar, Arturo. "Imagining a Post-Development Era? Critical Thought, Development and Social Movements." *Social Text* 31/2 (1992): 20-56.

Escobar, Arturo, and Sonia E. Alvarez, eds. *The Making of Social Movements in Latin America: Identity, Strategy, and Democracy.* Boulder: Westview, 1992.

Franco, Jean. "Death Camp Confessions and the Resistance to Violence in Latin America." *Socialism and Democracy* 2 (Spring/Summer, 1986): 5-17.

—. "Going Public: Reinhabiting the Private." *On Edge: The Crisis of Contemporary Latin American Culture.* George Yúdice et al., eds. Minneapolis: U of Minnesota P, 1992. 65-83.

Frank, Andre Gunder. *Capitalism and Underdevelopment in Latin America: Historical Studies of Chile and Brazil.* New York: Monthly Review, 1967.

—. *Latin America: Underdevelopment or Revolution.* New York: Monthly Review, 1969.

Fraser, Nancy. "Rethinking the Public Sphere: A Contribution to the Critique of Actually Existing Democracy." *Social Text* 25/26 (1990): 56-81.

García Canclini, Néstor. "Cultural Reconversion." *On Edge: The Crisis of Contemporary Latin American Culture.* George Yúdice et al., eds. Minneapolis: U of Minnesota P, 1992. 29-43.

—. *Culturas híbridas: Estrategias para entrar y salir de la modernidad.* México: Grijalbo, 1990.

—. "El debate posmoderno en Iberoamérica." *Cuadernos hispanoamericanos* 463 (enero, 1989): 79-82.

Gonzalez Echevarría, Robert. *La ruta de Severo Sarduy.* Hanover, NH: Ediciones del Norte, 1987.

Habermas, Jürgen. "Modernity—An Incomplete Project." 1980. Seyla Ben-Habib, trans. *The Anti-Aesthetic: Essays in Postmodern Culture.* Hal Foster, ed. Port Townsend, WA: Bay, 1983. 3-15.

Hinkelammert, Franz J. "Frente a la cultura de la post-modernidad. Proyecto político y utopía." *David y Goliath* 17.52 (septiembre, 1987): 21-29.

Holston, James. *The Modernist City: An Anthropological Critique of Brasília.* Chicago: U of Chicago P, 1989.

Hopenhayn, Martin. "El debate postmoderno y la dimensión cultural del desarrollo." Unpublished typescript, ILPES.

Huyssen, Andreas. *After the Great Divide: Modernism, Mass Culture, Postmodernism.* Bloomington: U of Indiana P, 1986.

Jameson, Fredric. *Postmodernism, or, The Cultural Logic of Late Capitalism.* Durham: Duke UP, 1990.

Laclau, Ernesto. *New Reflections on the Revolution of Our Time.* London: Verso, 1990.

—, and Chantal Mouffe. *Hegemony and Socialist Strategy: Towards a Radical Democratic Politics.* London: Verso, 1985.

Landi, Oscar. *Devórame otra vez: Que hizo la televisión con la gente, que hace la gente con la televisión.* Buenos Aires: Planeta/Espejo de la Argentina, 1992.

Larsen, Neil. *Modernism and Hegemony: A Materialist Critique of Aesthetic Agency.* Minneapolis: U of Minnesota P, 1990.

—. "Posmodernismo e imperialismo." *Nuevo texto crítico* 6 (1990): 77-94.

Lechner, Norbert. *La conflictiva y nunca acabada construcción del orden deseado*. Madrid: Siglo Veintiuno and Centro de Investigaciones Sociológicas, 1986.

—. "Un desencanto llamado posmoderno." typescript, Santiago de Chile: FLACSO, 1988.

—. "Some People Die of Fear." *Fear at the Edge: State Terror and Resistance in Latin America*. Juan E. Corradi, Patricia Weiss Fagen, and Manuel Antonio Garretón, eds. Berkeley: U of California P, 1992. 26-35.

Lipset, Seymour Martin and Aldo Solari. *Elites in Latin America*. New York: Oxford UP, 1967.

Lyotard, Jean-François. *The Postmodern Condition: A Report on Knowledge*. 1979. Geoff Bennington, and Brian Massumi, trans. Fredric Jameson, fwd. 1984. Minneapolis: Minnesota UP, 1989.

Moraña, Mabel. *Memorias de la generación fantasma*. Montevideo: Monte Sexto, 1988.

Slater, David, ed. *New Social Movements and the State in Latin America*. Amsterdam: CEDLA, 1985.

Smith, Neil. *Uneven Development: Nature, Capital, and the Production of Space*. Oxford: Basil Blackwell, 1984.

Sommer, Doris. "Rigoberta's Secrets." *Latin American Perspectives* 70 (Summer, 1991): 32-50.

Wallerstein, Immanuel. *The Capitalist World Economy*. 1979. Cambridge: Cambridge UP, 1987.

Woodford Bray, Marjorie and Jennifer Dugan Abassi. "Introduction." *Latin American Perspectives* 66 (Summer, 1990): 3-9.

Yúdice, George. "El conflicto de posmodernidades." *Nuevo texto crítico* 7 (1er semestre de 1991): 19-33.

—. "¿Puede hablarse de postmodernidad en América Latina?" *Revista de crítica literaria latinoamericana* 29 (1er semestre de 1989): 105-28.

—. "*Testimonio* and Postmodernism." *Latin American Perspectives* 70 (Summer, 1991): 15-31.

—. et al., eds. *On Edge: The Crisis of Contemporary Latin American Culture*. Minneapolis: U of Minnesota P, 1992.

ON WHAT WE DO: POSTMODERNISM AND CULTURAL STUDIES
John Beverley

in memory of Agustín Cueva

Almost a decade ago, Fredric Jameson argued in his postmodernism essay that the theoretical equivalent of postmodernism was poststructuralism; today we would probably say instead Cultural Studies.[1] What is evident in most of the papers presented at this conference, whose intention is to formalize Latin American Cultural Studies as a field or network, is a theoretically informed anguish over the cultural situation of Latin America, an anguish (the word *angst* is perhaps more expressive) that recalls above all the reaction of the Frankfurt School to the rise of mass culture in Europe and the United States in the thirties and forties.

In part, I share this anguish; in part, I don't. This ambivalence has to do, in turn, with what I will call, borrowing a phrase of Stuart Hall's, the political vocation of cultural studies.[2] Where the object of devotion for many of you

---

[1]This is a translation, slightly elaborated, of remarks I presented at the founding meeting of the Latin American Cultural Studies network, organized by Néstor García Canclini and George Yúdice at the Universidad Autónoma Metropolitana-Iztapalapa, Mexico City, May 3-5, 1993, with the support of the Rockefeller Foundation. It addresses in particular a paper by Teixera Coelho of the Department of Communications at the University of São Paulo on cultural pathology in contemporary Brazilian urban society.

As Gayatri Spivak has noted, it would be more correct to speak of *Culture* Studies. See her essay "Scattered Speculations on the Question of Culture Studies," in Spivak, 255-84.

[2]Admitting that even as coherent a model of Cultural Studies as the practice of the Birmingham School was constructed out of radically different conjunctures, concerns, methodologies, and theoretical positions, Hall asks:

(D)oes it follow that cultural studies is not a policed disciplinary area? That it is whatever people do, if they choose to call or locate themselves within the project and practice of cultural studies? I am not happy with that formulation either. Although cultural studies as a project is open-ended, it can't be simply pluralist in that way. Yes, it refuses to be a

here clearly seems to be Walter Benjamin's Angel of History, who moves backwards into the future with its eyes fixed on the ruins of the present, My Lady—Madonna—might be said instead to look directly at the ruins to come of an ever more horrible future with rose-colored glasses.

Some days ago, I had the chance to hear in my city Gustavo Gutiérrez, the founder of Liberation Theology. He gave three lectures on the topic of what he called the New Evangelism. It made me think that in a certain sense *our* church, or sect, is also bound up with a preferential option for the poor, and shares with Liberation Theology the essential methodology of "listening to the poor," to use Gutiérrez's phrase. At least if Cultural Studies is not a kind of preferential option for the poor, it doesn't interest me much. I'm speaking only for myself here, of course. But if you agree with what I am saying, it implies that Cultural Studies carries with it, and within itself, the necessity of defining a new relationship between ourselves and what Gutiérrez calls "the poor." For Gutiérrez the poor are those who have no significance, who do not "signify" (in the semiotic sense) as full subjects in the hegemonic cultural codes that we manage and perpetuate as academics or public intellectuals, codes like literature, or the discourse of public policy, or theory. The poor, in other words, are what the South Asian social historians who call themselves the Subaltern Studies Group mean by the subaltern.[3] We could use other terms in place of the poor such as the new social movements, or emerging transnational proletariat, or "the people," or (under erasure) the Third World, but the result would be more or less the same for our purposes here.

The general formula of this new relationship is to pass from an epistemology and politics of representation to one of solidarity. Gutiérrez insists, however, that such a passage must begin with a relation of "concrete friendship" with the poor; it cannot simply be a matter of taking thought, or of romanticizing or idealizing the poor (for the poor are also "poor in spirit"). He concludes that the consequences for us of a preferential option for the poor are best represented in the structure of the contemporary world by the asymptotic curve: we can

---

master discourse or a meta-discourse of any kind. Yes, it is a project that is always open to that which it doesn't yet know, to that which it can't yet name. But it does have some will to connect; it does have some stake in the choices it makes. It does matter whether cultural studies is this or that. It can't be just any old thing which chooses to march under a particular banner. It is a serious enterprise, or project, and that is inscribed in what is sometimes called the "political" aspect of cultural studies. (278)

[3]Those unfamiliar with the Subaltern Studies Group may find an introduction to its work in Guha and Spivak.

approach closer and closer the world of the poor, what the subalternists call its "radical heterogeneity," but we can never actually merge with it without losing our own identity.

The emergence of Cultural Studies as a field is in part the product of the impact of the commodification of culture in late capitalism on the human sciences, the same commodification that postmodernist ideology celebrates (or diagnoses) in its sense of the breakdown of the distinction between high and mass culture. In this sense, although Cultural Studies, particularly in its post-structuralist or "Birmingham" strands, has been politically connected with the Left and the new social movements, it also depends on the character and possibilities of capitalist production and circulation of commodities; it is something like a superstructural effect of economic deterritorialization.[4] In the emerging global society based on the control and manipulation of information and images, and the production of new, more highly-skilled forms of labor power, our location within the cultural apparatuses, particularly (for readers of this article) in higher education (which has itself become an eminently transnational institution), acquires a new and unexpected power of agency. Indeed, what is striking about the so-called "crisis of Marxism" is that it has taken place at almost every other level *except* that of culture and education.

On the other hand, our meeting here is framed by the rapid and spectacular breakdown of the socialist project in almost all of its traditional forms of political instrumentality, especially (but not only), the state socialism represented by the Communist countries and the international Communist movement. It goes without saying that the "crisis of Marxism" has been in some sense also a cultural crisis (or, more accurately, that cultural and economic factors are inexorably intertwined in it). I have argued elsewhere, however, that the cultural problems of socialism did not happen mainly at the level of high culture.[5] Despite all the well-known difficulties of censorship, bureaucracy, homophobia, and so on, there exists or existed a more or less adequate high culture in the socialist countries. The problems happened rather at the level of efforts to create a socialist mass or popular culture. The socialist countries, or social-democratic cultural projects such as that of Jack Lang in France, were, and are, not able to compete effective-

---

[4]In the United States, the work of Tom Wolfe and the New Journalism could be said to represent something like a right-wing populist form of Cultural Studies, frankly celebratory of the new forms of capitalist culture.

[5]What follows is based on Beverley 1992.

ly with capitalism in the creation of mass culture (wonderful theater and film, but mediocre television).[6]

In relation to this problem, the great debates which framed left cultural discussion, like the Lukács-Brecht debate or the struggle over the character of the Peking Opera that initiated the Chinese Cultural revolution, are not all that relevant. Stalinist Socialist Realism as much as left modernism, Collazos as much as Cortázar, the grass roots poetry workshop movement in Nicaragua sponsored by Ernesto Cardenal as much as the more cosmopolitan view of culture defended by Daniel Ortega's wife, Rosario Murillo, represent normative, pedagogic models of cultural activity, based in Latin America on a prolongation of a Eurocentric and class-specific concept of the centrality of written literature as a cultural form and its consequent institutionalization. This is not in essence a position all that different from that of nineteenth-century liberals like Sarmiento, who saw in the standardization of language and culture represented by written literature in Spanish the antidote to what they regarded as the continent's barbarism or cultural adolescence.[7] By giving the power of literacy to broader sectors of the population, the actual cultural policies which tend to accompany these debates, like the literacy campaigns in Cuba or Nicaragua, undoubtedly change the nature of the relation between Ariel and Caliban, intellectual and people, to recall Roberto Fernández Retamar's articulation of the alternatives in his famous 1972 essay, but they also reinscribe it by making literature and literacy again the privileged signifiers of cultural authority. Cultural Studies as a form of a preferential option for the poor, by contrast, would involve incorporating the logic of what Ranajit Guha, the founder of the Subaltern Studies Group, has called "a writing in reverse."[8]

---

[6]Someone will mention in rebuttal the BBC, product of the hegemony of the British welfare state in the post-World War II period. But if the BBC had been an *adequate* form of Labor-oriented mass culture, the political defeat of the British Left represented by Thatcherism would not have happened, or would have happened in a less virulent form.

[7]See Ramos.

[8]In his essay "The Prose of Counter-Insurgency" (in Guha and Spivak, 45-88) Guha criticizes the prejudice in South Asian historical scholarship on peasant rebellions favoring the written record. Such a dependency, Guha suggests, betrays a bias in favor of literacy as a cultural form and of foreign and native elites, whose status as such is partly constituted by their control of literacy and literature in the very construction of colonial and postcolonial historiography, a bias which, even in forms of historiography sympathetic to the insurgents, "excludes the rebel as the conscious subject of his own history and incorporates the latter

It is in relation to this cultural impasse in the socialist countries and left cultural modernism in general that I want to emphasize my difference with the somewhat apocalyptic picture of Latin American culture that many of the papers at this conference paint. I don't want to minimize the real problems and structural contradictions they address. The model of noxious culture that they deploy comes, as I noted, from the Frankfurt School, which identified conjuncturally capitalist mass culture with the rise of fascism and other forms of modern authoritarianism. In a similar way, in Latin America the dominant tendency on the Left has been to regard postmodernism as the product of a disenchantment with the "hot" politics of revolutionary nationalism in the sixties and seventies, and thus as the cultural accompaniment of the hegemony of neoliberal political economy in the eighties.[9]

But if I take U.S. mass culture as my object of study—that is the most powerful and international of all regimes of mass culture—I don't necessarily see this connection. Just the opposite, in fact. U.S. mass culture is undoubtedly an imperialist culture in many ways, but also one that generally favors democratic values and human rights, including racial and gender equality. The complaint of neoliberal ideologues that the mass media portray corporate culture in an unfailingly negative light is not without some merit, although it neglects the complex dynamic that may connect "making fun" of corporate culture to practical quotidian submission to it. A good part of the transnational appeal of U.S. mass culture may lie in the fact that it represents to international audiences, besides consumerism (but certainly connected to it), *relatively* nonpatriarchal (or at least less patriarchal), democratic, and secularized values—something like the Imaginary, in other words, of a more democratic and egalitarian society.[10]

In regimes of combined and uneven development where one form or other of precapitalist cultural stratification involving a marked separation between intellectuals and the popular sectors has prevailed (and among these would have

---

as only a contingent element in another history with another subject" (77). To recover the historical specificity of the peasant rebellions, Guha argues, the historian has to read backwards from the (written) historical record. My thanks to Patricia Seed for bringing this point to my attention.

[9]The classic statement is Norbert Lechner's "A Disenchantment Called Postmodernism." For this, and other position papers in the Latin American debate on postmodernism, see Beverley and Oviedo.

[10]Jean-Luc Godard, whose own artistic practice was directly opposed to that of mass culture, was one of the first to demand that we try to understand the nature of this appeal, which constitutes one of the primary forms of postmodern globalism.

to be counted the situation of intellectuals, both party and non-party, in most of the former socialist countries), the commodification of cultural production through the operation of the market and through the new technologies of commercial mass culture can be, *in some areas*, an effective means of cultural democratization and redistribution of cultural use values and commodities, allowing not only new modes of cultural consumption but also an increased access to the means of cultural production by subaltern social subjects. By contrast, we can observe in cultural policies undertaken by both the Soviet model of socialism and Latin American populist nationalism the persistence of an ideology of the literary, which, apart from conjunctural differences, maintains a close affinity with bourgeois humanism and, in the case of Latin America and the Third World generally, with colonial or neocolonial cultural castes. As Althusser demonstrated, in Stalinism this ideology, which depends on the efficacity of its claim to "represent" both politically and epistemologically the interests of the poor, combines with a mechanical notion of the development of the forces of production and a consequent political economy of so-called socialist primitive accumulation that entails a coercive action by the state and the party on the masses and leads in turn to their gradual alienation from the socialist project itself.

I want to stress that this recognition of the democratizing function of the market, while it shares certain elements with the neoliberal critique of state planning or control, is not a defense of neoliberalism; it points instead to the possible advantages of a mixed economy, but one that is articulated by the interests of the popular classes, that is based on popular sovereignty. To say that in certain conjunctures (for example, in Cuba today) the introduction of *some* market mechanisms can have a democratizing effect, certainly does not imply that everything, or even most things, should be ruled by the market and the logic of capitalist investment and accumulation. Despite the ideological claims of neoliberalism about the relation of market and democracy, we all know that there can be a harmonious fit between marketization and the most reactionary and authoritarian political forms, that in fact the first more often than not requires the second for its effective implementation: that is, after all, the "lesson" of the Chilean "model."

On the other hand, I don't think that the market is a phenomenon exclusive to capitalism, or that it is market relations as such that define capitalism. In that sense (recalling one of the issues in the debate over dependency theory), I'm a relations of production purist. While capitalism undoubtedly gives great centrality and power to the market (so that society itself comes to seem coextensive with it), the market is the medium for its particular regime of class exploitation, not its cause. Just as there can be forms of class exploitation that don't necessarily pass through the market (for example, feudalism), I believe that there can be market functions that are non-capitalist or even anti-capitalist. By the same token, however, I don't assume an automatic linkage between cultural commodification and democratization. This depends on the incidence of popular forces on the state apparatuses (including the ideological apparatuses) and civil society generally (the workplace, cultural institutions and industries outside the state, "common sense," quotidian patterns of behavior and expectations, etc.), and the effects of this incidence in the creation of leisure time, sports, popular festivals and entertainments, and the like.

If the formula of intellectual activism suggested by Rodó in *Ariel* was "the domination of quality over number" (*el dominio de la calidad sobre el número*), the aim of a Latin American Cultural Studies in conditions of postmodernity should be to favor the domination of number over quality. Or, better, to favor the development of a notion of quality and value related to processes of dehierarchization and democratization.

I pass, however, to something that will seem at first sight to contradict what I have just said. I believe that there is also the danger of a kind of cultural utopianism in the postmodernist celebration of popular or mass culture, a possibility that recalls Gutiérrez's warning that a preferential option for the poor does not mean romanticizing or idealizing them. The premium placed in Cultural Studies (here the impact of literary Reception Theory is evident) on analyzing the activity of the consumer and the nature of the commodities he or she consumes often leads to the claim—Canclini comes close to saying this at times—that consumption itself may constitute a particular realm of freedom and resistance in relation to the ideological forms or reality principle of capitalism.[11] Beatriz Sarlo spoke in her opening remarks here about aesthetic and theoretical populism, meaning by populism something self-evidently bad. I'm not sure this is the best way to make the point. In any case, I don't mind thinking of myself as a populist. As Laclau showed, the question isn't populism as such, but what kind of populism. I'm a democratic socialist populist.

The problem instead, I think, is that postmodernism may perpetuate unconsciously the modernist aesthetic ideology that it supposedly displaces (an ideology that Sarlo would presumably defend), by transferring the formalist program of dehabitualization of perception from the sphere of high culture to the forms of mass culture, now seen as more aesthetically dynamic and effective, more capable of producing *ostranenie*. But this is an essentially *intellectual* appropriation of mass culture, by intellectuals of the traditional type (to use Gramsci's category), which produces something akin to a "pop" form of the

---

[11]See Canclini 1991. I have not been immune to this temptation in my own work: see e.g. Beverley 1989. I owe these remarks to my friend Paul Smith of Carnegie Mellon University.

Romantic sublime. There is something of this, I believe, in notions of cultural hybridity, nomadism, transvestism, and the like, which make the situation of the transnational immigrant representative of postmodern cultural experience in general (I'm thinking in particular of the work of Homi Bhabha, which is known to many of you, and of some strands of *Culturas híbridas*, although Canclini has also been careful to warn against such a generalization of his hypotheses).[12]

U.S. and British-style Cultural Studies was in part the consequence of the deconstructive impact of mass culture itself on the human sciences. But to the extent that mass culture can be re-aestheticized as a sort of "supplement" to economic transnationalization, it becomes possible for the humanities and social sciences to regroup around their disciplinary specificities, against the threat that Cultural Studies was going to usurp their territory or blur their frontiers. The fact/value distinction, which previously determined the autonomy of the aesthetic and regulated the separation of the humanities from the sciences, and which it was the main challenge of what has come to be called "theory" to weaken, can now be reinscribed within Cultural Studies itself, which becomes an academically sanctioned and non-contestatory space for "interdisciplinary" dialogue, what I'm sometimes tempted to call an epistemological "Faculty Club."

But the point of Cultural Studies was not so much to create new forms of academic interdisciplinarity, as to challenge the integrity of disciplinary boundaries per se, in favor of the possibility of developing a *trans*-disciplinary practice, whose components included semiotics, feminism, postcolonial critique, new forms of Marxism and social theory, and the more oppositional forms of poststructuralism and deconstruction—discourses, in other words, that implied both the inadequacy of existing forms of academic disciplinarity and the need for structural transformation of the existing social relations. (The distinction between interdisciplinary and transdisciplinary I take to be homologous with the distinction between international and transnational: in interdisciplinary relations, the subject is still the disciplinary module, as the national state is in international relations.)

While in its inception Cultural Studies seemed precisely the pedagogic embodiment of the cultural and political radicalism of the academic wing of the generation of the sixties, now emerging in middle age into positions of authority in the university, its rapid institutionalization, represented in part by this conference, suggests that it may have become more or less compatible with a revision of the forms of academic knowledge in and around the humanities and communications demanded by the present stage of capitalism, however one chooses to characterize it. Jody Berland counters in her remarks earlier here that we should

---

[12]See e.g. his remarks in Mier et al., 40. For a critique of the immigrant model of postmodernist culture, see Ahmad.

not be afraid of being coopted, that cooptation is precisely the way in which our ideas and work begin to acquire a material effectiveness. I agree, and I welcome the support of (among others) the Rockefeller Foundation for this conference. At the same time, I do not lose sight of the fact that it is the vanguard function of institutions like the Rockefeller Foundation to anticipate the new forms of knowledge and power relevant to safeguarding the reproduction of capitalism as a mode of production. I may be in a minority here, a kind of quaint relic or "survival" of the sixties, but I still see our intellectual project as bound up with ending, or at least radically attenuating, the domination of just about everything by corporate capitalism.

The conversion of Cultural Studies from a form of academic radicalism—a "postmodernism of resistance," if you will—to the avant garde of transnational bourgeois hegemony must necessarily aim at diluting its potential to become a form of ideological-epistemological agency of the social groups and movements outside the university and the cultural establishment whose subalternity Cultural Studies was precisely concerned with theorizing in its inception. It seems to me, then, that the project of Cultural Studies faces or will face a kind of impasse as it develops. The university and the network of research institutes need it, because it responds to urgent shifts in forms of life and knowledge, but they cannot let it be itself: that is, something like the academic equivalent of a "liberated zone."

Unlike many of you here, my anguish is more over the inevitable deradicalization of the project of Cultural Studies than over the toxic effects of the actual forms of commercial mass culture or postmodernist high culture (seen as decadent, narcissistic, puerile, violence-promoting, or the like). Again hearkening to Gustavo Gutiérrez's warning and to my own point about a kind of pop sublime, I don't want to idealize mass culture or ascribe to it a radical agency per se. But in the long run I have more confidence in the proliferation of mass culture and its effects than in the scientific-humanistic culture represented by the university, which has a stake both in producing subalternity and in keeping things that way.

Like all populist enunciations, this one is slightly demagogic: I understand that the university and mass culture are not as radically separate as they appear, that *we* are also interpellated by mass culture, that all producers and consumers of mass culture pass through or are affected by the education system at some level, that the classroom is a place to negotiate the political and social consequences of the postmodernist "ecstasy of communication." But I also remain faithful to the initial thesis of Daniel Bell on the cultural contradictions of capitalism, a thesis that I believe defines the postmodern as such. Capitalism has produced/is producing forms of cultural and technological experience that no longer coincide with the capitalist work ethic or with the complex of capitalist forces and relations of production, in other words, with capitalism itself. What Bell, from a neoconservative perspective, saw as a problem, however, I see as an opportunity. Our job is to convert this virtual contradiction into a real antagonism.

Works Cited

Ahmad, Aijaz. *In Theory. Classes, Nations, Peoples*. London: Verso, 1993.

Bell, Daniel. *The Cultural Contradictions of Capitalism*. New York: Basic Books, 1976.

Beverley, John. "The Ideology of Postmodern Music and Left Politics," *Critical Quarterly* 31.1 (1989): 40-89.

—. "'By Lacan': Política cultural y crisis del marxismo en las Américas." *Nuevo texto crítico* 8-9 (1992): 263-69.

—, and José Oviedo, eds. *The Postmodernism Debate in Latin America*. A special issue of *boundary 2* 20.3 (1993): 1-17.

García Canclini, Néstor. *Culturas híbridas. Estrategias para entrar y salir de la modernidad*. México: Grijalbo, 1990.

—. "El consumo sirve para pensar." *Diálogos de la comunicación* 30 (1991): pagination unknown.

Guha, Ranajit, and Gayatri Spivak, eds. *Selected Subaltern Studies*. New York and New Delhi: Oxford UP, 1988.

Hall, Stuart. "Cultural Studies and its Theoretical Legacies." *Cultural Studies*. Larry Grossberg, and Cary Nelson, eds. London and New York: Routledge, 1992. 277-94.

Jameson, Fredric. "Postmodernism, or the Cultural Logic of Late Capitalism." *New Left Review* 146 (1984): 53-92.

Mier, Raymundo, Mabel Piccini, and Margarita Zires. "Figuraciones: las culturas y políticas de la modernidad. Conversación con Néstor García Canclini." *Versión* 1 (1991): pagination unknown.

Ramos, Julio. *Desencuentros de la modernidad en América Latina Literatura y política en el siglo XIX*. México: Fondo de Cultura Económica, 1989.

Spivak, Gayatri. *Outside in the Teaching Machine*. New York: Routledge, 1993.

BIOGRAPHICAL NOTES

ARTURO ARIAS. Professor of Humanities at San Francisco State University. He is a specialist on Central American cultural studies (*Ideología, literatura y sociedad*, 1980; *La identidad de la palabra*, forthcoming), and also a writer of fiction: *Después de las bombas*, 1979 (*After the Bombs*, Curbstone Press, 1990); *Itzam-Na*, 1981; *Jaguar en llamas*, 1989; *Los caminos de Paxil*, 1991, and winner of the Casa de las Américas Award and the Anna Seghers Scholarship for three of his books. He was also co-writer for the film *El Norte*. He was born in Guatemala, but lived for extended periods abroad (USA and Europe), until he established his residence in the United States. His current projects include a book on Central American cultural criticism (*Gestos ceremoniales*).

ROGER BARTRA. Full time Senior Research Fellow at the Instituto de Investigaciones Sociales, Universidad Nacional Autónoma of Mexico. He has published extensively on the question of political power and the agrarian structure, and also on Marxism and the politics of the Left. His book *La jaula de la melancolía* (1987, 1st. ed.) has been translated into English (*The Cage of Melancholy. Identity and Metamorphosis in the Mexican Character* (1992). From 1989 until recently he was the editor of *La Jornada Semanal*, the cultural supplement of the influential Mexican newspaper *La jornada*.

ANTONIO BENÍTEZ-ROJO. Thomas B. Walton, Jr. Memorial Professor of Romance Languages at Amherst College. A Cuban-born writer and critic, he has lived in the United States since 1980. In Cuba he was head of the publishing department of Casa de las Américas and Director of the Center for Caribbean Studies. Several of his works of fiction and criticism have been translated into English including, most recently *Sea of Lentils* and *The Magic Dog and Other Stories*. The article included in this collection belongs to *The Repeating Island: The Caribbean and the Postmodern Perspective*, which won the MLA Katherine Singer Kovacs Prize in 1994.

JOHN BEVERLEY. John Beverley was born in Caracas, Venezuela. He teaches in the departments of Hispanic Languages and Literatures and Communications of the University of Pittsburgh. He was one of the founders of the university's Graduate Program in Cultural Studies, and was a participant in the founding conference of the Latin American Cultural Studies network. He is also active in the newly formed Latin American Subaltern Studies Group. His own recent publications include *Literature and Politics in the Central American Revolutions* (1990), co-authored with Marc Zimmerman, and *Against Literature* (1993). He has co-edited with Hugo Achúgar *La voz del otro: Testimonio, subalternidad, y verdad narrativa* (1992), and with José Oviedo *The Postmodernism Debate in Latin America* (1993).

NICOLÁS CASULLO. Professor of Cultural Studies at Universidad de Buenos Aires. He has also written fiction. He has edited several collections, including *Política y comunicación: hay un lugar para la política en la cultura mediática* (1992); *Sobre Walter Benjamin: vanguardias, historia, estética y literatura: una visión latinoamericana* (1993); and *El debate modernidad-posmodernidad* (1993).

H.B. CAVALCANTI. Born in Brazil, he is a professor of Sociology and Anthropology at the University of Richmond. He has published numerous articles on religion, and on the political consequences of the economic changes in Latin America. He is currently working on the social conditions of street children in Brazil, and the relationship between the Brazilian Workers' Party and NAFTA and MERCOSUR.

SANTIAGO COLÁS. Professor of Spanish and Latin American Literature and Comparative Literature at the University of Michigan. He has published a book *Postmodernity in Latin America* (Duke, 1994), and several articles on Postmodernism and Latin American literature and culture. His current research projects include a book manuscript *There's No Place Like Home: Towards a Theory and Criticism of Latin American Postcolonial Writing Since Independence*.

VINÍCIUS DANTAS. Poet, critic, and translator. He has written numerous articles on poetry and literary theory, and a book on poetry in collaboration with Iumna Maria Simon, *Poesia concreta* (1982).

CLAUDIA FERMAN. Professor of Latin American Literature and Film at the University of Richmond. Her book *Política y Posmodernidad. Hacia una lectura de la Anti-modernidad en Latinoamérica* won the *Letras de Oro* Award, and was published by the University of Miami (1993). A revised and augmented edition has been published in Argentina by Almagesto (1994). Her current research projects include a book manuscript *New Localities for Cultural Production: Transnational Languages and Texts*, which discusses contemporary processes of dislocation and relocation of Latin American artists and cultural production.

TERRYL GIVENS. Received his Ph.D. in Comparative Literature, and teaches in the Department of English at the University of Richmond. He is the author of *The Viper on the Hearth: Mormons, Myths, and the Construction of Heresy*, forthcoming from Oxford University Press.

JORGE JUANES. Philosopher and fine arts critic, he teaches at the Universidad Autónoma de Puebla in Mexico. He has published numerous articles on art and philosophy, and a book, *Los caprichos de Occidente* (1984).

JESÚS MARTÍN-BARBERO. Professor of Communication at the Universidad del Valle in Cali, Columbia. He has published extensively on the politics of communication and the mass media in Latin America: *Comunicación masiva: discurso y poder* (1978); *De los medios a las mediaciones* (1987, 1991), published in English in 1993 as *Communication, Culture and Hegemony: From the media to mediations*; *Televisión y melodrama: géneros y lecturas de la telenovela en Colombia* (1992).

CELESTE OLALQUIAGA. A writer living in New York City, she was born in Venezuela. She is the author of *Megalopolis: Contemporary Urban Sensibilities* (1992)—the article included in this collection comes from this work. She collaborates in several important periodicals published in Latin America. Olalquiaga specializes in Cultural Studies and obtained her Ph.D. from Columbia University in 1990, and she is currently working on a book about kitsch.

NELLY RICHARD. Author of *Margins and Institutions* (1986), *La estratificación de los márgenes* (1989), *Masculino Femenino. Prácticas de la diferencia y la cultura democrática* (1993), *La insubordinación de los signos* (forthcoming), and of numerous articles on theory of the arts and critical studies. She is the editor of *La Revista de Crítica Cultural* (Santiago de Chile).

IUMNA MARIA SIMON. Professor of Literary Theory at the Universidade Estadual de Campinas (UNICAMP). Her books include *Território da Traduçao* (1986), and *Drummond: Una Poética do Risco* (1989), and numerous articles on poetry and literary criticism.

ROBERT SIMS. Professor of Foreign Languages in the Department of Foreign Languages at Virginia Commonwealth University. He has published two books on the work of Gabriel García Márquez entitled *The Evolution of Myth in Gabriel García Márquez from "La Hojarasca" to* Cien años de soledad and *The First García Márquez: A Study of His Journalism From 1948 to 1955*. He has also published articles in *Chasqui, Hispania, Revista de Estudios Colombianos,* and *Hispanic Journal*.

CYNTHIA M. TOMPKINS. Professor of Women's Studies at Arizona State University. Born in Argentina, she has lived in the United States since 1978. She has edited a book on Alina Diaconu's fiction, in collaboration with Ester Gimbernat González, and published several articles on South American literature. She is currently working on a manuscript on Postmodernist Latin American writers.

INDEX